Anatomy
of
Civilization

Anatomy
of
Civilization

by

Oscar Robert Strackbein

A World of Books That Fill a Need

Frederick Fell, Inc.   New York

Library of Congress Catalog Card No. 69-20379

Published simultaneously in Canada by
George J. McLeod, Limited, Toronto 2B, Ontario

Manufactured in the United States of America

To the stamina of man and to his
determination to fulfill the high
destiny for which his unique endowment has prepared him, this book is
hopefully dedicated.

Preface

Man is a creature that does not know whence it came, when it arrived, why it is here, or where it is destined to go. This state is a very peculiar one but would be of no moment were man not congenitally and incurably interested in and concerned about these very questions.

Long and minute observation has told us that we of this creaturehood are descended from the same stem as the lower animals. We do indeed give very impressive evidence that we have brought with us a veritable animal heritage that rules much of our behavior.

It is to this duality of our nature, which is to say the animal and the human, that we owe our most perplexing and challenging problems. Were we either all animal or all human with the animal heritage left behind, the outlook would perhaps be brighter; but we are not vouchsafed an option. We therefore have no recourse but making the most of our heritage.

We are, it appears, not without assets, conferred upon us by the endowment that set us upon the earth and favored us over the animals of the fields. This endowment, called the mind, has bestowed upon us the possibility of progress toward civilization, self-government and freedom. The endowment is a trust that we may honor and so survive and thrive, or waste and wantonly use and so destroy ourselves.

Shall the animal in us submerge the man or shall our higher endowment prevail? Shall we convert our trust into a shame and a shambles or shall we use it wisely, honor it and apply ourselves to harvesting the rich potentials that are seeded in our rich endowment?

We are a mixture made for trouble and possible disaster but also possibly for nobility, heroic responses and magnanimity. Have we the wit and is our mental and moral endowment sufficiently resourceful to temper the rude inclinations, the harsh usages, the cruel and selfish forces in us, to bring them under the sway of the gentler, the kindlier and understanding offices of good will?

The mind of man has great mathematical capabilities. Can it solve the equation of authority versus rebellion, freedom versus responsibility and obedience versus oppression?

Whatever may be man's mission he will himself, individually and severally, reap the consequences of the struggle's outcome. He cannot shift the burden elsewhere.

Knowledge of the nature, make-up, dynamism and comparative strength of the contending forces may be useful to him as a guide. It is the hope of the author that the analysis here presented may help to illuminate the premises.

Contents

Anatomy
of
Civilization

1.

Anatomy of Civilization

AT SOME UNCHRONICLED MOMENT OF TIME, lost in the silence of speechless history, at some unmarked spot, unhallowed, wherever it was, by memory or spoken word, man, as a new creature different from any ancestral being, appeared on this earth, marking a unique and radical departure. Did he but know it, he faced a head-shaking prospect, on the threshold of an uncharted future. The odds were tight; the prospects hedged by gut-shrinking probabilities. Easy disaster was ready on many sides.

Modern man, plucked out of his civilized milieu, softened these many years by the delights of his ordered comforts and conveniences in the midst of which he inclines to mutter over deficiencies: were he now set shoeless and shirtless among his most primeval ancestors, to live as they lived, in the white light of the world as it was, unmade, uncleared, and unplowed; a roadless fastness and trailless, in all directions fresh and raw—were modern man to be thus confronted he would surely shrink and quail at the prospect. If mankind had all been epitomized in one man, so that its whole history were represented in him, he, were he asked if he would be willing to experience the whole of man's career again, from the first year of his appearance on earth until this day, would surely shake his head in negation.

Without spears and tools, the first *Homo sapiens*, also speechless and friendless, faced a world he could easily have renounced as impossible, if he had had the option. Facing primitive man today, we can only remove our headpiece, lay it over the heart and say, "Ancient man was a hero!"

What was offered him in his new estate that first day in exchange for his pure animalship? What had he to gain if he ex-

1

changed his animal defenses and some of his surest instincts for
a light that would be hidden in his head, called intelligence? He
would give up fangs and claws, strong arms, and nimble feet for
a light of low candlepower that was more adept at discerning
difficulties and problems than at solving them!

Homo I, call him Adam, if you will, was a unique creation,
not of his own making, because before he was man he could have
formed no notion of what it would be to be man; nor could he
have been in the least conscious of what his lot as man would be.
His vote was not asked, as even today none of his progeny is
given an option about being born.

This truth seems to be self-evident: man as man was *put* on
earth. He neither created himself nor chose his place of settlement
in the universe. His origin was not a democratic option.

He was like a seed, with his inward wonders and unbelievable
powers of extrapolation concealed in the shell. The plant seed
comes forth with magic developments, unfolding dormant potentials of untold richness as it responds to sun, rain, and soil. Man's
soil was and is *time*. He was made to develop and unfold in time,
not only as an individual but as a species—not in a generation,
not in a century or even a millennium, but in bounteous time; for
he has much to unfold and perfect. Futurity is his medium, enlightened by the past.

From "out of the cradle endlessly rocking" he had a destiny.
Verily, the beginnings gave but little promise, and man could
surely muster but little hope. He had only the rudest powers of
measurement. He knew far from near, up from down, now from
before and tomorrow, but he knew little of beginnings and ends.
He had no history, no teachings, no codes, and no guides. He was
set upon his primeval course without language, without writings,
devoid of signs and references. He knew not what he was, who he
was, or where he was. The question of *why* had no reason yet to
be asked. Whither he was going was of no concern, and his whereabouts was not in question since it was not known. He was where
he was and he was alive; that was all. Without knowing it, he
wished to remain alive. Why, to what end, or even how long was
immaterial. The question was not formed. It was still buried
deeply in the seed of time.

His legs moved him, his rude hands grasped things, his eyes beheld what was about him, his ears recorded sounds, and his other senses informed or misinformed him of the kind of world in which he moved, even as the other animals are informed in like manner. Very well, even as these other animals made their way, so could man. Yet he lacked their fleetness, their toughness of skin or hardness of scale or shell; he was losing their nimbleness, lacked their weaponry or deceptive coloration or poison, and much else that stood them in good stead in offensive combat.

His originator was not so thoughtless, even so, as to leave him exposed to a hostile world without some compensatory assets. His hand was made for grasping in a unique fashion. His thumb's position in relation to his other fingers was a great asset. It represented his tool-handling potential; but that was not all. He was provided with the basis of intelligence, that unique and mysterious light that was to gain him dominion over the creatures he left behind. This precious asset was called upon to substitute more and more for instinctual guidance. As man became physically more helpless before the beasts of prey and other animals that looked with no favor upon him, he became ever more dependent on his intelligence to fill the deficiency.

What an odd creature indeed! That a small group of his species should some day sign the Declaration of Independence not even the hardiest prognosticator would have envisioned as a possibility when a sense of futurity first stirred his untutored brains.

"Out of the cradle endlessly rocking" man was destined to overcome or defend himself against enemies and obstacles that were more formidable than those faced by lion, behemoth, or tiger: for he faced his own kind! After a while, as he learned to fashion spears and other means of defense, the outer beasts no longer challenged his ascendance. They learned rather to stay out of his way; but his new enemy became more formidable, for he, too, had spears and clubs and shields. So began one of man's great problems. It was man against himself!

In this he was not so unique, for in the animal world some animals of the same species also fight each other, with both cruelty and lack of mercy; but man, having been vested with greater intelligence and learning power, was able to fashion more astounding weaponry than grew on the feet or heads or tails of birds or beasts. In fact, man seemingly devoted his talents quite generously to fashioning new and surprising ways of beating his special enemy, driving him off if he made the attack or making a determined effort to overrun and to take his territory if it contained anything of special value that was not available at home.

Of course, man had other reasons for developing his unique light. First, he had a living to make, even as all other animals. He needed to eat and drink, to cover and shelter himself against the elements, to pass on his life to new generations, and to ward off enemies. These concerns through long millennia exhausted all his time. Yet this was not enough to satisfy him. As he was more than animal, things were stirring in him—very vague yearnings, not yet clear enough to be aspirations—announced by flashes or glimpses that moved his heart in strange ways. What lay beyond the river, beyond the mountains, out there where his feet had not yet carried him? Perhaps there were wonders his eyes had never seen!

Out into the haze, there where the sun went down, it was a bit terrifying, and yet it was a lure. Here and hereabouts all things, as in lotus land, all things always seemed the same. Today was like yesterday and yesterday's yesterday. But in the night there were sounds that came from nothing that was ever seen in daylight; also there were things seen at night that never were. What could these things be? Things different, some beautiful, some grotesque, and yet others as familiar as daylight and not rousing any wonder. His dreams gave him another world and moved his imagination. Everything as it was about him was not as it might be. He had seen it in the night; but in the daylight it vanished. There were other worlds, hidden worlds, more fantastic but also more terrifying and forbidding. In his breast were the first stirrings of dissatisfaction that would always drive him—to the moon if necessary and even possibly beyond.

Then there was the sea, that great breast-heaving mystery; and the stars, blinking from far beyond everything; and rain falling from the skies, sometimes feeling so good and then also making angry torrents and sticky mud; and the animals, some so marvelous, so swift and good to see, but others, oh, not so good, in fact, ugly and obnoxious and even dangerous, knowing how to bite or scratch or sting. It was better to get rid of them if only it could be done.

The light from out of his eyes let him see all those things; but that other light gave him more than sight. He saw, even as the animals saw, perhaps not as well, but he could do more than see. He could make judgments; he could infer and, inferring, could soon see more than he saw before. By heavens! He could learn! And he could learn because he could remember. He was the same as he was yesterday and at other times. This he could see by looking back, thanks to memory. He could also make distinctions, and once upon a time it dawned on him that he was himself, separate from others of his kind. Did they see what he saw, feel as he felt, hear what he heard? How could he know? He had no words, but he could see faces, and he could see how the others stood or walked or squatted. Their faces were not always the same, nor their movements and postures. Even as he himself did, they made different sounds. Some of these seemed to be the same at different times, as the same things happened. He remembered. Different sounds meant different things. A growl was sure to mean "Don't crowd me," or "Don't think you can take this from me," or "Get out of my way." Other sounds were more agreeable and were more pleasant to hear.

Yes, those of his kind lived together, much as some animals lived together. And therein, in this odd fact, lay complications. Man was not alone. That he had others about him spelled trouble but also brought great joy at times and much that was warm and heartlifting. What a strange to-do! Sadness and grief could come seemingly from nowhere at any time. The heart could be heavy and torn, the eyes downcast when there was no joy. How could such things come to be? Yesterday the day was good and all was warm and fair. The world was good. Now, what a heaviness! All is dark! Time wore on slowly, pain smouldered, and the gnawing knew no end—so it seemed; and yet time was also friendly as the days receded, and then the sun came out again, and life went on. Wrinkles came and white hairs appeared. These things could be seen in others who had been around so long. After a time some of them could no longer run or even walk, and it was clear they would soon no longer stand or even sit; and they lay still and after a while moved no more. So it was. Would it also happen to those who were still here? That was how it looked!

When did man shed his first tear? No one knows. When did he first burst into laughter? No one knows. When did his cheeks form the first smile? That great event is also lost in the darkness of things unrecorded.

What a mystery that man's origin is lost in the mists of time, and how long it was before his curiosity was aroused! How strange that his earthly career should be lost so long. What a commentary on his station in the universe! Verily, the semblance of man's history as a species to his individual career, beginning with infancy and passage into childhood, adolescence and the state of adulthood, is cause for consolation, hope, and optimism. Mankind had its infancy, its childhood, and is perhaps in its adolescence.

The young species came out of the darkness even as the child emerges from animal nescience, knowing nothing, into the light by a series of glimpses, unconnected, sporadic, like flashes of lightning in the dark. Instantly but only momentarily the landscape was revealed only to be swallowed again in total darkness. Then again came other flashes interspersing unconsciousness at more frequent intervals, until, after a leisurely cadence, the light became continuous for a spell, only to be lost again. After further leisurely paces, the light remained connected in its revelation of the more obvious constituents of outer reality. Perception was yet vague in general, but a few standabouts and movements of the configurations had taken form. Time was not yet perceived. History could not yet take shape.

Of course, the modern child has its human elders to look after it and to guide or misguide it. Mature man as man, Homo I, had only nonman as a parent to look to for guidance and leadership. Beyond the instinctual guidance, he was on his own. How did he cut the umbilical cord that tied him to his animal ancestor? But for his unique endowment he would have been unable to move a single step from his anchorage. His special endowment, his newly-found sapience, was in the form of a small searchlight, so to speak, self-activated and powered from a source of which he knew nothing. Necessarily he was a clumsy groper. Many stumbles, bruises, and falls marked his progress, even as they also mark the emerging capabilities of the child as it takes its position as an upstanding and moving biped.

Adam *sapiens* was indeed something new whenever and wherever it was that he stepped forth, coming out of the animal world as a whale out of the sea. He came upon the scene with a most amazing combination of biological assets and liabilities, dependent for his survival on that indefinable sapience that was uncertain and peculiarly unreliable in emergencies and extremities, even as it is today, prone to flicker when it was most needed, and easily snuffed out by the sudden onset of fear and high passion.

He fell perceptibly short of perfection. In fact, he had barely seized the notion of perfection by the tail, and his hold was precarious. Like the child, mercifully not knowing what lay in store for him, he nevertheless went on his way. It is not the policy of the biological forces to open the book of the future. It simply says, in effect, "Go ahead," and man, after the manner of the baby, learned to walk and then to run, not knowing why but doing it because he was meant to do it and was made for such activity. His flashes of self-consciousness no doubt mystified him and troubled him. His limited understanding and fragments of knowledge sometimes helped him but also brought him puzzles, so often his knowledge fell short of what he needed to know. So he learned to suppose and to guess. At the earliest stage he had no one to ask but himself. He was his only counselor. Self-reliance was his only recourse.

As pure animal this new creature was but little different from the wolves, hyenas, apes, and gorillas that he encountered in his path as he roamed the land for assuagement of his hunger and thirst—a primitive economist who knew no price of meat, fish, or berries other than effort, sweat, cunning, tired muscles, and defensive powers.

His stomach told him in terms easily understood what he needed to do if he wished to remain as a living occupant of the domains where he had been set. He knew nothing of title to land. He found himself at the dawn of consciousness as a squatter, with holdings not from a title inscribed in a book, but directly from and in common with the great God who had made him, and he held his place by power of combat.

As an animal he knew by instinct what he had to do in order to live. Hunger and thirst left no doubt in his mind. If the sun was too hot or too cold, in the one instance he found shade and in the other, shelter.

Strangely enough the filling of his stomach with meat, fruit, grain, nuts, and whatever else he found of use was a pleasure. It felt uncommonly good to put out hunger by eating and thirst by drinking. That was how instinct worked. It rewarded man and animal for doing what they had to do in any case if they wished to survive. As a matter of reflection, they did not know that they were seeking survival when they ate or drank, even as the infant knows nothing about survival when its suckling efforts bring it sustenance.

Other activities also brought pleasure and were pursued because of the anticipated pleasing experience, but without thought or possibly even knowledge of the consequences. If not for this system of attraction and reward, Adam would have been the first and last man on earth.

Man did what was laid out for him even as do the lower animals, and he did it even as do these animals.

He was discouraged from doing what harmed him by suffering pain, discomfort, and other disagreeable effects when he trespassed over the guidelines. If he remained exposed to the chill wind, he was uncomfortable and became downright miserable if he did nothing to escape the misery inflicted by the congealing temperature. So he learned to do something about it.

If the sun blistered his back, assuming he was hairless dorsally if not ventrally, he also learned that it was better to come in out of the sun.

If, against the counsel of his future uncle, Benjamin Franklin, he gorged himself to fullness on a raw leg of venison or clusters of grapes when it befell his luck to have the opportunity, he became uncomfortable, and his inner governor shut off the appetite that led him to eat in the first place.

It was all so very simple!

Yes, it was all laid out, not in readable terms, but in feelable, visible, audible, or smellable terms, operating on the pleasure-pain principle.

Oh, there could be and no doubt were mistakes. A fruit that looked delectable might have hidden within it a lethal chemical. The hidden poison might be tasteless; and by the time it was swallowed it was too late. Alas, poor Oswald! Adam knew him well! He fell a victim to primitive error! If he had a companion who did not eat of the unmarked but forbidden fruit but beheld the awful consequences, the relation between cause and effect may have impressed itself on the onlooker and he might then have warned his other associates in his herd or tribe or band.

Today we recognize the devices by which man was guided during his childhood as a new species. We see his early kinship, in his way of making a living, to the animals of the field, the trees, and the streams.

When man was hungry he sought food, and when he was thirsty he looked for water. In these pages we expect to refer to such impulses or needs as the expression of primary *will-forces*.

Considering how poorly we do today with centuries of education, mental discipline, and spiritual guidance at our disposal, it must remain a cause of deepest amazement to reflect that man did indeed make his way with none of the "advantages" by which today we set such great store and the absence of which here and there we so deeply deplore. We reflect that no one could hope to surmount such deprivations as our far ancestors constantly overcame.

As primitive man learned by dint of wrestling and contending with the forces of nature as he found them, the world was no paradise but on the contrary so inhospitable and exigent of human strength and wit that only a tough breed, disciplined by wind and weather, fang and claw, thorn and stone, friend and foe, could have survived. The weaklings fell by the wayside.

Nature, of course, is profuse and wasteful in many respects—at least as superficially observed. A thousand seeds mature on racemes and spikes when only one or two are needed to reproduce the existing stock. Millions of fishes are hatched into the seas while only a small proportion survives the hazards of the watery environment. One would think the little fishes could escape the onset of the bigger ones since the water provides visibility and minimizes the possibility of ambush. Yet the toll is taken. There is alertness and also great wariness on both sides, but there are also lapses and momentary inattentions.

Peering a little below the surface of appearances, we can reflect that the seeming surplus of plant seeds do not really go to waste but help feed birds, mice, and other rodents. These, too, multiply in a prolific burst of life, but like the seeds, in turn, act as sustainers of yet other inhabitants of the land.

We may therefore take heart as human beings in the thought that early man needed manifold expectations to the end that at least a few might be fulfilled. Youth at all times needs lures and charms and tantalizing wonders to lead it through the rough paths that lie on the way. If youth is overlured, or in a sense promised more than effort will ever later achieve or possess, we may also reflect that the awakened desire and wonders themselves bespeak life and living, and even offer a species of satisfaction. Adults in retrospect, contemplating the youthful years "when to outstrip thy skyey speed scarce seemed a vision," as Shelley mused in his great *Ode to the West Wind,* may again savor the delights that never came.

> . . . If even
> I were as in my boyhood, and could be
> The comrade of thy wanderings over Heaven, ...

he adds, and continues,

> . . . I would ne'er have striven
> As thus with thee in prayer in my sore need.

Shelley, no exception, harkened back, as befits a poet, to his boyhood days, to recapture, even as Tennyson did later, "the wonders that would be," wonders projected into an untasted future by the bright imagination of ardent youth:

> Yearning for the large excitement that the coming
> years would yield,

Eager-hearted as a boy when first he leaves his father's field.

So reminisced Tennyson.

Saw the Vision of the World, and all the wonders that would be!

Well, how would you have devised mankind?

In the gravel and dust of battle midst stinging spits of lethal danger and spattering bursts of explosion all about, fulfilling not all "the wonders that would be" but shivering heart and guts with terminal thoughts, what a recompense for those early visions as they flit into unreality routed by the overwhelming facts of life!

Or, bypassed by battle and even the fell blows of misfortune, as a fully seasoned man bears the unoiled grindstones of stout responsibility, glancing backward to retrieve the gilded expectations of romance and heady adventures of early imagination, he mutters in rank disbelief and wonders whether he was deceived; whether the seed of hope and wonder was compounded of delusion or whether it can be redeemed by satisfactions of sturdier and more solid substance. As romantic love is recontemplated from afar, what was it but a lure to the threshold of the day when we would be stuffed into the meatgrinder of responsibility? Yet, who would abolish romantic love?

Ah, the delirium of it! The wanton luster and pearly halos about all reality as it broke dawnlike over the first kindling awareness of another waiting world to be born!

It is still difficult for the mellowed adult to close his heart to these early enchanting mysteries while beset by lusterless routines and abiding monotonies. The true romanticist never purges his heart of the sleeping remnants of the fairylands of long ago. Indeed, he, the romantic, regards his occupation and economic lock-step as unbidden masters to be eluded or put aside whenever such a happy possibility might present itself. The only real worth of life to the romanticist has its nest in the heart, in dreams and mists, and in dawns, moonlight, and dusk, rather than in the white light of noonday reality.

The "realists," those who meet the world eye to eye and walk a straight economic or professional line, dwell less in the past, and at the dawn of their world-awareness were not so enticed by the wonders that would be nor lured into the mauve-hued foot-hills of the future. To be sure, they too experienced the taboos and *verboten* signs that inhibited the pursuit of pleasure, but more readily than their more sensitive brethren accepted the leash and the collar of restraint.

So man moved forward, civilization still ahead of him, filled with all the wonders that would be. At what point man first looked beyond the horizon of the present, to be dazzled by the luminescence of futurity is not known; but he must from an early day have looked for and hoped for something better than the present.

To achieve its objective great Nature has revealed itself, as just now depicted, as something of a demagogic politician. It loads vast promises on youth and thus lures him forward. When he awakens to the rubble of broken promises, it is often too late. When it releases him by a gradual ebbing of his exuberant will-forces that spoke so pulsingly of passion, emotion, and romance, he is tamed to life as it is in reality and as civilization prefers it.

Why indeed not allow one person to live forever? Why pro-vide for a division of mankind into individuals? Could not one person alone experience the whole of life, without splitting the human entity into molecules for separate experiences? Even so, why, if man was indeed to be atomized into millions of indi-viduals, did his creator not set them all on earth at one time and let them all live forever, rather than dividing experience into generations? Each generation, as it was, lived only a few score years and was cut down, to make way for replacements that would start over again.

Was this good economics? The waste was obvious; and the process has not changed. It costs billions of dollars today to educate children. The lives of mothers were and are still spent in con-siderable part in looking after their young, merely to bring them up to where the mothers were, which probably was not so very far in any case. Instead of freedom to push forward, the mothers were and are greatly handicapped by using their time looking after the offspring.

As for the men, half their time, too, was and continues to be devoted to providing for their young. How much farther might they have gone had they but been able to look only to their own future? Again, what a handicap! Then, as the final reward, having struggled and fed their own minds and having arrived at some degree of competence and knowledge despite the handicap, having learned by experience much that was to be avoided and much else that was to be sought after so that they became wise in the ways of the world, they were and are cut down to give way to those whose minds were and are empty.

Again, what a waste! Why could not the procession continue without a halt, without a retarding recapitulation always starting over again from the beginning? Would not civilization be much farther advanced were it not for this system of annihilation and replacement and repetition? Or do we learn something of *process as end,* exemplified in what we observe in these seemingly impractical arrangements?

These are natural questions but they fall far short of exhausting all the questions that both afflict man and provide a reason for his continuing endeavor. If the full answers were provided for him, what would remain to hold his interest and to fire his zeal?

These many questions did not await the advent of the scientific age. They came before science. Man had wondered about his origin and destiny and purpose since the day curiosity opened its blossom in his breast and since his mind was able to distinguish between whence and whither, origin and destination, cause and effect.

Since he could give no final answer to such questions, they became the center of religions and philosophies, particularly metaphysics.

Man has the necessity of adopting an attitude toward phenomena with which he has to live. He must reach a *modus vivendi* or be forever bothered, tantalized, or terrified. Much the same holds true of his confrontation with the questions he cannot

answer about origins and ends. He, man, or some of his spokesmen, such as men of genius or of great depth, speaking as the
spirit of man or as his epitome, cannot avoid formation of an
attitude toward the unknown.

The numerous philosophies and religions that have expressed
these attitudes and accommodations throughout the world bear
witness to man's need to understand, to assess what he does not
know, to place himself, not only in relation to his physical environment, as he does in geographical expositions, but in relation
to his very being in terms of origin and destination; to orient
himself in relation to all there is, so far as he can, whether this
be in space, in time, in terms of purpose, or what not.

He is the personification in maturity of the questioning and
probing of the four- to six-year-old child that plies its elders with
numberless questions as its young consciousness seeks to know
and come to terms with its surroundings.

We perceive from these reflections that man has more concerns than merely sustaining his life by food, drink, and shelter,
even though these considerations come first. This is the field of
the primary will-forces, as has already been noted. By far the
greater part of man's career on earth has been devoted to these
concerns. It was only in recent times that he gained sufficient
surcease from gaining his livelihood that a few of his kind could
find time to devote to less pressing questions.

The pursuits beyond those called for by his primary needs
were in response to what may be called the *secondary will-forces.*
These will be given extensive attention later. They operate in
the purely human sphere and are not shared with the lower
animals.

The primary and secondary will-forces provide man with
much of his total motivation. Yet, these forces are not all the impulses that lure or drive him. We have observed that while man
is inevitably individual, he also lives with others of his kind.
While at first his numbers were sparse, in more recent times they
have grown by rapid progression, and there is no escaping the
social imperative. Yet each person is an individual. Within him
dwells a force that expresses his individuality and also relates him
to all those who are not himself. This is his *ego.*

The individual is obviously vastly outnumbered, but this fact escapes him when he first enters the lists of the living. Later he is impressed by its significance. Slowly, as a young child, and with varying degrees of pain, he learns that the world was not made for him alone—a sobering truth that is usually accepted only after a series of rather futile rebellions. His ego records the painful lessons.

The youngster unconsciously expresses his raw ego which is a rampant force that is almost wholly preposterous. How different this child from the newly-born solitary wasp that never sees its parents but goes its way unerringly by instinct! The child grasps everything within reach to appropriate and possess it. His judgment is a nullity. That he cannot have what he seeks overruns him with frustrations.

Negation, disappointment, defeat, and repulsion is everywhere! What cruelty, what shame! But the child is resilient and essays to do over and over again what did not "work" before. Evidently the child is not much of a pragmatist. Yet in time he drops some of the unprofitable ventures but finds new mistakes to make. The rebuffs do not wholly discourage him; and he learns to avoid favorite mistakes under tutelage and from experience. He also has a resourcefulness of his own. His ego is not yet clear-cut, but that he has one can hardly be doubted.

While man was still the product of a savage state, his ego sat in its raw housing. Its function was as primitive as the primary will-forces. It sought this and that and resisted what was not to its liking. If it dwelt in a person who had grown to the full stature of a man and who was well muscled for strength and agility, no less than massive of frame, the ego could display itself in its naked inclination.

If such a puissant specimen came upon appetizing food while he was hungry, he did not have to hesitate. His primary will-force would simply await the eye's survey and the judgment's decision to make its selection. Which bone had the most meat on it? Which fruit looked most mellow and tempting? Very well, take the best, fall to with relish and voracity, feed the hunger. Taste this and that and always select the best. Cast aside what the appetite disdains. Pay no heed to others who would intrude unless they are so ridden by presumption that they would venture to match your grasp and your reach.

Of such presumption make a memorable example. A sudden thrust with a bent elbow to the ribs might awaken them to their error. A shove in the face with a bare hand, enforced with a quick crash from flashing knuckles, might drive home the fact of relative dominion. Should your eyes fall on a favorite, someone you find pleasing to you, smaller and weaker than yourself, admit this lucky one to share with you. Now you could enjoy the envy and animosity of all eyes centered on you. You could bask in your high estate. Your ego could swell with pride. The more obtrusive the contempt you might thus heap on those you had pushed aside, the greater the swell in your chest.

This would be paradise indeed! Not only would the primary will-force representing hunger be gratified, but your ego would pulse at flood tide.

Why then all the fences and signposts and taboos in such a paradise? It is ridiculous. It is a snare and a farce! If you cannot seize and possess what your heart is set on when you have the power, what is the sense of having the power?

Thus spoke and still speaks the raw ego, and thus spoke also Nietzsche, the echo from the caves and the tree branches.

The ego, however, is not entirely of the primitive variety, although every child comes equipped with it. As the primary will-forces are overlain by the secondary level, so the raw ego is overarched by the tutored or refined ego. In it may dwell noble sentiments and even magnanimity. Nevertheless the ego remains a potent force, a moving force that activates men to various endeavors.

Once man moved farther afield into the secondary levels of both the will-forces and the ego, he was ripening toward philosophy and religion. The human mind went groping for meanings and explanations. It had little to go on until writing made systematic expression possible. The philosophies and religions of history that are familiar to us were already far advanced when they were given to the world. We can only guess at what went before, but that it was impressive we need not doubt.

These various philosophies and religions represented inter-

pretations of reality and attempts to come to terms with the laws
and forces that were abstracted from experience and observation.

The Stoics, for example, from Zeno the Greek, a modern of
about 300 B.C., to Seneca, Roman philosopher (approx. 4 B.C.-
65 A.D.), Epictetus, a Greek in Rome during the first and second
centuries B.C., and Marcus Aurelius Antoninus, Roman emperor
and philosopher, second century A.D., adjusted themselves to the
world by insulating themselves against both pleasure and pain. To
them materialism was a vacuous pursuit. They believed that man
should free himself of passion and not allow himself to succumb
to either joy or grief. On the other hand, he should be submissive
to natural law, and accept it without whimper or complaint.

This philosophy represented an accommodation of man to
the medium in which he lived by a negation of the rich world
opened to him by the senses. Evidently the Stoics mistrusted these
sense reporters from both the outer and inner world. They therefore pled for a way of life that would overcome or bypass the lures
of the senses. These could only end in a vain pursuit of a vacuum
in any case, in the Stoic's view.

Epicurus, Greek philosopher of the fourth and third centuries
B.C., had sought a different accommodation. Quite contrary to
the withdrawal from the sense world, as preached by the Stoics,
he saw in pleasure the very purpose of morality. He did not, as is
often so erroneously assumed, advocate gourmandising, gluttony,
or venery, but held that genuine pleasure could be experienced
only through the exercise of prudence, honor, and justice.

That is to say, Epicurus did not mistrust the senses and condemn them; he accepted them as the supreme good but held that
they must be treated in a certain manner. To abuse them would
be to despoil them and not only rob them of their supreme gifts
but convert them into sources of displeasure. In this he was
surely right.

He accepted the sense world and sought to understand it so
that the gift of it might deliver its maximum pleasure to man.
This meant prudent abstention but not renunciation. It meant
self-discipline and regard for others (honor and justice).

These two philosophies provide an example of the opposite
conclusions to which human reason may lead when it arises spon-

taneously from within a great thinker. The probability is that each such philosophy will express the temperament of the philosopher and the reaction of this temperament to the dominant conditions and problems, economic and political, of the society in which he lives. Early philosophers were in this respect purer than the later ones because they were less schooled by forerunners and therefore less influenced by other philosophies.

A hundred philosophies could be analyzed, from different parts of the world, but they would necessarily be found to revolve about two points, among others. One: what is man, his origin, purpose and destiny? Two: how should man live with his fellow beings in order to fulfill the intent of his creator and to gain the greatest satisfaction from life?

Two contemporaneous Orientals, Buddha (563-483 B.C.) and Confucius (551-479 B.C.), preceding the Stoics, enunciated principles of living that were designed to achieve results on earth most conducive to good order and genteel relationships, no less than personal good.

Buddha, like the Stoics, was concerned with escape from suffering, but he went beyond them by providing a species of reward in the form of a state called Nirvana. The way to this elevated state could be achieved only through an octave of right-doing, namely, right belief, right resolve, word, act, life, right effort, thinking, and meditation.

Confucius, on his part, built a system of ethics in which the principal virtues consisted of standards of behavior that were designed as a mode of living, with special emphasis on filial piety, benevolence, and fidelity, supported by intelligence, propriety and justice.

Mohammed, the Arabian prophet (570-632 A.D.), founder of Islam, the religion of the Moslems, held that there is no god but Allah and that Mohammed is his prophet. The Koran is the Scriptures and it contains the professed revelations to Mohammed.

That these philosophies and many others should have come forth from the minds and breasts of men is readily understood when we consider man's peculiar condition on earth, together with his mental curiosity and his probing nature. It might be asked what any creature so endowed and set on an island far removed from any other island would do under the same circumstances. To wish to learn more and more when the power of learning is given, together with an inclination to exertion, is not only natural but should be expected as an urgent inclination.

The sweep of recorded history leaves out we know not what of great interest that went before. Paleontologists, geologists, and anthropologists have been diligent in their endeavors to discover origins, growth, and development. Further unearthing of the deposits of time may tell us yet much more than we now know or presently speculate upon; but much that would be enlightening is inevitably lost forever.

Nevertheless man is still here, and he possibly has a vast future, if he avoids self-destruction. Therefore, the living, the present world, affords us scope enough for study and understanding. While the story of man, as recorded in history, is but a brief span, we have before us so much that needs interpretation and extrapolation that we should not want for raw material. Indeed the accumulation is so vast that a lifetime represents but a brief period for review, analysis, interpretation, and the formation of judgment.

The succeeding pages will represent an attempt to look not only upon man but into him and into his aspirations and relations, to achieve a perspective that may upon further pursuit yield some helpful guideposts.

The ultramodern pace is so swift that the question of its being too late for civilization to save itself for the rich future that might await it bears with oppressive urgency upon man. In the next chapter we shall examine man's ego, as representing his most formidable obstacle to intrahuman understanding and subjugation of man's destructive rivalries. Needless to say, the problems of man are herculean, and only the great spirit that guided man out of his most primitive beginnings, overcoming seemingly impossible and disheartening barriers, will guide him to conquest of himself. Therein lies the hope of civilization. Hitherto man on earth has surmounted whatever seeming impossibilities stood in his path. Are we not now so much better prepared?

2.

The Ego

MAN IS THE ONLY CREATURE inhabiting the earth that has an ego—so far at least as man himself is aware. Quite clearly, being what he is—an individual in society—he could hardly do without it.

Unquestionably the ego represents a guide, a motive power, no less than acting as a mischief-maker on its own account. It moves man to action when otherwise he might be dormant. It agitates him when he would rather repose. It spurs him when he would prefer to contemplate mysteries and to withdraw himself from the much ado about a variety of activities that claim so great a part of the lives of young people and of not a few who are older.

The ego is not readily defined because it appears in so many odd guises. At one moment it is modestly arrayed and gentle, even self-abnegating; but wait, it may soon defend the host in whom it dwells, quite ferociously. It hides, it stands forth, it cowers. But it may as readily growl and bare its teeth.

What would man be without an ego? Behold the gorilla—he has no ego. Is he then in a better station than man, or worse? Endowment by an ego has in man gone hand in hand with bestowal of a mind or intellect and intelligence as a governing influence.

Indeed, the ego is one of the characteristics of man that separates him from the lower animals. It dwells deeply within him, at his very core. Yet it is not the self, and is therefore something less than the "I." Otherwise I should be out of order in referring to *my* ego.

This strange indwelling source of energy and force, dormant or active, is in reality the defender of the inner person. Above all, it reflects the quite visible fact that human beings, while being

20

born and existing as individuals, must live with and maintain relations with a variable number of others of their kind.

It is an inner mirror of the person in which the attitudes of others who have to do with him are also reflected: showing toward him a warmth or coldness, esteem or dislike.

The person, as he is self-conscious, is seldom without awareness of his self unless he is deeply absorbed in some pursuit in the grip of which he loses himself. His own image floats in his consciousness, sometimes accented by special incidents or experiences, such as having been called a liar or praised as a light-footed dancer. The ego then either gnaws at itself with rancor or swells with buoyant pride. In either event, it is sensitive to its host's standing in the eyes and on the tongues of others.

Assume the first of the two possibilities.

A report of having been characterized as a liar may be expected to ignite a sputtering bundle of firecrackers in the one so accused, inducing fulminations and agitations within him that ordinarily might be regarded as unbecoming in others but as a sign of self-esteem in oneself. Either a torrent of blood might rush to the head, distending blood conduits in the neck, on the way, marking the location of the aorta unmistakably; or, in other instances, the blood might as readily race away, leaving a blanched spread of facial features, not always inspiring to behold, as evidence of specific displeasure over the report. Whether the flooding or the ebbing of the blood from the cranial and facial regions has a bearing on a possible feeling of guilt or of honest outrage has not been established. Quite clearly the process, either turning inordinately red or bluish, or on the other scale, ashen gray or livid, does reflect a direct hit on the ego and a certain lack of control under surprise attack. It also shows the great power of the ego over blood flow, not to mention breathing, muscular activity, sometimes evidenced by tremors and spasms, and bodily attitude.

The ego is strongly inclined to make a darling of its host; and the darling can assuredly do no wrong. This attitude often extends from the father or mother or both to the offspring and sometimes to the second or third generation. In the typically extreme form, the paternal or maternal ego is capable of exclaiming, as in the oft-repeated story about Sam who, marching in a company of soldiers was out of step, but who in the eyes of his doting parents was the only one in step: "Look, papa, everyone out of step but our Sammie!" The ego also extends to racial pride, nationalism, and to other sources of personal attachment or pride.

To say that the ego is a result of individuality is not the whole truth since other living creatures are also cast as individuals and may be differentiated from others of their kind even as are human beings. To be sure, the ego does have its home in the individual, and individuality is one reason for its being. Its responsibility springs from the fact that its habitation is very exclusive—that it alone and no other ego dwells in its premises. At the same time, it is inextricably woven together with its fellow individuals, as observed just now. The ego more than any other characteristic reflects the dependence of man on man. The gregarious inclinations of man, shared with some other animals, reflects the dependence of the ego on association with others of its kind.

Except as a recourse to a supernatural agent, individual man looks to someone or to a number of others to sustain and share his satisfactions. He does very little strictly for himself. Even the selfish person or the so-called self-sufficient person glances at the impression he creates on one or more other persons. He needs and craves an audience or a gallery, so to speak. A few rare souls may be willing to await the plaudits of history, but they must be few, indeed, if ordinary observation can be credited. Even the "tough" individual—the one who purports to scorn the opinion of others —is in fact and above all concerned about creating an impression. Otherwise, why bother about being "tough?" To be "tough" requires thought, study, and much self-direction. What is to be gained by an attitude that reflects this quality if no one is within reach to make a report about the person who seeks to be tough? Place him on an island by himself, left marooned, with no hope of escape. Assume that he can lay no blame on anyone else for his exile—that it came about quite by accident, with no possible malice aforethought on the part of anyone else. How long would such a person continue to be "tough" assuming that he had been of that turn of attitude before he had become marooned? To whom would he exhibit his toughness? For a while he might exhibit it to such nonhuman creatures as might inhabit the island with him; but, if he were endowed with ordinary intelligence, he would soon note the folly of his attitude. Habit would assure continuation of his pattern of behavior for an indefinite period; but that part of his toughness that had required effort and steadfastness would begin to pall after a season. Effort for its own sake, proving nothing to nonexistent observers, would lose its attractiveness. To be impressed with oneself would become an empty and tiresome pose.

Napoleon, it seems, continued a routine of pomp and ceremony after his imprisonment on St. Helena, and we may assume that he derived some satisfaction from the make-believe. But he was neither alone nor was he necessarily without hope of a second escape. After all, he had escaped once. Moreover, he had his eye on history in which he was assured a place. This assurance sustained his ego and called for reminders of the dignity to which he regarded himself entitled.

The man marooned in perpetuity on an island, without hope of again seeing anyone of his kind, would in time find all pretense fatuous and empty. There would be no occasion for strutting, no reason for posturing, and even the usages of dignity would depend for their preservation on self-respect. No point in dramatics, no use to salute oneself, and no use to address the trees, the water, the sand, or the rocks! Only religious persuasion could provide an audience for prayer, and only a profound faith would withstand the vacuity of existence.

The ego would be stripped naked. All its pretenses, attitudes, and simulations, and all its dissimulations would be left without meaning. The man would be face to face with himself, with no props to lean upon, no excuses to invoke; no self-justification to fabricate, no blame to shed or transfer and no honor to look after.

How long would such a man desire to live? What would the ego say?

It is characteristic of the ego that it does not say anything. It feels; it reacts in tonal qualities. It becomes buoyant and exultant if the stimulus is of the pleasing kind. It rebels, resents, and thirsts for repayment if the stimulus impinging upon it displeases or bruises it.

The ego cannot long feed on itself. It must finally stand mute if no stimuli from the outside impinge upon it. Memory would, under the circumstances imagined here, of course, stir it for some time; but would slowly lose its force. Aspirations would become useless since (again, outside of religious considerations) they would lead nowhere.

Would the ego then go sour? Or would it incline to become simply dormant? If there were no responses to make, it would seemingly have little reason for being.

The man would soon reach the estate of nonhuman existence (with the exception noted). If he had available to him without excess of exertion food enough and of a dietetic variety appropriate to good health; if the climate were mild and equable and therefore variations in the weather were readily bearable; if noxious insects were scarce and no source of danger, and no fierce beasts roamed the landscape or inhabited the forests or dens; if the water were plentiful and pure, free of harmful minerals—if all the physical environment were conducive to a happy organic interchange, so that the man were free of oppressive needs, experienced no undue harshness in providing for his bodily needs, what under these circumstances would he do?

His organic impulse would carry him forward. Biologically the will to live would override his loss of hope, and, supported by a natural revulsion from pain, he would continue to live. His hunger and thirst would bring him pleasure from eating and drinking. He would live the life of a hermit, of a natural animal cut off from its herd. He might even gain satisfaction from the healthy functional operation of his biological organism.

Without headache, without eyestrain, free of nausea and indigestion, with no ambition or aspiration to be shattered, no bitterness to be nursed over injustice, oppression, or treachery, and no burdens imposed by untoward events—no bankruptcy looming on the horizon, no catastrophe to blot out the placidity of existence, and no animosities aroused by stalemated negotiations, broken promises, dashed expectations or fraudulent behavior—freed from the tensions and pressures of civilization and the compulsions of human companionship, his ego would be unemployed.

No doubt his imagination would in the beginning supply his ego with vain exercises. No doubt, too, that he himself would be the hero in his imagined experiences, deeds, encounters, contests, or the like. He would outsmart his imaginary adversaries at every turn. He would win all arguments. He would stand high in the esteem of his friends, neighbors, his family, and, were he a youth, he would tower as a hero in the regard of some favored romantic creature dwelling in his heart.

Yet, in time the vanity of these imaginary pursuits would rise to mock the mental excursions, for they would never come to anything. Intelligence would say, "It is useless." The ego would yet not so easily resign; but surely after some years it would become subdued even as the ego in a lifelong prisoner. Without exercise it would perhaps atrophy as an unused and useless article of personal psychological equipment.

To be sure, the person would still be an individual, but his individuality would be meaningless: he would be at the end of the line, with no heirs, assigns, or survivors. The individuality that is of such concern to the ego would stand bereft of significance. The wild creatures would not care. The trees and flowers would be unaware of his presence. From whom or what would his individuality then distinguish him? His thoughts would end within himself. Flashes of brilliance, should they occur within him, would die with him, unheard, incommunicable to any living thing!

His appreciation of the universe, his reverence of the intricate wonders of the natural world as exhibited in the fidelity of means to ends in the instincts of creatures, the infinitely minute workmanship in the processes of nature, in petals of flowers, wings of insects, feathers of birds; his inexpressible awe over the tenants of the firmament, the island universes and the infinity of space—all this must be sealed within himself. Perhaps he would talk to the stars, recite poetry, and even sing—all without an echo from without him—unless among the creatures inhabiting the island with him he had made some friends, by feeding them special harvests he had gathered, and by treating them all gently, letting them know he meant them no harm and indeed had not harmed them and would not harm them.

Thus might he build another little world of his own, regarding himself as a benefactor, returning to his creatures for their trust in him, solicitude for their safety, help in their distress or disability. His ego would then regain a partial function in this shadowland of reality.

Oh yes, he could use words and sounds to communicate with his innocent friends, calling them to take food from his hands, shouting at violations of his rules of orderly conduct at feeding, or drawing a few pets to him after teaching them the pleasures of having their backs stroked or their heads, horns, or ears toyed with. He would protect the weak against the strong, the meek against the ferocious, and thus enforce to some degree the rudiments of justice. With sticks and stones he would institute the lessons of punishment.

Some of these activities would come from sources other than his ego, but they would bolster this self-regarding phenomenon.

So varied are individual human specimens that no one can know or predict what he himself or other individuals would do under the circumstances of living in isolation as pictured here. The function of the ego would nevertheless soon reveal itself, no matter what the individual traits of the person so marooned. It would stand silhouetted in its stark essence, its skeletal lines showing and exposing the inner mechanics of outward behavior. It would be a chastened, soft-breathing ego, tamed and tethered.

The ego, like the primal biological appetites, asks no questions. In its untutored and unbattered form it seeks free expression; and this would usually represent pure selfishness. The young child is a creeping, walking, running, and reaching exhibition of such pure selfishness. Were it not guided by its elders who protect it against one danger after another, it would not long survive its lack of intelligence and experience. It must perforce be restrained in one manner or another until its brain cells become sufficiently developed to recognize experience and to make possible the functions of memory. The ability to learn is not itself a part of the ego; but, rather, as lessons are learned through the combination of experience, intelligence, and memory, the ego comes more and more under the restraints of the mind that records the lessons. This process may indeed grow into a battle of bruising proportions. The ego by nature is restive under restraint, no less than the biological appetites and impulses. It bears the natural propensities to domination and autocracy. Under restraint it may uncover some very raw responses.

Some egos, from ordinary observation, are more amenable to restraint than others, just as the character of some individuals is more plastic than that of others.

Nevertheless the ego left to its own devices will soon provide exhibitions of itself sufficiently bizarre to convince anyone of the contrariness of human impulses. The modern-day youngster, one of the variety that is subjected to a minimum of restraint under the force of the quaint psychological principles that have flourished in recent decades, is capable of demonstrating in rather conclusive form the waywardness of the untutored ego, its richness in irritative attainments and unseemly violations of all canons of decent behavior.

No laboratory studies are needed to furnish examples of the untutored ego's astonishing achievements in crudely offensive conduct. None but an indulgent parent, either intoxicated from excessive doses of modern freebooting psychology or indulgent in any event because of laziness, can endure the products of an inordinate tolerance of egoistic tendencies. This phenomenon of endurance is itself but an example of the power of the projected ego of the parent as it is turned on the offspring. Frequently such parents find the children of other parents, who are products of similar indulgence, wholly intolerable; but, protected by their innate ego-blindness, they cannot see the monstrous quality in the behavior of their own darlings.

Almost anyone has within the range of his acquaintance homes that can readily qualify as laboratories for the study of freelance juvenile behavior. To be sure, it is not only the raw ego that contributes to the disarray and untidiness in behavior, but it is perhaps the more difficult to bring under control. Appetites and habits, once disciplined, may remain subdued for all future time, but the ego continues ready to respond in wayward fashion in numerous directions. It is more complex than the appetites and responds to many more stimuli. It may be called into action by a great variety of outer events under many different circumstances, and it does not age.

The sense of hunger merely reflects the emptiness of the stomach, and other impulses or desires are aroused only by specific inner or outer events of the same variety, but the ego is exposed to influences too numerous and varied to catalog. A remark by another person, a glance, manner of handshake, a particular facial expression, or a mere inflection of a word or two that might go unnoticed by the unsensitized—any one of a thousand nuances of behavior, attitude, address, or posture may reach the ego and affect it. Unless it has been insulated by conscious determination and practice, it is responsive to insult, actual or imagined, or flattery; to rebuff or amiable overture; to indifference or solicitude; to shout or whisper; censure or praise—in other words, to nearly all aspects of the manner and the means by which persons talk to each other, eye one another, express themselves by gestures to each other, by glances or by not looking, or by staring intently or absently.

The ego, unless it inhabits a veritable bovine or apathetic type of personality, records the impact of its *human* surroundings —the more acutely, the more personal are the relations.

Its antennas are very sensitive, and the messages they receive go far toward setting the inner tone of feeling. Even some half-forgotten remark may rankle long after its reception, or it may long buoy the spirit if it was tinged with praise or evidence of notice by one whose notice was particularly esteemed. The whole inner tone may be infected, and often the outer behavior is sufficiently changed to become noticeable. Acquaintances or intimates may remark on the buoyant mood observed or, if the case was negative, on the long face or brittle mood exhibited by the subject.

While not all changes in mood are traceable to the impact of human behavior on the ego, no other single source of mood modification can perhaps compete with the ego. Disappointments, for example, are bitterest if they reflect on the ego, either justly or unjustly. If the reflection is justified, the pain will be of one variety. Efforts will be made to conceal the facts. If it is unjustified, resentment and desire to repay the insult or denigration will combine to produce not only pain but an impulse to vengeance. This too will be painful if it can find no outlet or, if given the opportunity, the counterattack is bungled. The secondary pain may then even exceed the primary, especially if words designed as a rapier-thrust stumble over each other, bunch up around the epiglottis or spit out incoherently, while the face reddens and the hands tremble.

Such an ignominious exhibition will put the ego in double jeopardy, and if the confusion cannot be covered gracefully, the consequences in the form of fellow disesteem must simply be awaited and borne as best they can be. An ego so wounded may fester unless the mind laves the wound and cools the passion by dissipating the thoughts that would linger on the defeat.

The influence of the ego and its state of rest or agitation over the inner condition of feeling is not always so visible and overt. Secret ambitions, hidden aspirations, covert attractions and other tendencies may lurk unseen but may nevertheless be charged with amazing powers of affecting moods and momentary inclinations, aversions or apathies—by the simple fact of spraying the inner atmosphere with their perfumes or noxious odors, as the case may be.

The unexpurgated ego is not only vain; it is a rogue, a natural-born dissembler, and not infrequently a cheat and a liar. Meantime and concomitantly, it is sensitive as a forget-me-not. It deigns not to seem forward unless it is overpowered with desire, but prefers to don the robes of modesty to achieve its ends. Its success in this respect depends on the intelligence and discipline of its owner, i.e., the person in whom it dwells. If this intelligence is not impressively high, the dissimulation may become transparent, and the contours of the ego will emerge to full view, as it so often does in children and the unpracticed.

Yet, unseemly and egregious as the ego may be in the raw and untutored state, it is amenable to instruction and discipline. It may then, as remarked earlier, indeed become the fountain of noble ambition and high endeavor. It then supplies the unflagging motivation that subdues countless obstacles and seemingly hopeless odds. It gathers the satisfactions of success and holds in check the advocates of surrender or retreat.

At all times, sometimes far in the background, almost out of sight, hovers or looms consciousness of the regard or esteem of the self as harbored by others, friends or intimates, or more remotely but nonetheless sensibly, the public or even posterity. They seem to be there, listening, looking, indistinct, silent but sentient and responding, taking notes, perhaps betimes in an attitude of applauding or at least approving, with a connection to the self, a species of great mirror in which one's behavior is recorded.

So does the ego live in the regard of others; and that is why the question "What will 'they' say?" or "What will 'they' think?" comes to the lips when an action that is of doubtful ethics or conformity with opinion is contemplated. Were there no human wall of opinion, esteem, or disesteem from which to bounce an echo, much human behavior would deteriorate. If it were a matter of complete indifference to all and sundry what one might do, how would restraint of an impulse constitute itself (unless religion should supply an unseen audience).

The social sanction indeed is a sanction only because the ego is concerned about the opinion of the family, neighbor, community, or public. The *conscience* is the reflector of external opinion, and the conscience is seated with or in the ego. Its fear, and therefore its arresting hand, by way of the intelligence, is no more than the voice of the family, the community or the like, or that of a supreme observer if one is thought to exist. Conscience speaks from others to the self. What it says arouses apprehension or not according to the conclusion of the intelligence. If the latter has an irrebuttable explanation in defense against an accusation, the conscience will subside. If the explanation is only plausible but not fully exculpatory, the conscience will be apprehensive. It will harbor misgivings, bobbing on the edge of fear, and will be ill at ease. If the misdeed was of a regrettable magnitude, such as knowingly accepting a ten-dollar error in change, the memory may rankle even as the ego seeks to forget. While the intelligence provides assurances that no one observed the transaction other than the self and the one who made the error, which in any case was unwitting, the conscience will not rest. Something is not in accord with the code of conduct, with self-regard reflecting the opinion of others, with the echo of teachings absorbed in the past, or with the tutelary deity—if faith is present.

Conscience may therefore vary in sensitivity, depending on

the ruling attitude in the home environment in which the person made his way as a youngster. If the family would have condoned the dishonesty, the conscience would not record a sharp regret nor harbor a lurking fear—unless later, elsewhere than at home, a code of honorable conduct had been embraced. Even then the conscience would hardly react as sensitively as in the instance of a childhood inculcation of a code. The later accession would not be as deeply rooted as the family-implanted attitude. Young minds may be conditioned more surely to a permanent setting than adult minds.

The ego is therefore variable with respect to what will impress it. Its function remains the same; but what external message or circumstance will affect it and how, will vary from person to person according to early individual tutelage. What would offend one might not offend another. What would elevate the ego of this one might leave the other one untouched. A similar difference might be recorded within the same person. As his inner receptivity of outer events changed because of experience, new teaching, or self-development, the sensitivity of his ego would change; so also would the reaction of his conscience.

Temperament and character traits, such as might defy instruction, might also differentiate the response of the ego. There are those, for example, who are more impressed and some who are less impressed with the good opinion of others. The timid are usually more sensitive than the bold and forward. They are much more sensitive to the esteem or disesteem of others.

Yet, the bold, forward, and brash are not wholly beyond the remonstrance of conscience precisely because they may harbor a spacious ego. They may really not relish the disesteem of those to whose opinion they affect to be indifferent. Therefore their freedom from concern may represent so much bravado or simulated indifference. Without an appreciative audience, the brash and bold would have but little reason to be either brash or bold. After all, who would be impressed? The very words "brash" and "bold" come from observers and record or characterize impressions created by behavior. We may be sure that beneath the most ostensibly indifferent and impressive air of overt indifference a play is under way, and that the actor is deeply absorbed in creating and maintaining an appearance. Should the actor indeed arouse the indifference in others that he affects in his own behavior, he would soon drop the pose.

In order to maintain his style, to which he may become quite attached, his conscience will be sensitive to any shade of his own conduct that might undermine his "image." The typical response of the conscience is fear of being found out by companions or the community. Any danger of transparency will cause great circumspection and caution. Of all the departments of consciousness, the ego is the most discomfited by the reflection that nothing is hidden from the deity. The omniscient observer represents an unwelcome presence to the ego. Its shabby pretenses are quickly revealed for what they are. The pious know this, are well aware of it, and therefore practice humility. It is not too much to say that the quality of faith, in the religious sense, is tested by the degree to which the devotee is aware that he conducts his whole charade of behavior in a goldfish bowl. Indeed, desertion of religion may sometimes be traceable to the ego's unwillingness to live with a bad conscience. Foreswearing of religion then allays the conscience.

The hypocrite, of course, is the practitioner of piety, lofty principles, and noble pretension who inwardly believes that his motives, which are quite different, are locked within himself, concealed from all eyes but his own, and that therefore his only concern need be the quality of his cleverness at wool-pulling. His conscience will remain at ease so long as he is assured that no one suspects his duplicity, or, if someone does, the latter may be dissuaded from whispering by one move or another to effect a checkmate. Should damaging evidence of the duplicity come into the hands of a hostile person, our host's conscience would begin a characteristic process of fear-incitation designed to put intelligence and wit to work. A feverish search for means of retaliation would begin, hoping to find means of silencing the enemy by a species of blackmail, or, failing that, opening a conspiratorial gambit that would act as a bribe. Pious pretensions could then be continued, but always under the danger of exposure to the world.

The hypocrite, should the danger of exposure increase in spite of blackmail or conspiracy, might begin to question the quality of his own honor. So long as all had gone well, this question had not occurred; his conscience had remained dormant. Since he entertained no belief in immortality even if he might profess a religion, a profession he might make as a means of enhancing the value of his hypocrisy, he would be without a conscience that would respond to a violation of a creed. Conscience is not stirred unless some penalty is attached to any act that would invoke such a penalty. In absence of belief in immortality or in a code of behavior that would determine progress toward a desirable or undesirable state, an act or deed or chain of conduct that might be expected to prick the conscience would be without effect.

Yet, conscience in such a person is at home nevertheless to evidence of danger to the standing of the host in the eyes of those whose regard he esteems for whatever reason. This esteem might be very practical, as in any instance in which loss of good repute would entail loss of income; or merely human in the sense that human beings enjoy standing well in the regard of their companions and associates. It may be guessed that, of the two, the regard for the esteem of others is the more fundamental; for even fear of financial loss would lose much of its sting if such a loss did not also mean suffering a loss of prestige. Prestige, again, is registered more in terms of others than the self. It is a compound of what others think.

The ego is the substratum for conscience, and it, the ego, would be useless encumbrance if man were not a social animal. In like manner the raison d'être of conscience would also disappear.

The basis of conscience presumably exists in all men; but, without consciousness of a code of conduct or of principles of honor or decency or, in other words, of moral considerations, a pang of conscience would be as unlikely as a successful pull-up of the body by one's own bootstraps. Unless fear of discovery of some violation exists, the conscience remains dormant. Any fear must revolve about unpleasant consequences of discovery, and these might be formidable. The theft of money actually awakens pleasant feelings—indeed, very pleasant ones—and conscience can rear its head only if discovery of the theft is recognized as a proximate probability. Even the pain of conscience is proportionate to the probable punishment or other consequence.

Hunger, which is a primary will-force, has no conscience as such; nor does thirst, lust, or greed. They merely demand gratification. Nevertheless, the conduct elicited by any such will-force becomes the subject of a possible awakening of conscience. It is only the ego that is concerned. A sated stomach has no regrets; it is in fact gratified. But the ego may be concerned over certain facets of gratification once it has been tutored and has become aware of the meaning of the opinion of fellow-beings.

So, again, is the ego distinguished from the physiological sources of needs, desires, and impulses. These are neutral and indifferent to moral aspects of behavior. They make their imperious demands on the organism for action designed to satisfy them whether other human beings are present or absent. Hunger on an isolated island would be as real as in a crowded hostelry. The human environment would have no bearing on the need, no matter how it might affect the possibility of obtaining food. On the other hand, what the human environment consists of is far from a matter of indifference to the ego.

Were there present in a particular situation only old men or only old women or both; were there only children, or only boys or only girls or both; or were there present only feminine specimens of age twenty to thirty, and were these all comely and lively; or were the human environment thoroughly mixed in regard to age and gender, such as might gather on the sidewalks or on a beach on a holiday—it is clear that the individual ego concerned would be affected differently and that a further difference would be created by the age and sex of the particular person in question. In any instance, on the other hand, hunger or thirst would remain the same.

The ego is multivalent in its relations to other human beings and therefore highly variable also in its responses. The same cannot be said of the will-forces that speak for the physiological needs—with the exception of the mating instinct. But there the ego intrudes so closely that its influence becomes virtually inextricable from that of the primal force.

It is the ego that seeks dominancy over fellow men. It is the ego that exerts itself to the end that its host escape being placed in a bad light. Therefore it savors the advantage of his always being right, of his having always the best judgment and committing the fewest errors. It becomes very sensitive about these indexes of status and may build prolonged fires of contention in order to establish proof of relative freedom from error in contest with others. A high score at being upheld as right becomes a prized achievement. Respect for good judgment is gained from others, and acknowledgment of this high level of attainment has its uses. In contention, others will henceforth defer to the judgment of the one whose high repute has been gained over a period of time. He who carries such a high regard has less need in the future to marshal facts in support of his judgment and therefore will more readily prevail whether or not he is right in a particular instance. He needs to take less pain and has less occasion to repeat or offer proof. He is spared the bother that may be costly in time. Those who come on the scene late or without a backlog of impressive experience will have little standing before the established sage and will hardly enter the lists as a challenger.

The ego is aware of the loss of face that waits on him who is shown to be wrong. The penalty is that he subsequently must be thrice right before he regains his original standing. To appear to be right in the absence of proof, therefore, becomes a great concern of the ego. It will often go far afield to achieve success in a contention lest it drop a stitch and suffer an unravelment that may be difficult to repair.

Many a contention and numerous argumentative encounters become stubborn tests of endurance because neither of the contending egos elects to submit to defeat. The headstrength thus exhibited is but the measure of each ego's tenacity; for it senses that more is at stake than the bare bones of contention in a particular instance. The contest is over dominance or submission. Habitual dominance will be loath to relinquish the privileges that become associated with superior standing. By the same token the ego of the one contending against the reigning dominance at times tires of dog-eared submission. A veritable outburst with characteristics of rebellion may indeed occur when the cup is full and the erstwhile yielding ego decides that it is time to make a stand.

Each ego then enlists all the intelligence its host has at its command, including shrewdness, trickery, and evasion, and even obtrusive browbeating by the erstwhile wearer of the dominant colors.

In contentions of male and female, and particularly between man and wife, the former may be ignominiously beaten by a tract of broken logic that seems so outrageous to him that he is reduced to muttering bitter thoughts about feminine intelligence. He senses himself to be at bay, which he is, and he cannot, even with his obviously superior wit, upset his mate's logic because she has none. His helplessness produces a state of inner fuming that he will not exhibit externally lest he be accused of resort to brute force. If he elects a course of silence, on the other hand, he stands accused of pouting or his dignified aloofness is mistaken for submission. He is a whipped beagle, and he knows it. As a means of avoiding permanent damage to his hard-won status as head of the household, he may essay another ploy. This may, by stupidity of choice, perhaps induced by occlusion of his intelligence by his exasperation, take the form of an effort to inject a ray of humor into the contest hoping thus to divert the attention from his discomfiture; but the sally is doomed to failure, for the feminine talent at intuitive reading of the truth under such circumstances makes any attempt at humor not only silly but massively inopportune.

In a final effort to be disarming and to cover his retreat, he brings his whole countenance into what he intends as a shattering change of face and pace.

"Why do we argue like this?" he intones, not in an imploring voice but with the idea of conveying a reflection of "how silly of two grown-ups to act like this!"

"You ought to know! You started it!"

"Come, come! No more of this. Don't you know when to stop?"

This is an attempt at remaining in charge of the field as it is being evacuated.

"If you knew how to stop you wouldn't say another word!" Whereupon the idea of chivalry breaks into his head and he retreats with his ego in a new light—a distinctly dimmer one.

The usages of dominance fit so snugly and with such pleasing countenance that they are eagerly sought. Some stations or offices bestow preferments, and these are soon taken for granted by the dominant ones who enjoy them. The human elements thereabouts adjust to the deferences and privileges. However, in circumstances of equality where title has not been established, or where relations are unsettled, the emoluments of dominance become greatly prized and will be quarries of rivals and contenders, even as sometimes between man and wife. The ego in its *intuitive* sense knows what is at stake (even in the male) when will-forces collide in disagreement. The issue may soon be joined.

One seeks this path or that goal and prefers this or that means over others. The other ego disagrees. The proffered path or suggested goal is anathema to it. Nothing could be so ill-suited and outlandish! The battle erupts. The contest rages, lines advance and are broken; flanking movements are launched and repulsed, frontal charges are beaten back. No decision seems in sight, and weariness besets both sides, each wishing to break off the engagement but unwilling to surrender, well knowing what is at stake.

Future relations hang in the balance. Who will gain the upper hand? Who will conquer and who will give way? Not only for now but for other occasions of disagreement—that is the prize, and that is why the battle may continue to the point of a decision.

It is not usually the preference of the ego to go into the future with relationships in doubt, unsettled, and subject to misinterpretation. Often this inclination is a matter of temperament. The aggressive one, aware of the stakes, may seize the offensive and gain the advantage of prior occupancy. Who is then able to stare him out of countenance?

If the opposed temperaments, on the other hand, are of equal heat, the arbitrament of the wits, if not of the sword, is unavoidable. If, more happily, the other claimant is less aggressive, of meeker countenance, and more peaceful, the first arrival will the more easily establish his position and hold it. There may be a contest, but it will be of a different order. The meeker one (assuming both contestants are male) will seek to shift the battle scene to the theater of wit and vocabulary where he may predominate. The other will prefer to rely on brute strength or perhaps shrewdness or arbitrary challenge. The tempo will then come to a slower play. There will be more ploy and counterploy, more eyeing and appraisal in place of onslaught and reprisal.

The winner in either case will enjoy the fruits of victory; but like many victories, those won in this field are seldom permanent. New elements appear on the scene. Advantages come to light that were not seen before. Strength fades with changed conditions. New tests of prowess come when the vanquished one believes the table of assets and liabilities have changed sufficiently to indicate that a reversal of fortunes might be expected.

Some relationships, to be sure, remain quite unshaken over the years, and harmony replaces contest and battle; but new relationships are numerous in a highly peopled world and these changes call the ego back into service.

The ego we have before us here is the naked ego—not the disciplined ego or the ego modified by the kneading fingers of breeding, schooling, or piety. A disciplined ego is not so contentious and seeks to avoid emotional involvement by relying on reason and understanding.

The ego, as has already been observed, does not owe its constitution and its inclinations to physiological origins. It is free, therefore, to be much more diverse than the primary will-forces— not to say perverse or bizarre. It has its own zones of activity and may not be easily tamed or caged.

It may be satisfied and stand quiescent in one department and enjoy its state of dormancy while it is busy, perturbed, insulted, or beleaguered in another department. It may, therefore, be both happy and unsettled or even smarting at the same time. Should a particularly sensitive nerve, however, be pierced, the torture would soon preempt the whole field of consciousness, and the elation that may, for example, have greeted the receipt of a medal of distinction would be lost in the groaning affliction following the new pain. The negative would drive out the positive or at least bury it temporarily.

Even a pin prick, so to speak, may provide a spot of poison that soon will oust a balm of honor and sunder the soul in acidulous fumes. There is poor proportion in this wildness and no good sense of value. Sometimes a person's stature is measured by the threshold of his vindictiveness. Nowhere else in the world of cleavages and reverses, outside of the consonances and dissonances of romantic love, is such a ludicrous parade of disproportions encountered than in the raw ego, which is to say where small things assume overwhelming importance and fill the soul to the exclusion of all else.

Essentially the distinction between the will-forces and the ego may be sought in that which distinguishes man from the lower animals. Primary will-forces are held in common with the lower animals. The origin is biological. The ego is human, is sensitive to human relationships, and responds to consideration of the opinion of other egos. Therefore, the influences to which it responds, positively or negatively, are as varied as the human environment. It is not merely a matter of bread and meat.

The ego, for example, is not satisfied to remain in what might be regarded as its own sphere. It intrudes itself quite obtrusively into the field of the will-forces. That is why table manners prevent us from following the example of the savage and grasping food in all haste and ingesting it as rapidly as possible lest someone else snatch the choice viands away from us. The ego is concerned about the impression its host makes on other members of the circle. What will so and so think? it asks, and in so doing may lay a restraining hand on the reaching arm.

It is not too much to say that the ego is the medium of civilization. It is because it is amenable or may be brought to be amenable to the opinion of others that civilization becomes possible. But for the latent responsiveness of the ego to the needs, comfort, desires, joy, and pleasure of others, a chaotic or anarchistic society would prevail. Considering the variety of man's desires, attractions, and aversions, far beyond those encountered in the animal world, a constant turmoil of clashing rivals for the same goods would prevail. There must therefore be a social governor, and the ego is the potential instrument; for wayward, self-serving, and arrogant though it may be and often or usually is, it is amenable, as has been said previously, to discipline, modification, and attachment to self-sacrificing goals.

While it is the source of the so-called will to power, or will to domination, and while that is its natural inclination, its form may be given a different content by experience, as we shall see; for the ego is also the source of the feeling of inferiority no less than superiority. This may be a feeling that reflects the individual's own reaction to the "batting average" he has (in his own mind) achieved—high, medium, or low, in contests and rivalries, whether this average was accumulated in dispute, such as pulling away toys from another, in gracefulness of speech or posture or dance, or in meeting problems, answering questions, or in general being equal to the diverse situations encountered in the pathways of life.

These experiences as recorded inwardly produce an inner ambient or tone of self-awareness that accompanies the person wherever he goes or whatever his activity. Does he meet the world with a sense of mastery? Will he seek to dominate? Much will depend upon the record he has amassed. Was he competent in meeting events and demands for response, both physically and mentally? If so, he may be expected to have an inner sense of self-confidence, and be inclined to dominate where he excels. If not, or if his experience has been a mixed one, such as having met some classes of situations with credit and even with merit to spare, but not so adequate or nimble in others, perhaps even clumsy, so that an onlooker might dub him stupid—in such an instance the person will have a mixed inner tone, well acquainted with both victory and defeat. He might wish to dominate but has been chastened by experience. If his victories have come in the more important departments or what he has so regarded, he may inwardly yet be predominantly confident and unafraid of the world. He may, to be sure, still experience an impulse to escape if he glimpses out of the corner of his eye an approaching unwelcome situation. Having resolved difficulties before, even if somewhat awkwardly, as he thought, he may now steel himself and meet the unwelcome approaching unpleasant situation, whatever it may be, and determine to muddle through even if it is not the sort of situation at which he is at his best.

He has learned from his past adequacies not to be so greatly embarrassed when on occasion he meets a deployment that will not show him in a superior form. He will no longer so greatly care what others may think because his experience tells him that they too have their varying degrees of adequacies and inadequacies. His ego, by reflection, if he has indeed reflected, may have learned something of empathy and feeling for others when he sees them embarrassed. Even a ray of charity may penetrate his attitude toward others. The timid one may learn that a catch in his swallowing mechanism has been induced by a sudden onset of what might frankly be called fear.

When such an indignity befalls him as he approaches or is approached by someone else who happens to be fitted with a strong personality—or at least a strong one in comparison with the first person singular—under such a circumstance he will almost certainly, if there is no escape hatch in sight, essay a species of bravado in order to hide the uncomfortable but plain fact that he has felt that catch in his throat—a fact that he would under no governable circumstance wish the other person to perceive.

Strangely enough, of course, his own approach to another person might induce the same catch in the swallowing mechanism of the second person as he himself had experienced. It is a matter of personality versus personality, and this varies unaccountably. The same person may easily be timid toward one person and feel dominant toward another—so variable are relations and so variable also the media in which the ego operates. Once more the distinction between the ego and the primary will-forces is seen as one of species, but this does not matter so much so long as we do not confuse the two—an undertaking not easily carried out in practice because of the constant intermeshing of the will-forces and the ego. The field of the ego is so broad that hardly a facet of mind or feeling is free from its concern, penetration, or participation.

If, of course, an individual's experience in his younger days, as he met the vicissitudes of the world, were predominantly negative—which is to say that he found himself inadequate or clumsy or afraid in very many encounters—the ego would undergo a shrinkage, so to speak. It would seek to avoid the painful situation and withdraw within itself. It would also make excuses for itself, or rather it would call on intelligence to come to its rescue with explanations that would cover the obvious deficiencies. Some of these explanations might be far-fetched and even bizarre— but no matter, so long as they provided the ego with a refuge.

The ego of the poor dancer will prod his intelligence, and the latter will find as many deprecatory remarks about good dancers as it can lay its hands on. In time the ego will have been so well insulated that it will perhaps even take pride in the previously painful fact that its host, the person to whom it belongs, is a poor dancer. Many a great man was a clumsy dancer, it will whisper. The light-footedness of the fancy dancer, it may continue, may be an index to lightness in other departments as well, especially at the other physical extremity. Subtle footwork and the deviousness that accompanies it may be of a pattern that extends to nonphysical characteristics, such as the morale. So, therefore, to be a good dancer is not the most enviable social endowment, if the truth were known. Better to be solid, substantial, forthright—these are the building blocks of good citizenship and honesty! Such is the defense.

Very well, the ego has been bolstered and insulated.

Of course, if the inadequacies are too formidable for the intelligence, a dream world may offer the only refuge. The imagination may fashion a haven of its own, peopled not with the everyday variety of flesh and blood, not the obtrusive elements that make a nightmare of reality, but with those who *understand* and who appreciate those inner qualities one keeps hidden, those talents that will not come out, and those graces that lurk in the deeper recesses. This dream world is as the world should be—a world in which the ego can enjoy self-respect and look the world in the face.

Sometimes a tree is seen, knotty and gnarled, confessing its crippled but nonetheless sturdy form to the world. It has overcome or grown around borers, bruises, sere days, or other inhospitable acts of nature and it has survived. Had it an ego it would be proud and would regard with some degree of contempt the smooth-branched and symmetrical specimens of its species; for their character has never been tested by adversity—or how else could they be without these honorific marks?

The ego is indeed as resourceful as the intelligence of the individual in which it dwells; but it may overload the intelligence. It may adopt a posture of superiority when it most feels the lack of it. Lest others fail to recognize its host's attainments, the ego prods the tongue to traffic in names of personalities and to claim varying degrees of acquaintance or intimacy with such and such a vice president, chairman of the board, or head of the elegant names society—not, to be sure, obtrusively, but by subtle inter-weaving of first names or better yet, lesser known nicknames, such as referring to Sinclair Lewis as "Red." Thus the ego escalates its importance and hopes to bridge the chasm yawning beneath it. It simply cannot bear anonymity, and therefore it must press reflected glory into service.

Egos are lonely in their unassuaged ambition and soon scent a like loneliness in others. Be it by the tone of cynicism or frac-tious diction by which they are inclined to allude to achievements of the more advantaged few, they are quick to recognize the tone and to sense a kinship of spirit. They relish the acidity mixed with oblique references made to the "patent" inadequacies so obviously revealed by the clumsy handiwork of the so-called suc-cessful person. As a matter of fact, say these aching egos, social values are a fraud.

The tone succeeds in undermining the merits of the accepted and the promoted, as if there were some counterfeit or some subtle deception about the recognition. So goes the divestment. Otherwise, this or that person would not be where he is. Success is a case of flattery being rewarded or of some half-hidden league of mutual self-interest between the dispenser of recognition and the recipient of the accolade—anything but pure merit. Of course, since the first person singular would not stoop to such shoddy ethical practices or traffic in reciprocal favoritism, he is justified in regarding himself as superior in his unrecognized estate, lonely though the atmosphere may be. Better to hold oneself aloof than to seem to be available to similar means of personal escalation.

Of course, the fact that the opportunity might in any case not present itself to the first person singular, the ego thoroughly overlooks; and, should a similar opportunity, indeed, present itself to him, the lonely one's processes of rationalization might quickly go into feverish activity, directed by his intelligence, seeking out all avenues of self-justification for accepting the opportunity. It would search for differences between this situation and that of those who but so lately had come under the ego's searing fires of condemnation.

Thus would the ego betray itself and the shallowness of the previous reasoning by which the same intelligence had supported it. Now the intelligence would reverse its engines to give aid and comfort to the ego in pursuit of its hopes—and the ego would be mollified and its integrity saved (in its own eyes) for the future. The moral sense would be driven into a corner, unless, indeed, it had by nature a principality of its own or had gained one by practice, exercise, and growth.

In a predicament such as this, we may perceive the relationship between the ego and the mind or intellect. The latter is necessarily honest. Not so either the ego or the intelligence—the latter being of the nature of legal counsel, available, all too often, for a fee.

Whereas the intelligence would seek to rationalize the ego's inclination, the mind or intellect would penetrate the duplicity or at least cast doubt on the integrity of the proposed action. It might lack the degree of acuity in the particular set of circumstances necessary for a clear differentiation between desire and principle. It could, however, not deceive itself. While it might be deceived by appearances and by the cloudiness contrived by the ego, it would nevertheless be unable to conceal from itself awareness of what is present to it. There can be no cheating of self at solitaire.

It is this duality of pretense as distinguished from reality that reveals itself in shamefacedness. The truth, inwardly apprehended, reflects the duplicity of the ego and the intelligence. Unless facial expression, eye muscles, and posture are under uncommonly cool control, embarrassment will surface in the countenance and muscular tension. Conscience will be mortified and will assume as nearly an ambiguous posture as possible. Mind, reflecting the moral principles, if any, to which the person adheres, holds to integrity with a grip that often is only too frail to win the day; but without a pang.

The dependence of integrity on the strength of the mental-moral combination is virtually absolute. Many games of hide-and-seek are played between the inner desires that speak for the ego and the will-forces, on the one hand, and the "higher" elements that are commonly identified with character, on the other. The game may become quite spirited, and clever sallies may be employed by the ego to save the day for itself. For this reason, integrity lacks popularity within its own precincts. The ego has easily the most winning ways, and yet so variable is its attachment that under long tutelage and early guidance, it may indeed ally itself with honor and integrity and become their most stubborn supporters.

This empirically observable phenomenon again demonstrates that the ego and conscience are not integral entities but may carry a variable cargo.

What this cargo may be depends on both innate traits of personality and the experiences of the person, including his education and tutelage, as already indicated. The mind or intellect is the interpreter and the judicial arbiter, so to speak, when it is presented with questions that produce indecision. Many actions are virtually automatic responses, shaped by habit or conditioned reflex. A good habit begets a response in kind; a bad habit as readily begets an unsavory response.

The question arises: how is a morally neutral force, as we have depicted the ego, transformed into a moral sentinel? If the ego is as base as it has been pictured, moreover, by what alchemy can its spots be changed? How, furthermore, can a neutral force be converted into one that weighs alternatives?

The answer is that the ego continues to be neutral; that it does not change its spots, nor becomes a wary sentinel. The *contents* of the receptacle have been changed by experience, reflection, or tutelage. This transformation was the work of the mind, which includes judgment and the capacity to analyze, compare, and reconstitute. The force of the ego still drives toward achievement of its goal; it still wants what it wants, and does not reason; but a change has occurred. It has a different goal. It carries a different cargo, so to speak, but its function is unchanged.

Yet, what the ego causes to be felt as a result of its aspirations may in turn greatly influence the mind. Indeed, the mind in its opposition to the ego's impulse may experience difficulty in standing its ground. The contents it thought it had planted in the container may not yet have struck deep roots. The ego may still be tempted. If so, it has not yet been tamed and will be an insistent advocate in behalf of its own primitive goal.

If, on the other hand, a transformation has in fact occurred, the ego will fight the mind's battle for it, assuming the mind itself knows what it is about. The two will be in unison, and since the ego supplies the motive force, the mind will be credited with a score when it has done no more than to point the ego in the direction the mind wishes it to go.

Even so, the ego may still influence the mind if a question of means arises. We assume now that the ego is in harmony with the mind in principle, but that a choice of means must be made. The ego's predilection may then gain the day. It may wish the action, if it is a creditable one, to be witnessed by others because of the credit it will reflect on its host. Rather than choosing a more humble means, it prefers the advertising. The mind may resist but then weaken and give way simply because it has had its own victory in gaining the ego's consent to the action in the first place.

The proposal may, for example, be one of making a donation to some worthy cause. A moderate sacrifice may be involved or possibly one of some real significance. The mind, reflecting on the usages of charity or goodwill, nevertheless decides affirmatively. The ego, although revolting because of the sacrifice, may submit to the mind's inclination, but in so doing may insist on a reward for itself. It may call then for a gift openly and publicly made so that it might gloat over its host's generosity. The mind, overlooking the more admirable course of anonymity, or not averse to the pleasure of the ego, may then consent without much ado. Indeed the ego might have revolted against the combination of a sacrifice hand in hand with concealment of the good deed. It would indeed have been doubly pleased should its host have been credited with anonymity while his identity with the generosity would in any case come to light. To the ego this double credit would be doubly welcome. Indeed, this strange actor, the ego, is capable of just such a species of duplicity while simulating a piety that is foreign to it and that it therefore does not feel. It relishes the credit for modesty without in fact subscribing to its forbidding exactions in self-abnegation.

Yet, if the ego had been converted to humility by the mind, to the point of sincerity, it would insist on anonymity in concordance with the mind, and would gain satisfaction from adherence to the code. Indeed, conscience would now balk at the species of duplicity described above, such as would please the unconverted ego, and it would be on the road to sainthood.

Even after the ego's anchorage is changed by conversion, unaccustomed situations may arise in the course of events. It may then be tempted to revert to its original nature. Such recidivism is not unusual. The mental-moral team will be faced with another struggle. Oh, how the ego longs for the recognition to which its host is entitled as a reward for his anonymous modesty! It is so dependent on an audience! If, of course, the host adheres to a faith that makes it possible to await the verdict of a future state, in an afterlife, the ego may be more readily subdued. There would be more at stake, albeit farther removed in time. Its audience, so to speak, is transferred from the present world to the future estate wherein concealments, pretenses, secret exceptions, and dissimulations have no standing. Unadorned reality, having no ear for pleas and excuses, will there be the judge. Here at last the ego must be honest. Only a sublime faith, free of doubt, can provide such a medium.

More than any other endowment of man, the ego relishes freedom. So do the will-forces, but their domain is more restricted. The ego is reflected in self-respect and dignity, and the concern over such an estate may extend far beyond the first-person singular. As the mind meditates and elaborates the principle of freedom, it may finally encompass the whole species of mankind.

The ego, beginning with self-concern to the exclusion of others, nevertheless is capable of extending its horizon if properly led. Since it is the mirror that reflects the regard that the self begets in others, and since it wishes to stand in good esteem in these others, it is amenable to an extension of its interest beyond its own self-regard, as we shall have occasion to relate later.

It goes without saying that its progress will be greatly advanced if as a child it had the example of parental tutelage and genteel surroundings. The work of its mind would be greatly eased. While there is no assurance of guarantee in these premises, as the number of reputed black sheep attests, the probabilities will be distinctly enhanced.

Freedom may thus be seen as a species of paradox. This is to say the ego is naturally selfish and yet is drawn toward unselfishness by the plaudits that unselfish acts beget. Whether an individual will overcome the self-regard that is inclined to be exclusive and become concerned over the well-being of others, deferring to their desires and convenience, depends on his particular temperament. There are, to repeat, those who are not as responsive to the plaudits of their fellow men as others. Their egos' demands are therefore not as easily overruled as in those who are sensitive to their standing among friends and neighbors. Nevertheless, the magnetic force of praise and encomiums is seldom wholly lacking. It represents an accessible reward that may be enjoyed this side of eternity in the commonplace activities and routines of life. The notion of rewards and their propriety is deeply imbedded in man. It borders on the instinctive. We feel something amiss if a meritorious act is not recognized. Ingratitude is universally despised. One who does not render thanks for a favor received is regarded as rude and ill-bred. We say that he thinks only of himself; that he has no regard for others. Inconsiderateness is of a like order. It is looked upon as reflecting a lack of breeding or, worse yet, a cold heart.

The bearers of such dispositions or attitudes may be feared but they will not beget warm regard and affection. They are not esteemed because they hold no esteem for others. They have elected to live in their own premises, ignoring proffered hands and overtures lest they become involved in the tribulations of mankind or in those of their neighbors. They have allowed the shell of their egos to solidify, so to speak, and so may have reached a state that seemingly lies beyond redemption. They have locked themselves out of the companionship and fellowship of man; withdrawn from the species to which they were born. They seek thus to find freedom. They wish to leave others alone and to be left alone, overlooking the fact that they are not of the species of the solitary wasp, which was fashioned for a solitary mission. The wasp knows nothing of others of its kind beyond one other individual. This phenomenon simplifies its courtship. In due season, it lays its egg in a tarantula or caterpillar and dies, never to see its progeny. Such is its way; such its nature. It is seemingly free; it is footloose and need consider only its own ways and means to its goal. Yet it is not free. It moves from necessity.

Man, so be it, is not a solitary wasp. He has others with whom he must share his life; and this natural state of affairs makes a world for him that is different from that of the solitary wasp. Therefore any aspiration in an individual to the life of such an insect is essentially misdirected.

Freedom conceived as being no more than a condition in which a person is left alone, free of appeals to lift a hand in behalf of someone else, free from bothersome consideration of the plight of the less fortunate, and free to cater to one's own whims, predilections, and peculiarities, is indeed the freedom of the raw ego; but it does not represent the freedom of man.

Man, indeed, has the double nature that distinguishes him not only from the solitary wasp but from the remainder of the animal kingdom. He is not only a social animal, as are also the bees, ants, and social wasps, but has a special capacity for harmony and discord that goes far beyond that of his lowlier cousins. The special container and exponent of this capacity is, once more, the ego.

The twofold and somewhat contradictory relation of the ego to freedom, as noted above, is now clear. The ego does not wish to do what it does not wish to do, just as it wants what it wants on the positive level. To have its way might then be regarded as freedom; but more appropriately it should be considered as something lower.

It is true that freedom consists of absence of outer restraint that would hinder or prevent action designed to carry out the mandate of the ego or of a will-force; but not all restraint is oppressive. Freedom is compatible with restraint if the bridle is held in the hands of him who is restrained and if he manipulates it. This means that his mind is in accord with the restraint. It is then the mind's task to instruct the ego or the will-forces to obey the restraining voice. If such instruction comes from understanding and assent, the restraint, while drawing a limit on liberty, is not oppressive but voluntary.

It is when restraint is imposed not by the self but by an external agent or influence without good reason or justification that freedom may be regarded as suppressed, and the suppression becomes oppressive to the spirit. The mind itself, which is the seat of understanding, while not restrained, nevertheless is then under duress not to give its assent to the ego or the will-force that would defy the restraint and break its mandate.

When the ego has been bent to the mind's dominance, it will ally itself with the mind, as already related. Thus, the ego performs a double function. It is not only a source of temptation and even the spring of hatred, but once converted, helps the mind hold to a code of conduct that will often be in direct opposition to what the raw ego would propose or does propose if it has not been thoroughly disciplined.

We turn now to a consideration of man's early development in view of his extreme limitations and the rarity of special insight and originality.

3.

Anatomy of Progress

MAN IS A CREATURE that shuttles between certainty and uncertainty; and since he cannot stand still except momentarily, he must respond in one way or another to innumerable options. The lower animals experience some uncertainty, as may be observed in the behavior of a dog when he is not sure of his master's command; but the prevalence of uncertainty is of a much higher incidence in man's activity because of his greater release from instinctive guidance. He perceives much more and therefore is aware of numerous alternatives. The greater his powers of perception as an individual, as already remarked, the higher the number of alternatives he sees before him. This is a function of his intelligence.

Unfortunately his *judgment* does not always keep pace with his perception of alternatives. He may then be baffled by the number of possible paths that open before him. In some instances an individual, seemingly one of many, has the good fortune of having a power of judgment that guards him against common error in making his choice of alternatives. Even so, such an individual may be deficient in some fields of choice. His extraordinary power of judgment may be limited to a few segments of responses.

Mankind depends for its progress in this or that field on the superior perceptive powers and sure judgment of this or that individual who is gifted with originality. It is the rare individual who in some field of activity sees what others do not see and disposes of rare good judgment in his choice of alternatives. It is he who pushes the frontiers of certainty or near certainty beyond their current limits. Those of duller powers of perception in time

51

bring up the long rear column. This is a slow process; the slower it is, the more radical or revolutionary the departure from the accustomed. The conservative forces embodied in the primary impulses, as observed above, will usually resist the adjustment in behavior demanded by the new insight.

Those individuals who most nearly approach the trailblazer in perceptive powers will be in the best position to interpret him to the long column of nonseers who trail off behind. Those next in line of perceptive powers after the first interpreters will be the most apt in turn at providing the next step in the secondary and simple interpretations, and so on. Since interpretations consume time, obstructed as the path to new understanding characteristically proves itself to be, the process of progress is necessarily retarded, and sometimes virtually hopeless unless time is measured in eras rather than in mere centuries or decades.

Only in geologic time, were there such a timekeeper, could the pace be regarded as of sufficient speed not to try human patience. The snail's pace from the human point of view is not necessarily absolutely slow. We carry one particular type of chronometer. It measures time for man, and this is not surprising because it was contrived by man. After all, man is not much solaced by his appreciation of geologic time, not to mention cosmic time.

Consider man's station! In his original naïveté he regarded himself as the center of the universe. Therefore a minute was a minute, an hour an hour, and a day a day. This datum of knowledge was clear and understandable. Also, up was up and down was down. East was east and west was west, and obviously the twain could never meet.

Then, as man pushed his knowledge in many directions, he became disconcerted over the undermining of his comfortable certainties. He found it necessary to reinterpret many commonplace "certainties" and he was at sea with Columbus and other navigators.

Luckily mankind numbered in its ranks a few—really a very few—intrepid souls that dared to look new hypotheses and ideas in the face. The process of following would have been much simpler and without so much heartache if the seers had all been "right." Unfortunately for such comfort, seers could be and often were wrong! Or, they were "right" to a degree—only so far, but not beyond that. Followers then experienced an initial exhilaration only to be rebuffed by the reality that lay beyond the limits of the seer's vision.

Naturally, skepticism and cynicism followed the disappointments. After all, it was the comfortable, everyday known facts that were the best! The primitive will-forces and the instincts of the primitive will-forces and of the primordial ego "knew" this all the time! The "progress" of man was thus hedged in an almost impossible array of positive, negative, half-positive, and half-negative notions and ideas.

Because of the paucity of "certainties" and the instability of some of these, and the prevalence of erroneous judgments, he was, as we have observed just now, impaled on the horns of varied opinions.

Opinion! Opinion!

Quite understandably man began to doubt the existence of any "eternal verities."

The source of opinion, of course, lay in the absence of certainty. Each opinion was eager to establish itself as certainty; and all men who had opinions, it seemed, claimed a patent on certainty! Not only that, but attachment to their particular opinions became a matter of stubborn loyalty. This style of loyalty was the work of the ego. Opinion could ripen into belief and thus involve the ego yet more.

Since error was as ubiquitous as evil, which was a species of error, opinions could be as varied as ideas and nearly as numerous. To be sure, not all ideas were wrong, but how was one to distinguish the right ones from the errant ones?

Disagreement under the circumstances was *prima facie* inevitable. Not everyone who disagreed with each other could be right, but everyone could be wrong, at least in some opinions.

The lower animals do not disagree. They may fight one another in pursuit of the objectives of their primary needs, but they have no opinions. Without opinion there can be no disagreement.

Man has opinions because he has mental perception. He sees alternatives and encounters uncertainties—sometimes many of them—and each of these may have supporting evidence as reported by his senses; but he seldom sees all there is to be seen, or more surely, never! Yet, he has a great conceit that his view encompasses total reality. Moreover, he is under a species of compulsion to be positive lest he be thought a nincompoop.

As a species, man is one, a unity, as we have had occasion to remark; but each little light of life represents an individual. There the trouble begins: Each individual a sovereign entity! More or less! And each an opinion-holder! Each also an ego-owner!

The mystery of how virtue can make its way in a territory that is so densely beset by countervailing will-forces and egoistic aspirations (of the primitive variety) is matched by the mystery of progress. The odds seem preposterous! (Surely someone will call for a definition of progress at this point!)

How then do we proceed? How did man proceed to "higher ground"—if the metaphor will withstand the barbs of the skeptics?

There is no "proof" of progress in the mathematical sense. It is a question of opinion. Therefore we must proceed, if we are to proceed, on an assumption that lies beyond proof.

If we *assume* progress, the question will arise how the upward movement has been possible, in view of the rugged nature of the terrain that lies and long has lain in its path.

The beginning of man's trek, being lost, as it is, in prehistory, we may guess that the mandates of the mind encountered seemingly insuperable obstacles. The arbiter, as previously indicated, had of necessity to be experienced. The capacity to profit by experience, again, depended on innate ability to learn, as previously noted. Evidently the disciplinarian was the external world —the harsh exactions of "nature." Only in this way, it seems, as a matter of opinion, could man have concluded that one course of action under particular circumstances was superior to another. First it was a matter of opinion: that of one man or of several against that of another or of several. The outcome of following this opinion or the other was noted, and conclusions were reached, supported by the senses. Men could see; they could discern the difference between one outcome and another. After many instances of trial and error, certain of the opinions became established as superior to the opposing notions. In time this approach or this manner of meeting a problem became accepted as the standard. Certainty, it seemed, dislodged uncertainty. Children were taught by their elders what these had learned, so that the offspring might be spared the ordeal of learning it all over again by trial and error.

The upset came when new situations arose. Such emergencies or transmutations were rather merciless. Poor man, after much trouble, heartache and strife, thought he had found eternal answers to certain common problems! Poor fellow!

Now he had it all or much of it to do over again! Opinions that had previously been laid low and brought under the sway of wisdom now broke loose and ran rampant once more. Bewilderment struck to the very bones! What of the wise ones? They could now only speak with the *tone* of authority while inwardly shaking their heads; but the tone of authority rang hollow when the common intelligence perceived that it had lost its link with reality—with the plain truth that the eyes could see or the mind comprehend. It was even worse when the "plain truth" was upset by science!

Fear and bewilderment were then perhaps the common bond and offered the only salvation from despair. New certainties were needed, and they were forthcoming.

Well, evidently man was more than a mere Sisyphus, who evidently is still engaged in rolling a huge stone up a hill only to see it roll down again—no tidings having yet been received reporting the remission of his sentence.

Unquestionably many a huge stone rolled uphill by man has indeed rolled down again; but man is not the victim of such an unrelenting and malevolent nightmare as would condemn him to a permanent Sisyphean state. What style of unconscionable creator must we presuppose or presume as the originator of such a diabolical scheme?

Notwithstanding the latter-day humanists who would credit man with the powers of creation, logic seems, as a matter of opinion, to demand something *given*. Long before man was able to form a concept of progress, he was already the product of it— if it exists at all. He had to progress to the point of appreciating progress before he could even form a concept of it. This reflection leaves us face to face with the bootstrap operation. Even if man fashioned the bootstrap, his capacity to fashion it must have arisen from some source. If he knew nothing of it, if he had no notion of it before it *occurred* to him, how could he occupy himself with the act of designing it?

Man has invented a word or two in explanation of the phenomenon. *Teleology* and *vitalism* are the words employed. They express the opinion that "the processes of life are *not* explicable by the laws of physics and chemistry alone and that life is in some part self-determining—opposed to mechanism." (Webster.)

Thus we move once more to the sphere of metaphysics and leave the land of proof. Also, we are back again to the element of purpose. This is not to say that no development could take place without purpose; for this might be possible in the sense that a particular event was irrelevant to the origin or course of another. It is to say that science cannot discern or test purpose, because it is not physical. Like *meaning,* it is without body. The scientist is prone to conclude that anything that cannot be measured or observed in some physical manner does not exist. That is his privilege. He may hold to his *opinion.* As an opinion-holder he is, however, no better than the nonscientist. He cannot prove the verity of his opinion! Therefore, it should not be regarded as existing; and, if it does not exist, it can hardly be defended or held to be right! Thus, the scientist should sentence himself to absolute silence to avoid branding his words in this sphere as absurd.

We may say then, as nonscientists, that progress in man can be recognized only as the development of something given— something not created by man but carried out by him. He may use the potentials given him and exploit them just as he uses electricity, nuclear power, or other properties and forces provided by nature. Man does not create the properties and forces of the physical world; he utilizes them when he learns the laws by which they operate.

How, for example, could man move from one manner of using objects supplied by nature to a better method did he not have the power of learning? Yet this power is given. He does not create it. He may indeed not use the power or exploit it to the highest degree, even when he has it, but it is at his beck and call.

The reality of the power to learn is so clear that its existence will hardly be denied, and that it is given is equally clear. The human infant is helpless to a high degree. It awaits growth and development before it becomes capable of performing certain acts. Yet the potential was inborn.

No great difficulty should therefore be encountered in assuming that the human race is capable of development and progress, and that the potentiality making this possible is *given*. It is certainly given in the human offspring!

If this conclusion is accepted, the dark figure of determinism immediately stands before us again. If man simply develops his potentials and if he cannot develop in any direction except as is ordained in the seed, what becomes of his freedom?

His freedom, as has been said here more than once, lies in the alternative routes that he has come to discern in front of him. As has just now been said, some of these alternatives are superior to others. Some, on the other hand, are not only inferior but downright destructive or injurious. These encompass the evil alternatives, although injury and evil are not synonymous.

In the physical world, the alternatives are numerous, and man spends much time learning which are the better ones. His will-forces no less than his ego have much at stake. If man's livelihood depends on his skill and prowess as a hunter, the superiority of one method of hunting over another makes a difference to his welfare. His primary will-forces prod his intelligence with the trident of pain to improve his methods. The will-force has no idea itself about methods. Intelligence, which is in the same field of consciousness, tells itself in response to the will-force that in order to assuage the cry of the will-force it must do better. Scarcity has a hand in the demand.

Probably one of the first results was the use of stones for throwing or sticks for beating, instead of depending on the naked-hand methods. That these acts of intelligence themselves depended for their very execution on the properties of matter and physical laws did not occur to man. He learned from an inner light that enabled him to perceive certain physical possibilities that were already present.

Why would he pick up a stone in the first place? A horse does not pick up stones. It has no physical equipment for doing so. It has no fingers and no opposite thumb. There would be no good sense then in the horse's having an idea about picking up a stone. This act would therefore never occur to it. It would be a totally useless idea.

Man, having an opposable thumb along with fingers that would make it possible to pick up a stone, might at some moment in time come upon an idea of doing just that! Who? When? Where? Why?

We do not know who it was that first picked up a stone. We do not know when it was; nor do we know where it was. Do we know why he did it? We do not; but we may have an opinion because we have the mental equipment that manufactures opinions. We can *believe* that at first the act represented no more than unconscious curiosity, such as may be observed in a young child. An inner "urge" manifested itself. It was perhaps no more conscious to the first man than the act of picking up a toy is to a young child. We grope here in a field of uncertainty.

If man picked up a stone for no reason at all, he perhaps soon dropped it again or pitched it away. When he dropped it, he observed the force of gravity without knowing it, and he would see innumerable things fall to the ground through many centuries before one of his kind would draw the conclusion that some unseen force accounted for the falling. Isaac Newton was the hero.

If our early man pitched the stone away, he possibly noticed that it made a noise as it struck the ground, or that it kicked up dust, or that it bounced or rolled. None of this meant anything to him until he pitched or threw a stone at someone else—without malice, without intent to inflict pain, and without any other intent. If the stone hit the other person, a scream of pain possibly rent the air. Possibly cause and effect were linked closely enough for him to learn that throwing a stone and striking someone with it caused an outcry. An outcry already had a meaning. It meant pain. Therefore stone-throwing and pain began to have a relationship.

Perhaps the man who first picked up a stone carelessly dropped it on his own foot instead of throwing it—if not the first time he dropped it, then possibly on a succeeding occasion. He then learned at first hand that a dropping stone caused a pain if it struck his own foot. How long was it then before he learned that if he dropped the stone on the foot of someone else it would also cause pain to the other person? Perhaps it took a considerable period to learn that the other person also felt a pain, as reflected by his outcry, but not so long a time before the other person reacted in a fashion that conveyed to the stone-dropper the idea that he should cease and desist from further concentration on the particular target. Again, it is not recorded how much time passed before it occurred to the one on whose foot a stone had been dropped by someone else to turn about and pick up a stone and drop it on the foot of the one who had done it to him or on the foot of someone else. It was a rather complicated equation.

Much depended, as it does quite normally, on the brightness or stupidity of the victim and secondly on the relative size and relationship of the two primitives involved in the interplay. If the victim was stupid, he may have suffered a number of bruises before his intelligence responded to the suggestion of his primitive will-force to resist by swatting the aggressor or tossing back the stone. In order for him to conclude that such a response was a good idea, he had to reflect. If the one or the other reaction took place at all, it was at first perhaps more nearly automatic. Animals often do to one another what they do not want others to do to them and get repaid by a reciprocal act that leaves its mark on the aggressor or is "intended" to do so.

As stone-dropping on feet developed into a fine art, variations occurred, possibly for one of two or several reasons. In the nature of things given, there were other ways of doing things (alternatives) different from the original. Therefore one person might go about the same act in a different manner. He was free to do so. There were also other possible targets for stone-pitching or dropping; but variations of the act awaited a brilliance that was not ubiquitous.

Another possibility was that error or poor aim or poor execution brought about a variation. If it was a matter of dropping a stone, it might miss the foot. Lack of skill would thus have manifested itself, and the need for practice might even have been suggested; but, again, to suggest this is to assume a considerable power of reflection in the primitive. One of them may have had such power and used it; while yet another one may have drawn a shrewd inference.

From dropping a stone on another's foot, a really clever denizen of a cave or tree-nest may have employed the law of gravity under a different circumstance. Seeing someone asleep on the ground, he may perhaps have formed a notion to drop a stone on the recumbent one's head! The consequences could have been swift and farther reaching than had been contemplated, again depending on the relation, respective size, and other variations between the *dramatis personae*.

Possibly under a different circumstance, the dawn-man took a stone up a tree with him, as a child takes a toy to bed, and, on a suitable occasion, wondered how it would go if he dropped the stone on the head of someone directly beneath him! Such a notion, of course, assumes again an advanced degree of knowledge or of intuitive capacity. Moving from dropping a stone on someone's foot on the ground to dropping it from a tree implies the drawing of rather complex inferences as well as good aim if a successful denouement was to be expected.

In any event, several useful lessons could thus have been learned. One would have been of the kind that animals learn or, rather, come by instinctively. This one would have said, "Do not walk under a tree without first looking up. Be careful!" Another possible lesson could have come from the same source, depending on who it was that dropped the stone and who got hit by it on the head. This lesson could have been expressed later in words somewhat as follows: "Whatever else you may do, do not drop stones from trees on anyone bigger than you or on anyone else unless he is a known enemy, and then only if the stone is large enough and your marksmanship good enough."

To be sure, these words would not have been used; for at that time there was not yet, we may believe, a language, much less English; but the sense of the lesson would in general terms have been something of this nature.

Now we may guess that it was again some time, such as centuries, before some primitive Phi Beta Kappa made the mental transition from beings to nonhuman objects with his stone-throwing. We assume that he had graduated from the pitching stage and mastered the technique of throwing. This, too, involves a very complicated act of execution that must have occupied man in the meantime for numberless years. This conclusion comes from the reflection that throwing is not instinctively executed and that therefore it was a representation of cooperative muscular and skeletal movement that required thought and guidance.

Special brain activity was needed, such as no horse or dog possessed. Since these have no hands, knowledge of how to use them would be a wasted gift. Yet, even though man had the special brain-capacity he needed for thinking, much of the muscular and skeletal coordination he would use was supplied by innate capability. Man did not, for example, find it necessary to think out each movement, nor even the stance he should take if he were to throw a stone to good effect. He did not have to say to this muscle that it should tense itself, and to that one that it should relax itself; or to another that it should maintain equilibrium and to yet another that it should relax immediately after a forceful arm-thrust had been accomplished. He did not have time to send all these messages to hundreds of muscles involved in the act of coordination. Even if he could have communicated instantaneously, he would not have known what orders to issue to each muscle or group of muscles. Had he tried consciously to do so, he would only have been repaid by a very clumsy and awkward performance.

The thinking he did was directed into the noninstinctive and nonreflexive channels, such as whether he should or should not throw; whether at this instant or after further observation, as a means of determining the best moments how hard and how far he should throw; in what precise direction and, perhaps, what size and shape of stone he should use. Here was scope for free choice after thinking. Being thus occupied, his brain had about all to do that could be expected of it. The throwing act had to be virtually automatic. While it did not represent an instinctive act, the potential was present in an implanted form so that upon a decision made by the mind, a semi-automatic response could be achieved.

Be that as it may, we may conclude that man did learn how to throw stones and that in time he learned further that stone-throwing held some useful and even valuable possibilities. After graduating from the stone-dropping stage and from what was possibly the next stage, which is to say stone-throwing at others of his own kind, he began to draw more inferences. He now had a fund of knowledge about stone-throwing that was at his brain's disposal for a diversity of purposes.

Someone had to draw an inference that indicated that if a stone could hurt a human being, it could also hurt a wolf or a fox. A stone well thrown might help ward off an animal attack by reaching the attacker before he was even ready to spring. This was a great advantage. It lengthened both the time and the distance separating attacker and attacked. The latter's defense was greatly improved. A well-aimed stone of the size of a fist could discourage an attacker from a direct onslaught. Progress at defense was under-way. Thoughts about the antimissile missile are not so novel!

Another inference could be drawn from the arsenal of knowledge drawn from verified experience. Why not use a stone to bring down a rabbit or some other animal that could so easily outrun man that he had difficulty capturing it? The will-force of hunger called for food and at times made peremptory demands upon the organisms to provide it. If one method failed, something else must be tried.

Had hunger not been thus demanding, had it indeed not had a persuader in the form of discomfort and pain, it would not have had a whip or other instrument needed to prod and drive the intelligence. The latter would have been lackadaisical and the organism might have starved. Hunger needed to drive with a veritable imperative if it was to be obeyed considering the dangers, the hardships and the pains endured in providing food. It needed a particular kind of pain—not such as one inflicted by a cut or bruise, which merely stung and throbbed, but a gnawing, insistent style of pain that stirred up the whole system and was armed with an aim dedicated to putting down the imperious demand by satisfying it—thus expressing the function of a primary will-force.

Very well, the force of hunger, which is to say, a primary

will-force, prodded the intelligence to do something for the organism that it guided. Unfortunately if the individual intelligence was ordinary, no new method would have been divined and devised. A thousand possibilities of doing better than had been done up to now lie all about man, but his routine intelligence does not discern them; but if the will-force does not relent, one day a more gifted confrere will see what even he himself had not hitherto seen, and a new discovery is made.

So it no doubt came to pass that some primitive discoverer in a flash saw that a stone could outfly the pace of even a rabbit; or better yet, the stone could be thrown some distance ahead of a rabbit. With the proper lead it would strike the running creature broadside and bowl it over, stunning or even killing it.

Such an extraordinary calculation called for rare insight indeed. The execution was something different. Once accomplished and more or less perfected, the method could be repeated and then adopted as a useful means of increasing the food supply. The new method, again, represented progress, this time in the material field of subsistence. Man had employed a physical object that was not a part of his own body to accomplish a mission that resulted in assuaging the imperious demand of his stomach.

He had the necessary equipment of limb and members, arm, hand and fingers; he had the intelligence; and he had the inner need that called for satisfaction. The need supplied the motivation or demand for cooperation of the intelligence and the physical equipment. The combination brought down the rabbit that otherwise was so highly elusive.

Characteristically this step in progress did not solve the food problem. Rabbits became wilder; people, more numerous; not every throw brought down a rabbit—far from it; but the discovery marked an improvement. "How," asked an ancestor of us all, "did we get along before the great Alec Stonehurler discovered the modern way of bagging rabbits?"

Stone-throwing was only one of the bright discoveries of early man; nor was it necessarily the first useful discovery. The use of sticks was no doubt a close competitor of stone-hurling as one of man's first maximations of his physical powers. Grasping a stick came naturally to a hand that *mirabile dictu* was shaped

and fitted admirably to this very act. To think of man as not
picking up sticks when they were within reach would be to see
him in a state or stance not natural to him. Man no doubt picked
up sticks long before he had any idea what use to make of them.
At the outset he perhaps did no more than to poke the ground
with them. He stirred up a little dust or scattered pebbles with
the end of the stick. In executing such aimless acts he possibly
stumbled on an idea or two awakened by what he had observed,
much as he learned something about the behavior and property
of stones through idle play and manipulation.

A stick obviously extended the reach of the arm. To observe
this as a useful fact, again, required the power of reflection and
reason or the power to draw inferences. If the stick could reach
the ground, it could also reach outward and upward. If something desirable, such as a fruit, nut, or berry, was a foot or two
out of reach, the stick might act as an extension of the arm and
bring the tidbit within reach. It has been recorded that even
chimpanzees have been observed employing a handy stick to reach
a desirable morsel and manipulating the stick with sufficient intelligence to bring the item of food within reach of the natural arm.

From using a stick as a rake, its employment as a means of
beating a lazy person, an adversary, an intruder or attacker was
no great distance away. Who knows? The stick may have been
used in that fashion before it was employed as a rake.

Be it stick or stone, man's physical equipment, which was
suitable for the manipulation and use of these common objects,
was accompanied by an inclination to exercise these physical resources. The impulsion to use was the natural outcome of the
suitability of the instrument (arm and hand) to the manipulation
of the outer object (stone or stick) to an end perceived as useful
toward the satisfaction of a biological desire. Man unknowingly
was fitted with arms that ended in prehensile digits, suitable for
grasping, picking up, and holding. Lo and behold, there were
sticks and stones within reach. Did the presence of sticks and
stones generate the limbs that could use them? Also, man had
needs that could be served by putting hand to stick or stone. With

the assistance of intelligence or the ability to learn, he put two and two together and was on the road of progress.

From stick to spear and from stone to hammer and axe may seem but a short step. Yet it can easily be imagined that the distance was much greater than might be fancied; for to use a stick as a spear, for example, needed more knowledge than was required for merely teasing a fruit from its twig or beating an incalcitrant adolescent to make him behave tolerably.

Also, the use of a stone as a hammer or an axe represented a distinct step forward. The manipulation of the stone in this fashion made it possible to do much that bare hands were unable to accomplish. With a stone a man could crush hard nuts and seeds, and break shells, and bring these edible gifts of the outer world into the service of man's needs. The battle against nature's parsimony to make it yield what it held so tightly to its bosom, by using other objects of outer nature, got underway. Man's range of goods suitable to his needs was widened.

The humanist exclaims exultingly: "He did it, the clever fellow!" and so he did. Let him have some credit; but let us not extend too much credit! Inflation of man's self-esteem is no better than monetary inflation. If we reflect, we quickly see that man used what was given, provided for his use if he had the wit to take advantage of the bounty, and the energy and endeavor to convert it to his needs.

Oddly enough, the properties of matter that he encountered were miraculously adaptable to certain uses; as were certain behaviors detectable in things man could use. In fact he could use them precisely because he detected these manners of behavior. Some things fell to the ground under easily seen conditions; some bounced, some rolled, some plopped. Some things were sharp, and could cut or pierce if they also had the hardness. A stick could be swung or used this way or that. It had length and strength. It could be used to pry loose a rock.

Nature was really a wonderland of possibilities. Man no doubt learned much about it before he so much as knew that he had learned anything. The commonalty of man was not self-conscious. Again, when it was, or where, or in whom the stir occurred is not known, but at some time self-consciousness lit a lamp, as in a young child today, that shone mysteriously in the dark and carried light inwardly as well as outwardly. Man could begin to communicate his experience only because he could remember his experience and was able to reconstitute it later after a fashion.

It goes without saying that communication was essential to progress. Not all of the members of a group would experience the same encounters, and some of these were dangerous. Some of our lowbrowed forerunners were no doubt clawed and torn or crushed and eaten by marauding carnivores; others escaped, either whole or damaged. If those who got away could not communicate their experience to others of their menage, these would have been fated to repeat the error, and to use unimproved methods of attack and defense. Progress would have sunk in its tracks.

How language could have come about where there was none must remain a mystery. We can only guess that as it comes forth in youngsters in modern man in a remarkably short time where it did not exist at the outset, it could have come forth initially for the same reason: the potential was given and the need for its exercise was present in many demanding circumstances—circumstances that would draw forth any supporting potential that might also be present.

The sound-forming capacity was present in man, and it sat there awaiting development by outer encounters that would embody a need for using the sound potential: a danger, a need for warning, a need for help, a demand that something be done or not be done or the like.

Without the potential no response could be made. With a potential but no need for its use, it would have remained dormant and in time might have disappeared. With a combination of a potential and a need for its development, the way was open to what may be called progress, whether for good or evil, with or without moral implications.

This equation is not a fulfillment of the conditions of determinism, which denies any scope for "free will"; but it does deprive man of some of his presumption and self-congratulation. It dethrones him as a creator and establishes him as an explorer, inventor, or discoverer. He becomes an inquirer, a pursuer; he is an analyzer, rearranger, and synthetist. He may not only use but also contemplate, savor, and compare. His field opens to meditation, enjoyment, and aversion. He may applaud and accept, criticise and reject, but he can do no more than inspire awe in his fellow man through his originality and genius. His "creations" must always be secondhand.

As man learned from experience, because he was able to learn from experience, and was minded to exert himself in response to his needs, by going outside of himself for extension of his powers, he expanded his dominion over the lower animals and outer nature.

While he did not know it, through tools and implements, the greater scope of his dominion over the external world gave rise to more internal problems than he had theretofore known and problems of relations with his own kind. Inner problems were relatively simple the nearer he was to his animal ancestry. He had much less to think about. It was a question of garnering enough food for his stomach, providing shelter against the inclemency of weather, mating, and guiding his offspring in the same simple routines. His human relations were guided by relative size, ability, native intelligence, strength, and similar natural differences. Obedience was not taught formally; it was imposed by the seniors.

After the use of primitive tools was discovered or invented, his powers over nature brought him greater bounty. Who was entitled to what beyond the bare necessities became a question of some importance and concern. The concept of merit raised its troublesome head. Disputes never before thought of arose over questions of entitlement; but these disputes caused difficulty only if two or more claimants of equal strength or nearly equal strength confronted each other. Otherwise the victory went without much ado to the strongest and most aggressive. If strength, wit, and agility were more nearly equal, disputes could hardly be avoided. The will-forces in the opposing claimants had no idea of compromise or submission to an impartial referee.

Each wanted what it had in hand, and there was little or no disposition to share except with mothers in the stage of childbearing helplessness and young offspring. The weakness of these was recognized even as in some animal species, and the claim to protection was recognized as by instinct. As between two equal claimants, the conflict in other fields was not easily evaded until, as noted previously, external authority was instituted. Even then, we may be sure, relationships were not noted for their unbroken harmony.

As the range of choice increased in questions of relation of tools and weapons, the play of intelligence also gained wider scope. The raw ego then had occasion to assert itself more frequently. Opportunity for diversity of opinion and therefore of disagreement also became more frequent. The effects of differences in range of intelligence came into greater prominence. The usages of authority as a means of subduing dissidents became more exacting and more rigid. Dissension, though more frequent, became a luxury that could be tolerated less and less because of greater dangers from external attack. With the stirrings of more ego impulses, the more uneasy became the crown of authority.

As the will-forces and the scope of the ego expanded, the prerogatives and emoluments of authority waxed somewhat in proportion, and this development opened the sluices of envy. Hatred found new dimensions. Greater knowledge, abetted by intelligence, opened the way to intrigue and conspiracy. Will-forces and active egos groped for and found alliances against obstruction. Disagreement broke more easily into savage controversies and tests of wit and strength. Man was launched on a course undreamed of by the lower animals that were destined or doomed to continue their simple conflicts of claw, stealth, deception, and fang. Man had risen to a higher estate of animadversion! He had come to know so much more about self-defense and conquest! He established himself as the lord of creation! In so doing, however, he found a new enemy—one that was so much more resourceful than the animals he had left behind, namely, as already observed, his own kind!

Nevertheless, at some point in his unique progress, he had come to a state of consciousness of his superiority over the lesser animal world, and as evidence of his advancement he measured his distance above the nether creatures. From his advanced state, he could accuse members of his own tribe as being "brutal" or "bestial"; as still much later he could hurl epithets of "savagery" against those who stood in his way athwart the path of "progress."

The sublimity of self-righteousness was essentially a function of his almost universal ego-blindness—a characteristic that he has been helpless to shed from his illustrious shoulders even to this day.

Thus, man appears to be both a victim and a beneficiary of progress. His progress has been universally accompanied by a pride or haughtiness that scatters scorn or contempt on those who continue to struggle on the lower slopes, whether these be of his own tribe or race or of an alien human aggregate. The quality of the scorn is not visibly diluted even if the object of it is his brother tribesman or cousin.

A combination of primary will-forces and egoistic aspirations and pretensions, laboring under the ruling principle of scarcity of need-satisfying means, begot a species of rivalry that shattered the claims of brotherhood. The claim to unity and cooperation had occasion to assert itself because of the obvious advantages discovered in teamwork by the primitive intelligence. If a hunter felled a bear he needed help to transport it. If a stone weighing more than one man could move lay in a path that had no detours, the cooperation of several hands could achieve what no grunts of exertion emitted by one man at top effort could accomplish. Primitive cooperation, therefore, was itself an aid to progress, and it was so accepted by men's early light.

Rivalry was not specifically the opposite of cooperation in benefits since it often led to great exertion by groups in competition with each other; but it could and did dissipate the fruits of cooperation on many occasions and substituted disruptive dissension.

Inside a group, two subgroups, each led by someone whose ego was expansive, might pull against each other rather than cooperating toward the same end. Thus the greater interest of the comprehensive group might be sacrificed. Each ego would summon to its support such intelligence as its own host possessed plus that of his supporters, and a contest of shattering proportions might break out.

Man on his early way, as conscious reflection opened greater vistas of the world to him, soon encountered the problem of disobedience. No other problem was destined to burden him with more disconcerting puzzles and to open more bitter recriminations than this phenomenon.

Once the raw ego of this or that low-brow, assisted by an intelligence of dim lantern-power, began to feel an inner ferment for recognition, the passive role of obedience lost its attraction. The ferment stirred amorphous ambitions, prodding the unknown but human unit to come out of the shadows of total anonymity. Intelligence intimated possibilities. It whispered of opportunity. It observed means and methods, and saw that meanings could be conveyed in glances or concealed and yet communicated by lowered eyelids. It perceived the possibility of silent conspiracy as a means of gaining advantages and calling attention to self.

Obedience, however, was an obstacle to self-advancement, or so it appeared. Obedience had little to offer the ferment of the ego. It pointed only to the homage that must be done to the one who stood first in the community.

Intelligence, of course, saw the advantage of the principle of obedience to the one who stood first. However, invocation of the principle of obedience produced the dichotomy that has stood as a mystery ever since: the use of obedience as a principle of unity and of necessary coherence and order, on the one hand, and its use as a means of quelling dissenting opinion and suppressing uncomfortable suggestions of change, on the other.

Those whose interests, comforts, welfare, and happiness coincided in greater part with the ascendant position of the one who was Number 1, upheld the principle of obedience, and they could point to the disruption and chaos that so often rode with disobedience. Obedience, they could stoutly maintain, was the cornerstone of stability. If everyone who had an opinion contrary to the accepted methods were privileged to disobey the rules and principles upon which they stood, anarchy would be enthroned; and it would last until another ruling power, possibly much worse than the current one, were established. Then a new order of obedience would be instituted, and it might have no tolerance at all for opposed opinion.

On the other hand, those who were not so comfortable under the power of the existing Number 1 or who, enjoying a very moderate degree of it but not knowing to whom they owed it, were fair game for the words or signs of another whose ego persistently prodded him to seek ouster of the old Number 1 and substitution of himself in his place. This aspirant's ego, served by his intelligence, sought the glow of inner exultation and the warmth of adulation on his cheeks that being Number 1, as he fancied it, would bring him.

Looking about, and groping for weakness in the high adversary, this intelligence discerned the Achilles heel. Number 1, it perceived, had put obedience on a high pedestal because by invoking it as something sacred, his position could be held against challenge. What a fraud!

"Follow me and I will oust this mountebank; and you will share in the glory. He has preyed long enough on your docile obedience! Be men! Stand up! In me you will have a true friend! Follow me!"

Man has been puzzled ever after by the enigma of obedience versus disobedience. Each side has its spokesmen, each its defenders and each its detractors. In the end, having reached power, if success crowns such effort, the newly enthroned Number 1 will soon in turn preach the virtues of obedience; for the ego will have achieved its end and will now wish to bask long in the glory it had sought and achieved.

The human irony of it: the detractors and disrupters of obedience finding it sacred so soon after becoming dependent on it for their own perpetuation and so soon enforcing it upon their own followers with an iron hand should they seek to take the road of disagreement!

Some of these followers soon enough will have cried loud and long in disillusionment: "Was it for this we followed him? Arm-in-arm we went against the chains of obedience. Disobedience was our fire—it inflamed ardor and lifted our hopes—now, now, what do we find? *Obedience* has become sacred under our new leader, and disobedience is now as bad as the old Number 1 had always said that it was in his hateful, growling way. What then have we gained? We have substituted one tyrant for another!"

Seldom, of course, is reasoning so clear and so soon unified in a larger society as the foregoing suggests. So long as a new regime, a lustrous new Number 1, succeeds in filling the needs of the primary will-forces of the populace, he will find few enemies. Even if another surging ego, such as his own, should arise, driven by ambition to displace him, the new aspirant would find little combustible tinder responsive to his torch. Satisfied will-forces offer poor kindling for external ambition to inflame. Rather, they offer the torch-bearer a damp mass, a spongy asbestos that takes no fire.

Obedience is, of course, of two sorts. One is voluntary; the other, enforced. Because voluntary obedience of wishes and orders is the most trustworthy, it is sought after; but when it cannot be won, different degrees of compulsion may be adopted.

It goes without saying that without obedience, human government would be impossible. Even voluntary obedience will be chosen as superior to disobedience by those who wield authority; for much force that could be directed toward more fruitful economic ends is dissipated by diversion of energies to the imposition of obedience and the suppression of freedom of expression. The latter becomes anathema to the primate because of the diversity of opinion it would promote and the disagreement it would trumpet to the world.

A difference should be drawn between mere free expression of opinion, which the primary will-forces and the raw ego of the ruler instinctively distrust, on the one hand, and the actual mounting of a rebellion or insurrection, on the other. It is fear of the transformation of the former into the latter that underlies the distrust of freedom of dissent and criticism, and history lends support to the fear. In nearly all regimes, be it a tribal authority or a broader and more advanced center of power, there is sufficient potential discontentment at almost any time to form a force of respectable magnitude should a leader organize it and lead it in opposition to the suspected source of dissatisfaction, which is to say, the current ruler.

When will-forces are not satisfied, the source of discontent nevertheless is not always known; the failure to provide satisfaction is not always imputed to a particular source; but either a true objector or a simulator harboring ulterior motives would be in a position to precipitate and shape an accusatory attitude by pointing to a supposed villain. It would matter little to the holder of power whether the accusations were justified so long as they are believed. Therefore freedom of expression should be suppressed!

To prevent the precipitation, many measures of precaution might be instituted. This action would be prompted by the primary will-forces and the ego operating in the holder of power and also in those whose interests are intertwined with his, either by contrivance or naturally. A defensive and offensive alliance in these circumstances forms as readily as clouds in the sky on a warm humid day.

Is obedience then good and disobedience evil? Or is disobedience good and obedience evil? Does the answer depend on the circumstance of who is in power?

Since inculcation of obedience through superstition and ignorance may be the weapon of tyranny, it might be concluded that obedience is indeed an evil or that it lends itself to manipulation by evil powers.

On the other hand, disobedience may also be employed by evil men of ambition as a means of stirring rebellion and wresting power from the existing regime be it ever so faultless.

Yet again, obedience is indeed essential to tranquility and peaceful advancement. When it serves that purpose, no higher end could be served by inducing rebellion, and disobedience then is not a mark of virtue but rather of folly, envy, and tragedy.

Finally, obedience serves no good end when it suffers an oppressive regime to maintain its power. Contrived docility may be suspected of ulterior manipulation by the intelligence of a ruling group exercised in behalf of self-perpetuation. It becomes nothing better than acquiesence in a status quo that would consent to no change lest its comfort be disturbed.

The enigma that has claimed numberless victims revolves about the question of who is right. Obedience to a just, sensitive, and progressive ruler represents a wise course, no less so than does disobedience of a tyrant. By inversion, disobedience of a wise and benevolent governor represents folly, as also does pursuit of a false leader in search of the prerogatives of power.

The equation is thus seen to revolve about what is desired as essential to good or evil.

In the absence of a final referee, the answer can never rise above the level of opinion. That being the case, the opinion that achieves the most powerful support will triumph. Good and evil are then relative desiderata.

If, however, a superhuman referee is invoked, the authority vested in him will demand obedience without question. If the referee is thought to be the fount of eternal and final wisdom, no other course would be open. Complete obedience would not only be justified but sanctified.

Difficulty would still be experienced in relating new circumstances to old rules. As man made his way, numerous new and unfamiliar circumstances loomed before him as original minds made new discoveries. If the omniscient referee was not present in person at such times, questions arose about the proper course to be followed. As human intelligence had long demonstrated its fallibility, a variety of disagreements naturally divided judgments, guided in high degree by the importunities of the several diverse will-force and ego interests. These could not be exorcised or evaded because of their intimate relation to thought, amounting virtually to parenthood. But for this diversity of the will-force and ego interests, difference of opinion would have begotten no heat and raised no pulse beat. Yet nothing is more familiar than the vehemence attending arguments over belief.

Therefore there would still be occasion for disputations even if a superhuman referee were invoked as the final arbiter. Indeed, the ego would see to this. In the absence of certainty about the truth, opinion must act as a substitute. *Whose* opinion should then be uppermost? Great thinkers might happily agree; but they might also disagree. In the happy circumstance of agreement, followers would have little to worry them. In the absence of agreement, the followers must choose sides. Neither of the dissidents would be inclined to bow and say "My opponent is so right! I defer to him!"

Should one of them do so, that might be the end of it. He would perhaps be willing to sacrifice his ego, to efface himself; but an able and forward follower might not elect to be so accommodating. His own ego might not tend toward pliancy; in fact, it might elect to seize the opportunity to be the group leader in place of the one who had bowed. His ego might urge him not to let so happy an opportunity slip by. "What better turn could have been hoped for?" it would ask its host. Through the intelligence serving it, it would observe that such an opportunity comes only once in a lifetime. How stupid then to let it slip by! To be presented such an unexpected bonanza might indeed be evidence of providential interference! Perhaps the occasion called for humility! To be thus tapped could be significant of great things, and it behooves one to be humble under such awesome circumstances!

Leave it to the ego! It soon builds castles and monuments for itself. After an excursion of the fancy, it finds the plodding and obedient world drab and unexciting. If obeying is a virtue, as it may well be, the ego in these circumstances soon asks, "Why should I not be the sublime recipient of a call to exercise its stern devotion?"

Disagreement with eminent authority may thus be the very circumstance that an expansive ego has awaited. The alternative— that of agreeing and obeying—as the other group leader had agreed, was the way to oblivion. No true ego seeks such a relinquishment of self-expression!

Napoleon is reputed to have waived aside a suggestion that he halt his conquests at a point that would have left his name to history as a great conqueror. He was not satisfied. In a thousand years, he is reputed to have reflected, he would claim only one page in a universal history! His ego craved more than one page! It hungered for more than so paltry a mark of awe and respect! It wanted not one page but tens of pages, perhaps hundreds of them!

Of course, not all egos suffer from megalomania, and those that do are not always served by an intelligence of sufficient wattage to light the winding way.

If, in the instance here described, no such ego had interposed itself to give a negative answer, self-abnegation by the one who bowed might have opened the way to peaceful acceptance of the superhuman referee. Yet history would show that self-abnegation while not lacking among men, nevertheless may accomplish no more than stepping aside to make way for one who is not sacrificially minded and whose ego has little but contempt for the self-effacer. This very reflection, namely, "If I do not step in, someone else will—and I have a good idea who it would be," may be offered by intelligence as an act of rationalization and justification. Such a thought, moreover, may be expected to open the door to a burning draft of envy that might quickly foreclose any hope of sidestepping.

Richard III, according to the Shakespearean version, was possessed of an ego that brooked no interference. Not only envy but a wounded ego begging for compensation drove him to high crime and despicable chicanery.

Again, not every crisis precipitated by disagreement at the head table has a Richard III as one of the participants. Obedience means subordination of the will-forces and the ego to the perceived interest of the organized group or to a principle. An act of unselfishness may then be hailed as a noble retreat. The egos of the onlookers and participants in interest recognize the temptation that was resisted and may wonder whether they themselves could have acquitted themselves so creditably.

Reflection by intelligence on the possibility that a retreat might be so interpreted might indeed help the ego reach a decision to be unselfish—thus demonstrating its awesome capacity at duplicity. "Be unselfish while everyone has eyes on your behavior. There may be great credit in stepping aside!" Such an unworthy thought, while truly unworthy, is nevertheless never far away, even if it is not welcome and is regarded as vitiating goodwill.

That man has recognized the need of a final arbiter as a means of getting on with the process of living and pursuit of legitimate goals is supported by much evidence. Recognition came, no doubt, from observation of the consequences of unsettled disputes. When the dissidents were of equal stature, neither one could impose his preference on the other. The strife or cold war that ensued interfered with the peaceful processes of living, and many onlookers and many who were discomfited or damaged by chronic discord became disenchanted with the issues and felt themselves victimized by the stubborn prolongation of the quarrel.

In the judicial world, courts of last resort were created, and the force of law was committed to the execution of their decisions. Even in the world of religion, final referees were recognized as a means of bringing bitter disputes to an end. The interests of the many in the peaceful process of living came to outweigh the interest of the few.

Needless to say, when many became implicated in a dispute because their interests were rooted in the one side or the other, the discord was without restraint, and only force could be invoked as the arbiter; and this was civil war or, what is called more grandiloquently, internecine warfare.

Obviously, if the community's greater interest in the peaceful pursuit of life's affairs was to prevail, a greater force must be contrived—a force great enough to subjugate any lesser group of dissidents. This was government.

In a sense it was a compact, if not a specific social contract, that reflected the common interests of the will-forces and the ego in going about their concerns without disturbance or disruption by private disputes of others in which they themselves were not implicated.

Why should you or I or both of us and many others similarly situated be deprived of water, bread, or meat because access is blocked by private disputants who bar the way? Let them put down their disputes or we must find means of doing it for them. Within us our will-forces clamor for satisfaction, while our egos ask, "Who are they that presume to deprive us of our 'rights' of access?"

Clearly, we are activated, as man has always been activated, by the inner forces that call for satisfaction. Without them he would not know what to wish or desire. He is given his tentative orders by them.

As already observed, these wishes cannot all be gratified because of the scarcity of the means of satisfaction and because too many of us seek the same thing even as we may differ acutely on details. We cannot possibly be in the same place as anyone else, nor can we possess and consume the identical thing of another's enjoyment.

Moreover, because of error, lack of penetrating insight or

want of information, the goals sought by the will-forces and the ego will not necessarily be the best. Even given good will, disagreements will occur about what is better or best.

The need for a final referee can hardly be avoided if an orderly society is to prevail. In a small society, he may be a chieftain who has gathered the elements of power into his hands. He metes out decisions according to his own light; but as his lights also reflect his own interests, his decisions do not always represent justice. They may be tainted by injection of selfish considerations, such as the desire to maintain his position and to that end of discrediting those who might aspire one day to fill his shoes.

It is precisely because man is subject to error and enjoys but few certainties in proportion to his uncertainties; it is also because the elements of nature that are needed for man's sustenance, shelter, and progress are scarce, and beyond being scarce are subject to wear, breakage, and disrepair, thus aggravating the initial scarcity; wherefore for this reason man must exert himself to the end of gaining satisfaction of his will-forces, he encounters rivalry, opposition, deceit, and trespass; further, because of limited intelligence and doubts, he must often be satisfied with mere opinion; and since opinion often attracts disagreement, overt conflict becomes inevitable if the will-forces and ego are stubborn, as they are by nature. This then is to say that conflict is unavoidable among human beings who are wholly ruled by primary will-forces and impulses of the raw ego. Force, assisted by intelligence, deception, and vigor, will win the day. Justice will have no hand in shaping the outcome.

Such a world, it seems, was the world of Nietzsche, who looked upon sympathy and kindness as weakness and decadence. To him strength and the ruthless exercise of power were the supreme good. His world, it becomes clear, was that of the primary will-forces and the raw ego. He called this philosophy one of "yea-saying" to life.

While Freud did not subscribe to the Nietzschean philosophy, the consequence of his psychology also betrayed a strong bias toward the expression of the primitive will-forces and the raw ego and an aversion to restraint or discipline.

Yet it must be clear that no civilized society could possibly

endure without discipline, without learning the value of obedience and without establishing the office of final referee. So great
and numerous are the potentials of conflict that self-abnegation
and deference to principles become indispensable to an orderly
society.

Mankind itself could not have survived had the raw ego and
the primitive will-forces not been accompanied by a saving grace
that tempered these raw impulses and appetites. Intelligence,
which is neutral, was as much at the service of the moderating
influences as it was available to raw impulses. But for this neu-
trality and equal service, moderation would have died aborning.

Once more, reflection and the power to learn from experience
helped in the processes of restraint. Even a dim intelligence would
sooner or later reach the conclusion that there are others in the
world beside oneself; also that these others could not be treated
according to one's selfish inclinations without begetting what
might in some instances be unhappy consequences for oneself.
Therefore, the idea of self-restraint, when it occurred, could on
occasion find acceptance.

Such supposed initial restraints were themselves selfish and
were not exercised, we may believe, for the sake of the other person. Such consideration could come only with the development of
the secondary will-forces and the education of the ego.

The secondary will-forces represented a potential bestowed
on man when he was separated from the remainder of the animal
kingdom as a very unique species, *Homo sapiens*. These forces
will receive more attention later.

Man, endowed as he is with a great variety of characteristics,
capacities, and inclinations, is also an imitator. The early learning
process, noticeable even in the animal world, leans heavily on
imitation; and so with the human young. Nor does imitation
cease with adolescence. It follows into adulthood and is everywhere apparent.

One hirsute, low-browed stone-thrower having restrained his
arm when it was about to pelt a neighbor, as a result of a reflection
that the act might bring retaliation upon himself, may have been
noticed by the intended victim of the aggression and by others.

The more pleasant consequence of not throwing the stone

may also have been recorded on the dim consciousness of the observers, including the intended but spared victim. Those who would merely have been upset or perturbed by the outbreak were perhaps thankful that it did not occur.

Later, similarly tempted, the observers of the act of restraint and its agreeable consequence may have been moved to imitate the example. No doubt this was not an easy endeavor, and it may have failed, not only once, but time after time. A raw will-force is not so easily curbed that it readily obeys a notion to imitate someone.

Slow as the process must have been, the advent of the secondary will-forces no doubt had their beginning in some such fashion; for always, according to the finite human mind, there must be a beginning.

Imitation is not always conscious and indeed may be regarded as instinctive. Its role in spreading the good or evil innovations of original genius can hardly be exaggerated, but we must credit the original with the pioneering act. The first restrainer of impulse then deserves the credit if he was observed; or if he persisted in his practice after the first instance so that he may have been observed later if not in the first instance.

We are now back again to the given! The idea of the restraint here depicted arose within the early primitive specimen of man much as an original seed has to be generated. The idea occurred to him. The seed either prospered or died. Many seeds die; some proliferate.

An idea, especially a novel idea, has peculiar characteristics. It seeks expression. It yearns to be tried. It fires the imagination and begets dreams. It does not readily settle down to sit quietly in a corner to be ignored and discarded. Curiosity seizes it by the hand and dances circles with it. A ferment, a restlessness and eagerness to do something fill the inner awareness and goad the hapless originator of the idea to action.

Any idea of self-abnegation, if finally executed, represented the expression of a secondary will-force. It was more than mere inaction. It was a holding back, and no primary will-force voluntarily halts itself. Its function is to carry out its purpose, and it can be arrested or frustrated only by external force or circumstance or show of force or by an internal countervailing force.

But for the development of these internal restraining forces, man's total conduct would have been ordered by his primary impulses and appetites with no possible interposition of internal opposition, except such as would occur when one primary will-force, such as fear, stood in the way of another, and thus inhibited its satisfaction.

If primary will-forces, however, depended on other primary will-forces alone for restraint or moderation, total restraint and moderation would be quite limited. Fear, for example, is not always present.

It is the function of the secondary will-forces and the cultured, educated, or civilized ego to raise other considerations than those provided by countervailing primary and raw impulses as restraining influences.

We will now turn to a consideration of these forces.

4.

The Secondary
Will-forces

BEYOND ACTING AS RESTRAINING INFLUENCES on behavior, the secondary levels of the will-forces and the ego also have functions in the field of aspirations and endeavor. On occasion these may moderate the primary impulses. They provide the element of will or impulsion in spheres where the primary forces would be wholly at a loss.

What, for example would the primary will-force of hunger do with the concept of justice? The two do not go hand in hand. Justice lies beyond the province of the primary will-force. The same is true of other considerations that may exert a strong influence on conduct or endeavor.

The various moral virtues supply an array of considerations that bear heavily on conduct. Again, these considerations are not confined to the negative or restraining influences. To be kind or considerate calls for positive action, not merely restraint. To be honest is also a positive consideration. Honesty may require more than merely avoiding fraud or deception. It may require positive identification of facts that are not merely not deceptive but useful for avoidance of concealment. Therefore honesty may require more than mere silence. It may call for uncovering of facts that if left concealed would mislead.

Clearly, when man was endowed with potential powers that were capable of leading him far beyond the cave, out into the open, onto the plains and plateaus, he needed something more than primary impulses and appetites. To regard primitive man as a noble being whose state should beget a nostalgia in his civilized successor, as Rousseau was inclined to do, is no more than a romantic flight into unreality. Primitive man needed long years of experience with the nascent secondary will-forces and the refinements of the ego before he could achieve a mode of life in which high sensibilities could find themselves at home rather than being ridiculed and rejected by the primitives as unworthy of masculinity.

The struggle against scarcity, the slowness of the struggle and the price exacted, retarded the growth and refinement of sensibilities. Gentility is not the companion of the spear; nor does a gnawing stomach hunger look with patience on politeness and the amenities of deference and protocol. Rude surroundings, destitute of comfort and the accoutrements of relaxation, do not promote refined thoughts or their expression in measured and modulated terms.

Scarcity was a jealous master. It demanded full-time devotion to the pursuits that were indispensable for the provision of food.

Yet, progress was made. How was this possible? How was it possible in the nature of things to "get ahead," to become considerate and genteel, when the most pressing problem was the one of staying alive? How could time be found for any other pursuit—for play, for recreation, for mere politeness and culture?

Evidently man had in him a ferment of dissatisfaction. Also, as he learned, his desire for more knowledge grew even more rapidly than his means of reaching more of it. Yet he was not merely trying hopelessly to catch and possess the rainbow; for this rainbow was potentially within reach.

As he achieved satisfaction of one range of desire of the primary level, he sensed how much more gratification lay untouched beyond his present means of reaching it. Recognition of the unrealized possibility provided him grounds for greater effort.

Greater physical effort would be helpful, but he needed more. *He needed the help of thought.* He needed to examine how he was doing the acts that brought him the means of subsisting. If he was not satisfied with his present lot and the meagerness of his satisfactions, he must devise better methods. If he had his eyes open, he might make an unexpected discovery or two, as already described. Had he not learned about stone-throwing or use of sticks, he would have been condemned to remain in the same state forever, even as the oyster or the hermit crab. His status would have been frozen.

In order to discover something new and helpful, he must have had the capacity of recognizing the character of the new, or its usefulness would have been lost. He also needed memory so that on the morrow he would still know what he had discovered yesterday. To summarize further, he also had need of capacity to let others know what he had learned or the discovery would have died with him, and his originality would have been of no avail. Yet, further, his fellow primitives must have powers of comprehension or his lesson would, again, be lost.

Oddly enough man had these various capacities in varying degrees—at least to the degree necessary to move forward, however slowly—or he would not have moved out of the cave or the jungle.

There was that in outer nature that responded to man's intelligence. He had but to make discoveries and use them. It was as if nature beckoned to him, saying, "Look me over, explore me; probe me in many directions. You may be surprised what I can offer you; but you must not relent, for I am not a pamperer. My riches are sometimes deeply hidden, my wonders outwardly invisible; but they are there for the finding."

Man could learn from trial and error, from observation and other acts of inquiry, and he was encouraged or prodded, first, perhaps, by curiosity and then by the usefulness of what he learned to do or to use.

To gain time in struggle against scarcity for probing and exploring was one of the problems. Without time to devote to observation and study, little could be learned, and without learning no progress could be made. This was the problem of research. However, there was a loophole. The tight circle might perhaps be now and then broken by the gratuitous nature of some discoveries. They might break on the mind in the very process of routine effort, without conscious reflection. If the meaning were grasped, a new and better method might soon replace the time-honored routine. Progress with the new method would release a little time for further probing or for engaging in other pursuits.

The further probing might, of course, be fruitless. The one discovery might have exhausted the stock of originality of the particular discoverer. In time, possibly a hundred years, another discovery might be made in the same department or in another field. The struggle with scarcity might then gain another advantage. More food or better shelter might now be provided than before, or the same amount with less time and effort. More time would then be gained for yet other pursuits if anyone could think of something else to do.

Carrying small things in quantity in the hands was always an awkward method because of the law of gravity. Things slipped off the hands and fell to the ground, especially if one tried to save extra trips by loading on as many things as possible for each trip. This slippage was disconcerting and annoying. Yet the temptation to overload was nearly overbearing, and one succumbed to it, always hoping that a careful act of balancing would avoid the avalanche, which it seldom did; for saving of a few extra trips was always worth the risk.

One day an idler observed a bird's nest. It held several eggs, and the eggs did not roll over the sides and fall. What a phenomenon! How clever! Why had this not been observed before? Birds' nests had been around for thousands of years, but no one had observed one with the same inner disposition as our discoverer. He had a need or at least he was aware of a nuisance or an annoyance that he would have been happy to eliminate. He could use a container that would keep the small things from falling to the ground when he wished to carry many of them so that he could save a few trips.

Here it was: a basket! How miraculous! How wonderful— and how ingenious to see the possibility in the bird's nest! Here was both a time-saver and a means of gathering more of the little things than ever before.

The need was there; the means of meeting it was there, provided by nature. Lacking was the thought that brought the two together; and this was provided now by the rare observer who saw as a seer and not as ordinary man.

The question now was how to contrive something like the bird's nest, but bigger and stronger. Our discoverer did not have much time to go around finding the means of reproducing the nest. He studied the mode of its construction, the materials used, and how they were held together. He tried to find suitable materials, such as the bird used, but the quest was not quickly rewarded. His hands, moreover, were clumsy. He could not make the materials stick together. They too easily fell apart. Perhaps he became discouraged and dropped the project and forgot about it. Then it might be a very long time before someone else made the same discovery. On the other hand, he might have laid the idea aside for some years and then returned to his interest when his annoyance over his small carrying capacity prodded him once more to make further effort.

Perhaps he then rededicated himself to his project. His earlier effort had made his fingers a little more adept at manipulation. This was noticeable and it gave him a hopeful impetus. He felt the thrill of skill and mastery. This feeling held him longer to his effort. He looked more intently at the construction of the nest. He learned that not all nests were constructed in the same fashion. His interest in nests had grown, and he examined a variety of them. A fascination grew within him. It helped him to persevere, to keep on trying. Today he saw what he had not noticed yesterday. He became aware of a certain lacing effect in the construction of the nest and sought to imitate it in putting materials together. Hitherto he had merely pressed them together and they did not stick suitably.

He had patience but was not aware of it. He was merely following his inclination, driven by his fascination. Beside patience he had determination. This was provided by the desire to find a better way of carrying a number of the small things at the same time so that he need not make so many trips. Sometimes he had a dream about his nest-copying and saw more clearly than when he was awake. On the next day he would try out his dream. Alas, it was not as wonderful as it had seemed! Difficulties were in the way. Reality was less pliant than dreams would have it appear. Too bad!

His cave- or tree-mates thought he was peculiar and shook their heads at his silly obsession.

One day he perceived that one of his difficulties lay in the small size of the nest. If he made a bigger one, his fingers would not be so cramped in their manipulation and he could make it stronger. This was a bright thought, and it once more buoyed his spirit.

Alas, the larger size brought some problems of its own. Things came apart more readily. Each time he thought he had the problem mastered, some new difficulty reared its head. It seemed he needed more hands than he had. Two hands could do only so much. It occurred to him to try to induce someone to give him a hand, to hold a strand or a strip in place while he used his freed hand to secure it. It became obvious that three hands might be better than two and four better than three—if the hands belonged to someone who was not sundered in clumsiness and who had the patience to engage in what appeared to be a useless exercise. It was not easy to find such a willing helpmate, but with persistence he might gain at least some help. One or another of those who had helped him soon turned away when he approached. They did not share his vision and determination. Some became disgusted with his folly. One of them, annoyed by the pest's persistence, offered a helping hand only to grasp a half-finished nest from the weaver. Having got possession of the handiwork he threw it in the air several times mockingly and then catching it, tore it to shreds which he cast off to the wind!

The act was applauded by some of the others who were at the spot. They had had enough of the simpleton's haunting them. He, in turn, stood with his mouth open, amazed, shocked, and disappointed. His face formed strange wrinkles; his mouth closed and opened but no sound came out. Drops of water ran from his eyes and trickled down his cheek into his beard. A great roar of raucous laughter from the onlookers rent the air. He felt an inner chill, and that was the end of his nestmaking!

In his many turns at his task he had been aware of a ten-year-old lad who had sometimes stood close by watching intently as our artificer wrinkled his brow while he worked with his hands so carefully. No words or grunts passed between the two, but a community of feeling held them together.

Our would-be basket-maker died of natural causes at the advanced age of twenty-five. No one mourned his passing. His silly obsession was forgotten—or so it seemed.

The youngster who watched in fascination was eager to try nestmaking on his own, but he was careful to be out of eyeshot when he turned his hands to the task. He had no desire to be regarded as a silly follower of a silly old man. Unlike his forerunner, he could start near the point where the other one had left off, thanks to the many times he had watched him. He remembered he had been tempted on occasion to show the old man how to do a turn a little more handily, and he remembered what the movements were. Now he could avoid the mistakes the other one had made and could improve on the effort. His progress was more rapid, and the bigger nest was taking shape. One luckless day the one who had seized the nest from the old man espied the youngster intent on his own project. Stealthily he made his way to the side of the new artificer with intent to repeat his foul act of seizure and destruction, but his foot snapped a twig on the ground and his plot was betrayed. The youngster whirled away and was quickly out of reach, clutching his prized possession, but his tormentor was in pursuit. The youngster ran, dodging skillfully and made his getaway. Inwardly he felt a loathing of his fiendish attacker and thereafter avoided him, guided by a natural wariness that served his purpose.

He hid his unfinished work and left it concealed for many days lest he fall victim once more to the evil one at a time of concentration. Later when he returned to the hiding place, the nest was gone! He grieved over the loss and hunted for the remains of his many hours of effort, but it was nowhere to be found. Much later, when he was learning to hunt, he saw at the foot of a tree in a clump of dry grass something that looked familiar. He stooped to grasp it and recognition of the rude handiwork loosed a rush of blood from his heart and he shouted in glee. Quickly he checked himself lest his elation attract attention. The nest had held together and he thrust it under his arm.

A secondary will-force, a desire to finish his work, activated his intelligence. This desire was not like hunger in the sense that life depended on its execution. That is why we call it secondary. But it represented an impelling force nevertheless. He took pains to keep his devotion from further discovery.

He, too, became aware of the greater mastery that his fingers now possessed and the easier manipulation to which they responded. He knew better where to find the needed materials, and busied himself at his resumed project. He hid the nest more carefully than before, and it was not lost again. In time he mastered the technique of rounding the shape, even as the birds had known from instinct without observation or study. After all, he was not an instinctive nest-builder.

Time had little or no meaning to him. His patience did not count the hours. One day he looked critically at his handiwork. It was big enough; but how could he round it off so that it would not unravel or fall apart? Once more he examined the artistry of the birds. His power of observation had become more penetrating. His capacity for scanning the details of construction had been sharpened. What had been so difficult now seemed much easier. He had become a veritable artisan. Improvement had attended his obsessive efforts. A pleasant inner feeling etched by a final eagerness accompanied his application to his task.

Lo and behold, one day there it was, finished! His feet stomped around in expression of satisfaction. He swung his arms in a great arc and shouted in exultation. He did not care now what anyone would think. He had done what no one else had ever done! The thought swelled in him. He knew nothing of his ego, but it was in a veritable palpitation.

He now was eager to show his handiwork and did so without fear of ridicule or attack. The effect, sad to relate, was somewhat less than he anticipated. His art aroused little comprehension and not much wonder. What kind of hunter was he likely to be: that was the more natural question. No one lifted eyes to him in admiration; no one danced a jig. No one shouted as he had. He was without honor in his own cave!

For that matter, he himself had no idea of any use to which his creation could be put. His predecessor had not communicated to him the purpose he had in mind in embarking on his endeavor. The youngster had not worked at gathering little things in his hands to carry them from here to there.

The connection between the original motive and the contrivance was lost! His idea had not been original and his efforts were an imitation. Here was the forerunner of the basket and no one knew what to do with it!

The finished nest lay about here or there and was soon left unnoticed. It disappeared ingloriously in the expanse of time and was forgotten. The youngster grew up and became a hunter. He also lived to the ripe age of 25. No monument marked his passing. The silent universe looked on saying nothing. *Sic transit gloria mundi.*

The tribe did not become basketmakers. This honor was left to a later date and to a place far away.

Nevertheless, someone had learned that a combination of striving and repetition, which is to say persistence at an endeavor, brought *improvement* and a sense of mastery. The experience brought a joy and satisfaction that enveloped the whole being and kept it concentrated in pursuit. Aim, objective, purpose—all formed around and promoted the task. It must get done! Thus was born something that was not pointed toward a direct satisfaction of an organic need. To be sure, there was a connection, but it was indirect and roundabout. There was a will-force, but it was *secondary* as distinguished from the primary which had a direct object, and represented a peremptory demand.

The secondary will-force could wait, and failure to satisfy it was, to repeat, not lethal. It was more diffuse and subtle, more long-suffering and less easily gratified in one sense than the primary variety. A good meal would sate the appetite completely for a while, but a secondary will-force, not so pre-empting in its demand, it was ever present even if dormant at times. It was not connected directly with a bodily need. Its expression was in the nature of an aspiration. It played not with appetites and organic impulses so much as with the mind.

It was the stirring in man of the aspirations that would carry him far beyond the animal world of the beasts and birds. Its fortunes were the fortunes of civilization. The emergence of the secondary will-forces was at the scene of man's climb. The refineable ego was the companion. The combination of secondary will-forces and ego gave man conscious purpose in one of numerous directions.

The awakening, we have been at pains to say, was slow, halting, and doubtful. Early gains were repeatedly erased and lost, but the pursuit was not abandoned. Man had an inner ferment, an absorbing interest, epitomized in rare individuals that moved him on, constantly renewed by the accession of youth. He was destined to develop the potentialities that were stored deep within him.

It is the lot of man to be an imitator to a very much greater degree than to be original. It may be guessed that more than 99 per cent of man's actions represents imitation. Originality is a rare jewel. Sometimes it represents nothing more than the power of observation, which is to say, the ability to see relationships, meanings, trends, possibilties, qualities, or characteristics in a new light or juxtaposition. Once discovered, noticed, or invented, the new may become obvious to the many who had eyes but did not see, or ears but did not hear.

Some discoveries are more intricate or technical and are not so easily understood by those to whose attention they come. Such new insights may require much explanation. Other times, again, it is only necessary to give accent to vague ideas or abstractions by dressing them in concrete terms. They may then be more readily understood. Yet, again, organizing diffuse data, using analysis and synthesis, and presenting them in support of a meaning may be necessary to give life to an idea.

The question may be asked whence the desire to explain, to present new ideas, to teach, to instruct arises. There must be an impelling force. Were such a force not given, there could be little advancement in the arts of civilization. The ability to learn and to improve at skills is, of course, also a *sine qua non* of progress; but this capacity would not move far afield were it not given impetus and purpose by an inner force. Understanding would stand still did not some individual break the existing limits; and since imitation itself would not know what to imitate but for teaching, explanation, or other manner of communicating ideas, the ideas, the dependence of progress on the secondary will-forces and the tutored ego is inescapable.

As man extended his knowledge from stone to tool to implement, he extended his dominion. More people were able to remain alive. Their relationships became more numerous and complex. The number of desires increased with the proliferation of alternatives of gaining satisfaction. Learning became more important as more tools and other helpful external devices were fashioned by man for his own use. The question of entitlement developed more facets as more articles were created for use and comfort.

The primary will-forces and the raw ego were no longer equal to the demands of the manifold relations that came with the more varied activities and broadened horizons.

Time came when it was no longer merely a question of food and drink. Man had growing sensibilities that called for satisfaction, but sight, hearing, touch, and smell began to intrude their secondary interests. Food must not offend sight or smell too obnoxiously; nor was the function of body cover to be enjoyment of warmth or dryness alone, completely indifferent to the offense it might give to eyes that had a strange delight in beholding some of the graceful forms and sublime coloration offered by outer nature. Even the ears revolted against grating noises, screeching sounds, sudden assaults on the tympanum, and general din.

There was something in man that urged him to aspire to delights of the senses that were not necessary for the sustenance of life but which filled his heart with a warmth that felt good. For the eyes this meant taking note of form, graceful lines, flowing turns, proportion, color, even manner of movement, stance, physical attitude.

In relations of the one person with others and among others it was no longer elbowing, jostling, beating, pulling, pushing, biting, kicking, or scratching that produced the most satisfaction. Animal-like behavior, for reasons unknown, were offensive to refined man. Freedom from the rude and bestial behavior of savagery found appreciation in the human breast. Refinement therefore represented avoidance of the displeasure caused by the animal-like behavior of the primitives.

Departure from the harsh practices of the primary will-forces and the raw ego depended on the refinement of the sensibilities and the awakening of the senses to elements of beauty, grace and gentility. The nascent and developing secondary will-forces were the pioneers. It was these that revolted against the harsh and unredeeming features of primitive behavior that took its cue from the primary will-forces and the raw ego. They had something to get away from!

It was also the secondary will-forces that represented aspirations to cleanliness and a desire for order. An instinctive inclination to cleanliness is notable in certain animals, such as cats, and bees are clearly very orderly. Nevertheless the refinements of both cleanliness and orderliness in man depend on conscious sensibilities of both positive and negative qualities. Cleanliness attracts while the unclean may cause revulsion. The well-ordered array pleases while the jumble of disarray and squalor repels.

As man's sensibilities were pleased in varying degrees by cleanliness and good order, and repelled by the opposite, he had two sources of impulsion toward what is regarded as evidence of civilization.

5.

Nature's Discipline

THE LIVING OF LIFE, if attended by good health and periods of calm, no doubt justified itself in a feeling of well-being and at times in a joyous appreciation of nature's moods, its atmosphere and pleasant creatures, its plants and fragrant flower, songbirds and sunsets. There were also the joys and delights of mating, of the play and laughter of little children, and the rare succulence of fruit or other sparse pabulum. Memory of the joyous occasions might be sufficient to carry the spirit through bad times, storms, and ugly weather, animosities, losses, and privations, always buoyed by hope that the dark days or nights would pass, as somehow they always had. The sweet stood as a beacon against the bitter. Hope was the carriage—hope that the satisfying intervals borne in memory would surely return.

Man's clinging to life, harsh as it was, was the result of the two influences, one negative, the other positive. The pain and fear of death on the one side were joined by the intervals of buoyant joy that said that life is good.

The Zend-Avesta of Zoroastrianism expressed the duality by which man was beset as an endless war between the lord of light and goodness and the forces of evil. In such concepts, man personified what his intelligence learned, not only from observation of the changing forces of nature, which at times were so obviously kindly and benevolent while at other times cruel and seemingly malevolent; but also from his observation of man's own behavior. He had but to take note of the expression of the primary will-forces and the raw ego to see both good and evil clearly expressed.

The condition under which man trod the earth, so utterly dependent on its fruits and so inescapably victimized by its rigors, had, of course, to be taken for granted. Reality was reality; and so it was. Quite naturally man sought means of communicating with the unknown, the unseen, and the sources of events he could not understand. He was surrounded by a thousand mysteries, some of them wondrous and gratifying, others terrifying, relentless, and destructive. Overwhelming outbursts of nature could reduce man to a state of helplessness, fear, and awe. On the other side, nature's benevolence at times smiled benignly, showering on man gifts that he had done nothing to deserve!

What to make of such an inscrutable state of affairs?

Man, vaguely aware of purpose in himself, was prone to impute purpose to outer nature. The mixture of the benevolent with the cruel, the alternation of smile and scowl, and the unpredictable and unfathomable changes in nature's mood were a puzzle, an impenetrable enigma.

The origin of religion may be traced to man's woeful insufficiency. His mind did not penetrate the mysteries. Some of these remain as impenetrable today as they were when they first stirred man's questions into conscious inquiry. What little he did learn, what the rays of light shining from out of the genius of some rare specimen revealed, as surely gave rise to yet more questions. The quest, frankly, had all reason to seem hopeless. The view from one mountain top only revealed more vistas from yet other mountain tops. Man, it seemed, must be a long-suffering slogger on earth's surface.

Yet the glimpses! What wonders, like hints, lay just beyond the horizon! If only they could be captured and possessed, pressed to the breast, even as a baby, and sucked of their goodness!

Oh, yes, the lure was there! But why a lure? Was the lure deceptive? Was the view from the mountain top an *ignis fatuus,* a false lure? Or did it represent an earnest fee deposited by the promise of progress? The question was perhaps never as explicit as these words suggest, but there was possibly a hint that the whole process was a fraud. With all the failures that man experienced after taking the bait, disillusionment more than once, we need not doubt, overcame hope and left nothing but bitter dregs.

Yet, then again, the seeming fraud at times was converted into an honest actuality!

Time, of course, could consume generations with little concern. From the time when Galileo Galilei looked through his telescope at the moon and described the landscape until the pictures transmitted by space vehicles confirmed some of his speculations, some three hundred and fifty years elapsed. To man this span of time is oceanic in its expanse. To geological time it was but a moment.

Man's impatience measures his patience. The fact of patience has a significance of its own, related to the question of the fraudulence of the lures that lead man to prove the mysteries.

Patience, which no doubt made itself felt in early man, revealed his hopefulness, and his hopefulness rested on faith. He had learned from experience that it was more likely that man erred rather than nature when intent was frustrated or when his endeavors failed. Nature was hard and exacting, but it soon gained a reputation for immutability in its fidelity to cause and effect in visible and verifiable events.

But for this established fidelity in the verifiable spheres of action, hope could have gained no foothold because there would have been no ground for it; and without hope, patience would have been irrelevant and self-deceptive.

Hope, however, to repeat, was justified by experience. When events seemed to be perverse if not indeed diabolical, there could be hope that it would not always be so because in the past good had often replaced the hostile and malevolent. As nature had exhibited an honesty in the past, it could do so again. The ground for hope was therefore not a mere figment of the imagination but rested on a sound probability.

When events brought adversity, hope and its handmaiden, patience, could come to the rescue; and man need not, as he obviously did not, succumb to suicidal despair.

Patience is in the nature of a control exercised by the mind over the will-forces and the ego. Mind, using experience laid before it by events, preserved by memory and interpreted by intelligence, curbed the impatient will-forces or the ego through faith in the laws of nature. If a storm seemed endless, it was well not to respond to the baleful distractions of despair; for fair weather was likely to return. It had always done so in the past. Faith supported hope, and hope sustained the counsel of patience.

That man was driven to despair or near despair more than once on his way, in one region or another, at one time or another, may be assumed as a natural consequence of the seemingly hopeless conditions that fell to his lot many times.

Individuals not infrequently bow their heads in recognition of their dependence and helplessness, thus confessing to the unseen powers their recognition of this state of affairs, as a sign of humility. Why the posture of bowing should represent a recognition of dependence, rather than some other posture or physical attitude, is not clear, but it seems to express what man feels when he recognizes his weakness and limitations.

Weeping also represents a surrender and a confession of helplessness, mingled with a degree of self-pity and supplication. It rises characteristically in fitful gusts from an aching heart that is unconsoled by the seemingly stern and cruel realities that will not yield to mercy or understanding. Time, however, reduces sorrow, and weeping is not perpetual. It subsides as memory fades.

It is characteristic of man that he becomes humble in adversity and haughty when fortune smiles upon him. The reason for this strange characteristic may be found in the natural inclination of the primary will-forces and the raw ego to ignore the counsel of the mind and to brush aside restraint. When events are adverse, the mind more easily imposes its restraints because intelligence, neutral force that it is, then supports restraint. When adversity seems far away because fortune has smiled so continuously on us, the primary will-forces and the raw ego may find intelligence on their side. This is to say, intelligence may be more readily deceived when the wish is the father of the thought, the wish being the product of the impulses. The mind then finds the restraints and reflections recommended by it more easily dismissed as unnecessary. Man's buoyancy may rise to such a height that the blind will-forces and the untutored ego, carried along by a strong draught, even as a roaring fire creates its own draught, cannot even be brought to listen.

We need have little doubt that in the unrecorded history of

man, one or another tribe or group on occasion found itself so favored by circumstances that complacency found its way into the general attitude toward discipline. Relaxation of the rigors of restraint gained support as no enemy seemed to lurk in any direction and as nature made her bounty available with a minimum of effort.

Why, asked the appetites and the inclination to indolence, so much discipline and exertion when there is no need of them? Discipline for the sake of discipline is irksome to the indolent and complacent.

When a drouth struck or an enemy appeared seemingly from nowhere, the means of survival had been weakened. A drouth then took a toll much greater than it would have if preparations had been made for lean years. The onslaught by the enemy warriors was perhaps ferocious and irresistible, but it might have been repulsed had indolence not sapped the strength of the defenders and had optimism and complacency not corrupted discipline. The result was no doubt panic, defeat, and capture. If the circumstances were propitious, the captives were perhaps not slain but pressed into hard labor as slaves.

A history of adversity inherent in the vicissitudes of nature might have spared the tribe its debacle. As previously observed, the will-forces and the ego would under such circumstances have been more amenable to discipline. This is not to say that an unbroken regimen of discipline would give assurance of perpetual security against defeat from without; for Sparta, the home of rigorous discipline, did not prevail against its neighbors. Other factors may overcome the asset of discipline in preparation for combat; but discipline is designed to obtain the highest yield in combat strength from a given number of combatants. Discipline would produce greater unity of striking power because all combatants would be turned toward the same end with the least waste or dissipation of energy.

The divisions of mankind that lived under the need of continuous discipline, such as that imposed by the descent of winter year after year, would have been expected to be stronger and more amenable to restraint than those that found nature continuously indulgent, as in the tropics. The will-forces or the appetites they represented would have felt the whiplash of necessity in the northern climes, for exertion was the only passport to survival until springtime. Adversity made the necessary discipline within the tribe not only more bearable but intelligible and therefore more acceptable. In areas where winter's lethal breath did not reach, the optimism and complacency that reflected the ascendancy of the will-forces and the ego were left relatively unrestrained, and efforts at discipline lacked the support of intelligence when the question arose. Survival was not at stake in the struggle with nature to a degree remotely comparable to the inexorable requirement in the areas where frost, sleet, and bitter cold halted the vegetable sources of sustenance over half the year.

Winter was an ally of the inner voice that counseled exertion and foresight in the higher latitudes. Complacency and indolence represented the forces of extinction in those areas rather than survival, and man's power of learning from experience showed him the path to survival. Those who disobeyed the meaning of the lesson courted extinction, while those who obeyed vastly increased the probability of survival.

The races of man were differentiated, it may be guessed, to a great degree by their fated residence in areas that either exacted or did not exact restraint of the appetites in behalf of survival through seasonal deprivation. In the one area, indolence and indulgence of the appetites would be sinful and the object of tribal or group sanctions; in the other, the same discipline would have been unintelligible and frowned upon. No tribal or group sanction in support of discipline would have found justification in the common intelligence. In the absence of such support, the primary will-forces would have enjoyed much greater scope of indulgence—assuming the absence of slavery or despotism.

Indolence would not have attracted the frowns of companions and the spur of the overseers. No one would have asked whether nuts and grains had been stored in sufficient quantity to last until springtime again offered substitutes. While scarcity was not a stranger in the winterless land, it was not more pressing in one season than the other. Moreover, such scarcity as did intrude its gaunt figure seldom did so except to say that if anyone should have desires beyond those that could be met by ordinary effort,

he must exert himself to a degree that was above and beyond the
call of duty. Only if one sought more than enough to live from
day to day would he find it necessary to put forth special effort.

Such an option would make little appeal to the primary will-
forces since they would be satisfied with the simplest fare that
had the power to put down hunger and thirst. The option,
however, could offer an attraction to the ego because of the distinction that special possessions would confer on the owner. The
idea of standing out among his fellows, while meaningless to the
primary will-forces, might nevertheless occur to anyone whose
ego had sufficient development to produce the satisfaction that
is characteristic of distinction. If such a craving would arise at
no other time, it might appear on the scene during periods of
rivalry in the attraction of a mate. Again, since not all inclinations are equally distributed among members of a community, a
few in any group might be endowed with a more lively ego than
others. Their ambition would then provide the prod for special
effort.

The powers of the secondary will-forces, as distinct from the
primary variety and also as differentiated from the raw ego,
might in the state assumed here still be poorly developed, precisely because need, espoused by scarcity, is the cradle of invention. As we noted in considering the stone-thrower or stick-
wielder, these inventions or discoveries were in response to
pressing needs, and their successful prosecution and employment
released more time for other pursuits and led finally to refinements of the crude fare and elements that were good enough to
sate the stomach or cover the body but fell short of gratifying
the more refined sensibilities that were awakened as man's potentials responded to development and progress.

If the environment was sufficiently liberal in its supply of
what was needed by man to assure his survival, and if the goods
needed could be gathered without extraordinary effort, the incentive to invent or to discover new methods of doing what
needed doing was comparatively weak. The situation then did
not produce the ferment and alertness that drove those who were
hard-pressed to gain relief from the unremitting effort; for there
was no need for such strenuous effort.

After much time of exposure to the two sets of circumstances, the communities of primitives that strove under the stern exactions of nature to survive both scarcity in general and climate-imposed deprivation in winter, on the one hand, showed more progress and improvement in tool manipulation and other aids to production than those who were favored by liberal provisions furnished by nature, on the other. By much time we mean not merely a few generations but tens of thousands of years.

Man is not naturally inclined to exert himself more strenuously than the king of beasts. The lion has a vast preference for a prone position so arranged that muscles are relaxed and sleep easily pursued. Only when hunger drives him does he go afield to forage for food. Even then he sends for the lionesses while he waits at the banquet table to have a zebra or wildebeest dragged before him for his delectation and engorgement.

In the absence of the secondary will-forces which may stir a man to great activity, man would engage in no greater exertion than that necessary to gratify his biological hungers.

After the development of a variety of secondary will-forces, these prod him into activity on their own account, but with a demand less peremptory than that prepared for him by the primary will-forces. If the latter are gratifiable in the environment without extraordinary effort, man will not cry out for more effort. He will assert his kinship with the lion. Under the circumstances there would be little occasion for development of the secondary will-forces. They would represent excess equipment for which there would be little use. Nature is not inclined to be wasteful in this respect; for excess equipment may be a handicap. Why should the horse have claws or the earthworm have eyes?

Why develop secondary will-forces when they would be a nuisance and a goad to unnecessary activity? Why store nuts and fruits where no cold freezes vegetation to a standstill? Why worry about the morrow when it will be the same as today to all intents and purposes?

Secondary will-forces arose, seemingly, as we have noted, in response to a need. Having arisen, they began to exercise their function. This was to prod man to satisfy the secondary desires even as the primary will-forces impelled him to do what was necessary to satisfy the primary and inexorable needs.

There were, of course, areas where the rigors of winter were too harsh and the cold seasons too prolonged to release man from endless activity to sustain himself. In such areas development beyond the primitive was blocked by insuperable adversity.

Also, nowhere was abundance so rounded that man was wholly free of scarcity or adversity. He still had enemies. The balance in nature might be deficient in certain elements necessary for maximum physical well-being. Adversity might take a different form from its characteristics elsewhere. Disease might be more prevalent. Malnutrition might take its toll in the midst of abundance. Lack of certain minerals in the soil or protein deficiency would represent a form of scarcity.

However, this style of adversity would not be expected to exert the same influence toward progress as the adversity generated by scarcity that could be overcome by skill and special effort. Disease and malnutrition do not provide a prodding effect as does superable scarcity.

Nevertheless there was a common denominator running through the premises no matter where man resided. This was the problem of getting along with his own kind, and also the question of the meaning of life, its purpose, and the mystery of destination, if any.

It could be imagined that primitive man who was surrounded by relative plenty would have had at his disposal an abundance of time to pursue inquiries posed by the mind—time that the man who was beset by scarcity of the material goods found it difficult to find.

Yet, as remarked above, man is not naturally inclined toward unconstrained exertion, and constrained exertion in the primitive stage is in response to the prodding of the primary impulses. Man is not prodded to exertion by malnutrition or disease. Quite the contrary. He is debilitated. He is prodded to effort by an inclination to overcome the need of disagreeable effort. He may work harder to avoid work than engagement in the work he seeks to avoid itself entails.

It seems from these reflections that man needs to be prodded if he is to develop and make progress. It further seems that scarcity of the need-satisfying means in the form, place, and shape making them suitable for consumption is one of the primary prodding agents. If man is to live, he must expend effort if nature does not hand him his sustenance for the reaching.

Next it seems that the scarcity must not be excessively austere and oppressive, as in the polar and subpolar regions. Man there has no recourse beyond devotion to his task of gaining a livelihood. Moreover, despite the whiplash of cruel need, nature provides him with very little in the way of vegetation and other materials out of which to fashion tools or other aids to productive effort.

Finally, it seems to follow that if nature is generous enough to supply man what he needs to fill his stomach and provides a climate so gentle that he needs no cover against so much as a chilling breeze, the agent necessary to incite effort is virtually absent. The secondary will-forces will not then be called forth from their potentials; and not being called forth from the cradle, they will make little or no stir for anything beyond what satisfies the primary will-forces.

Yet, as already noted, the ego is different. It thirsts for distinction and plaudits of human companions and fellow spacefillers. Not infrequently indeed does a capacious ego pair itself with a singularly meager aggregate of capabilities. Such a one would have all the plaudits and distinctions without earning them. He craves the prize but despises or shrinks from the effort of entitlement. He would place the crown on his head without accepting the rigors of discipline. Indeed, the resentment of free men, especially self-made men, over hereditary monarchy and hereditary wealth reflects the revolt of the secondary will-forces against the ego's pretensions when it aspires to distinctions and an eminence to which it has little evidence of an earned title. An outraged sense of justice stirs the inner premises.

It is possible, because of the separation of the ego from the will-forces, closely allied as they often are, that pretensions and aspirations of the ego may easily outrun the realities of entitlement. Much trouble indeed flows from this inclination of the ego to pretensions, especially because other egos may be expert

at detection and determined toward demolition. A rivalry of
pretensions among avid practitioners is not uncommon. Behold
sundry politicians!

We have already said that the hungers of the ego, so to speak,
do act as a prod to man; but without the parallel impulsions
provided by the secondary will-forces, in the form of aspirations
fathered by special talents or creative abilities, the ego would not
travel a steep gradient, were the elements and the constituents
that give title to distinction and eminence not scarce or even rare.
The ego by itself would be lost in paradise, out of place, a misfit.
Over what would it beat its breast, over what flap its wings?

This side of paradise, man in nature is an overcomer; and
he will never want for something to overcome, thanks to both
outer nature and to man's own nature. For example, he engages
the problem of scarcity and as he gains a step—two steps—he
can be sure that tomorrow there will be more steps yet to be
taken; for he is on the trail marked for him by his secondary will-
forces. Refinement uncovers previously unseen crudities, and so
opens new worlds to conquer. Nevertheless he gains satisfaction
on the way and also in retrospect.

Of course, he has not only scarcity of the means of satisfaction to overcome but excesses as well, principally, to be sure,
excesses of evil in one form or another; but on occasion also an
excess of good, because usage may and often does convert a good
into an evil.

We are, however, moving ahead of our caravan, into the land
of secondary will-forces and their relations or interlacing with the
tutored or refined ego.

Man is in difficulty and will always be in difficulty because
of what he is and the conditions under which he inhabits the
earth. He can never be what he would like to be, and yet he
would be much less than what he is should he cease his efforts to
attain what he seeks. There are enough examples in what is
called "skid row" and elsewhere to eliminate any need to resort
to a laboratory test for verification of this observation.

Man's predicament is indeed such that logic is all but driven
to the conclusion that he is under test or on trial. His very values,

at least in the Western world, are laden with considerations that take their cue from the measures used in the test. Deficiencies, for example, are measured according to the degree or extent of shortfall from certain standards. Standards, of course, are the very substructures of tests or trials. We measure by them.

Man navigates in greater or lesser degree by values, even if often unwillingly or under protest. Sometimes the values are imposed by those who are in a position of dominancy.

The standard of excellence is taken from what is considered necessary or desirable to fulfill an assignment, implicit or explicit, that involves action, modified by method or behavior, whether this be in the performance of a task, filling an office, or otherwise answering a need or aspiration. In the process, an array or sequence of relationships is momentarily opened and usually closed, but sometimes with a wake or trail of variable duration.

The question is how well or creditably or abominably an individual acquits himself. An answer to this question demands a determination of what constitutes deficiency or fulfilment.

But for man's peculiar and overdeveloped capacity for error, but for his consequent uncertainty at many turns, and beyond these liabilities, but for his limited penetration of mind, imperfect judgment and other disabilities and shortcomings, such as insufficiencies, he would not be confronted with the problems that are uniquely human.

He either seeks to overcome his natural deficiencies, which lie in all directions, or he does little or nothing. His status will to a considerable degree be determined by how he acquits himself. His repute, his esteem or disesteem, will be determined by these measures even among his own kind. His innate capacity, if ascertainable, may be taken into account.

Man judges man, in a mundane sense, by the values derived from his relations to nature and to others of his kind. First come his primary will-forces.

So far as these primitive forces are concerned, the degree to which he satisfies them is the measure of his competence as a procurer. Thus is his physique tested—his skill, his strength, his wit, his agility. Only practical considerations enter into the equation. Values here are pragmatic values. There is no question of justice, mercy, kindness, or honesty. If he meets the test, he survives; if he fails, he perishes.

However, confronted with a possibility of error that was assured of no small degree of actualization, and with demands beating upon him from the primary needs, he was born for difficulty in the field of the secondary will-forces and tutored ego. His intelligence and adaptability could carry him far beyond the range of eagle or tiger, but it soon encountered baffling options and dazzling allurements that often turned out to be false gold.

The baffling options came from his uncertainty, and this uncertainty, in turn, was the price he paid for the relative freedom from instinctual guidance in many fields. It was the price exacted by the precious gift of freedom. If man were always certain of consequences, he might indeed still exercise his options; but his estate would be vastly different from his actual estate on earth. Much of his endeavor on earth, as it is, is directed toward the very end of overcoming uncertainty while exercising options would still remain. Suspense would perish. Life would be deprived of much of its zest.

His procedures in all directions would be very different from what they are if he were always sure of the outcome of his choice of action. The two eventualities of which man is said to be sure are not such happy ones that he would elect either of them if he had a choice. Yet some certainties are approached with impatient glee while others are anticipated with dread.

Uncertainty affects man's behavior even in the prosecution of his efforts to gratify his primary needs. Judgment is the special mental equipment given him to cope with uncertainty, and it is a variable gift. Its quality determines in a high degree his record of accomplishment. Other qualities of the mind and body will play their part, to be sure, such as purpose, health, strength; but judgment is the great divider between feasor, nonfeasor, and misfeasor—judgment nudged by the will-forces and the ego.

If man's trek through the haze on earth were not a test or a trial, why should he be placed on a special plane "above" that of the lower animals, confronted with options of a thousand varieties, each of which harbors the possibility of error? Why, furthermore, in the selection of alternatives among the options, should uncertainty attend nearly every consideration to be weighed by judgment?

The elections or choices made among the options may carry weighty consequences, depending on the action proposed. A decision to shoot or not to shoot, to wed or not to wed, to buy or not to buy may affect life's very future.

The feasor or doer may then be asked, "Why did you choose to do what you did, when you might have done otherwise?"

In replying the feasor again has an option of one of many responses, if his mind is prolific. He may say that circumstances were such that what he did seemed to be the best of the options; or that he did not at the moment know what he now knows; or that he forgot something, which had he remembered, would have changed his choice of alternatives. Again, he might plead ignorance of certain aspects of the subject, as for example, not knowing that the gun was loaded.

If a nonfeasor or nondoer is asked, "Why did you not do what you were told?" he also has one of a number of possible responses. He may allege that he did indeed do what he thought he was told, thus indicating faulty communication or misunderstanding. On the other hand, he might retort that in his judgment the suggestion or command was unwise or did not meet all aspects of the situation, or reflected ignorance of the circumstances, or represented bad timing, or did not go far enough or too far.

The ego is usually quite adept at deflecting blame; indeed, doing so is one of its prime functions.

Counterintelligence may, of course, undertake to dispose of the responses. At stake is the question of proper action judged by accepted standards. Did the feasor or nonfeasor meet the requirements?

If he did, very well! Thanks may or may not be added. If he did not, disappointment or regret or outrage, and punishment may or not be prescribed.

The *mis*feasor or wrong-doer, faces a similar act of justification or confession. He too may exculpate himself; or if he is truthful, he may confess but offer extenuating circumstances. His ego will ask his intelligence to supply these as his counsel for defense.

As noted earlier, man holds his fellow earth-inhabitants responsible for their acts, with certain quite definite exceptions. The result is that all those who qualify as responsible are on trial in all they do, usually implicitly but often explicitly as well. Often, too, the individual is aware of the tentative character of his standing or repute. He is aware that a lapse or two, a few missteps or culpable error will alter his "image" in the eyes of those who are affected by his behavior or performance.

Man's fellow beings, of course, can never render a *final* judgment on one of their kind, except for practical social purposes, as exemplified by restraint, incarceration, or execution. This incapacity is not surprising for several reasons.

No one can read clearly the intent of another, nor weigh the quality of his judgment, or feel the impact of a provocation as it strikes. No one can replace the inner deployment of will-forces and ego responses of another with his own. The two will never be identical and may indeed be radically unlike. Could we transpose two consciousnesses, each aware fully of the other while not relinquishing its own, we could achieve a better appreciation of the differences in motivation and emotional responses; but such merging of two sets of consciousness is not possible. Moreover, the quality of an act cannot always be judged by its consequences.

We may assume a *gestalt* or configuration of circumstances that to an observer might spell danger or imminence of undesired events unless steps were taken to prevent such an outcome. If the preventive steps were indeed taken and should beget the result desired, it could always be alleged that the preventive action was unnecessary, that the danger was vastly exaggerated or nonexistent, and that therefore the alleged preventive action was but an excuse invented to hide an ulterior motive. Events cannot be reversed and then moved forward again without intervention of the preventive action as a means of proving or disproving the need or lack of need for it. Whenever preventive action succeeds, it is subject to challenge, except under some clear circumstances of physical relationship. If one person pulls another precipitately from the path of an onrushing heavy object, it may be quite obvious that the preventive action was indeed decisive in preventing disaster; but if a political executive invokes police power to prevent a riot and does prevent it by his action, it can be claimed that harsh measures were employed when they were not necessary, and were therefore oppressive of freedom of demonstration. Who will pronounce judgment?

Human insight into human motives is often clouded or distorted by the reaction of the will-forces or the ego, in terms of emotion, within the observer. Procedures governing the administration of justice are designed to guard against such distortions, but the precautions are seldom proof against the penetrative powers of the volatile emanations, so to speak, released by the will-forces and the ego.

Nevertheless man does hold man responsible for his acts with the exceptions noted earlier; but cannot aspire to eternal justice because of the limitations to his powers of observation and the implication of his emotions and predilections in his assessments of intent. Man does subject his fellow men to mundane judgment in many directions, and on many more occasions out of court than in court, as a matter of practical necessity; but the final judgment in the nature of infinitely detailed fidelity to justice is beyond man. Whether man as an individual is eventually subjected to such judgment is a matter of belief, not of factual demonstration.

If we incline toward extrapolation of what we see on earth into possible extramundane existence, we should no doubt be led to conclude that such justice does await man since we place him on trial throughout the course of his mundane existence.

In the modern world, man tests his young as they move through their schooling, plying them with tests and examinations and grading, or otherwise weighing their performance against presumption to advancement. We follow this testing routine through secondary and higher education. Before we permit a physician to put his store of learning into effect, we demand official certification that he has met the qualifications or standards established for the purpose. We establish similar qualifications for those who are to teach our young and our adolescents. We demand of our practitioners of the law that they successfully pass prescribed courses in accredited schools, which is to say, tested schools. Pharmacists, engineers, and many public employees must also satisfy prescribed standards measured by tests. Clergymen are tested before they become duly ordained as ministers of the gospel.

Today one great exception may be noted. No course of prescribed study or certification is demanded of those who practice journalism. In view of the great influence that lies in the hand that writes the news and interprets it to the public, the oversight, if oversight it is, beggars explanation. Perhaps the exception fills the function of proving the rule.

Man is a testing creature and he proceeds characteristically by the process of trial and error. Reward and punishment, as previously noted, are closely related to how well the individual fulfills what is expected of him.

In the physical world, as in the animal part of it, the test is provided by nature. The quality of man's acquittal of himself determines his fortune. This test, however, does not extend to the inner disposition of man's own assessment of his place in the world and the ordering of his reaction, which is to say his behavior, including his conduct toward others of his kind.

So far as his primary will-forces and his raw ego are concerned, man is directly under the discipline of nature.

In the other sphere, his secondary will-forces, his refined ego and his mind, as arbiter, determine his fortune. This sphere is not independent of nature, is indeed greatly affected by it, but is not finally anchored there; for man's mind has the power to interfere with nature, to redirect its blind forces; in other words, it enables man to set up a semi-independent world of his own, using nature's properties to his own end.

He builds a world within nature, at nature's sufferance, so to speak, dependent on nature in its physical aspects, but turned to man's nonanimal existence. He has a nest in nature, so to speak, and uses nature while at the same time he is at its mercy. How he will acquit himself in his own nest depends on himself. He has certain special assets as well as special liabilities in this sphere. He is still leashed to nature, to be sure, but even as we see in medicine, he is able to emancipate himself from many of the elements of harshness in nature. He has a franchise, as it were, to reach beyond nature. How he uses it depends on himself, individually and severally.

Man has built expectations with materials derived from both worlds. These expectations reflect his reaction to nature's discipline and to his relations with his own kind. They represent to a degree both what he thinks may befall mankind and what he hopes as a result of his estimate of man's potentialities. He inclines to convert the potentials, as he assesses them, into what ought to be, and may transform them into moral demand.

6.

Primitive Bases

of Freedom

HUMAN EXPECTATIONS represent an invisible and often an unexpressed force or influence in human behavior. They reflect what has been taught formally and informally as modified by personal experience and interpretation. In a sense they sit silently at the base of judgment-formation and contribute to the shaping of mental attitude; and, needless to say, mental attitude is the arbiter in many decisions. As previously indicated, what is in the mind may be decisive in the application of value-judgment. If the mind has some reasonable control over the primary will-forces and the raw ego, its contents, while not assured of supremacy, will nevertheless exert a strong influence on the options. The contents of a weak mind will have less influence, and the will-forces and the ego will dominate the disposition of the options or choices.

Expectations are not only internal but external. The internal ones may indeed be shaped by or greatly influenced by the external ones. The latter reflect what other people—members of the family, the community, the nation, or the world—expect.

Some of the external expectations become converted into social conventions and act as habitual guides to conduct. Such conventionalities may indeed take the place of reflection and may on occasion act as an irrational restraint on freedom. On the other hand, conventions may have the virtue of economy, in the same sense that habit represents an economizer of mental energy and time. As not all habits are blessings, not all conventions are without blemish. *Comme il faut* may in time suffer from obsolescence or anachronism.

In the days of childhood, parental expectations are most immediate and possibly also most influential, although the disappointments frequently encountered may raise questions as to their potency as an influence. Later, the expectations of friends or the community rise to a higher level of influence on behavior, and ultimately, particularly if public life is entered, as in politics or through the professions, a wider area of expectations may be recognized. The attorney becomes aware of the expectations of the bar with respect to his behavior; so also the physician learns of the expectations of his profession. The statesman's horizon may extend to the whole nation and then beyond that limit to the expectations of other countries. In some instances, even the expectations of mankind as a whole, the species, *Homo sapiens,* may exert an influence, if anyone knows what these expectations are —if, indeed, they have taken shape or found expression. The latter development will depend on influential writings and philosophic interpretations as these may be expressed through an international organization, or otherwise.

Whatever their source and territorial scope, human expectations reflect the standards and values or mere conveniences and codifiers of behavior that have been adopted either explicitly or implicitly or even perhaps subconsciously, as by instinct.

Internal expectations may reflect those of external origin by adoption or assent, active or passive. The inner expectations, like those regarded as being an aggregate of the community, nation, or the like, may, of course, not be directed toward quality of conduct, but toward events, such as expecting rain, war, or an improvement in economic conditions; but the expectation here addressed, is concerned with standards of conduct or achievement. The word to be used would be contained in "ought." In this sense we expect someone to do this or that because he ought to, not because we think we are so intimately acquainted with his cerebral processes that we think we can successfully predict what he will do. It is in the sense of "ought," that we use the word "expectations" here.

Yet another sense intrudes itself. It is expressed in the

phrase so frequently applied to modern trends among people of the so-called underdeveloped or, more kindly, developing nations, namely, "the revolution of rising expectations." In this sense, expectations express a claim provoked by some species of implicit promise that has aroused anticipations that should be fufilled.

The expectations that are relevant to the present discourse reflect the existence of standards of human conduct. The saying that the public expects every man to do his duty would express the variety of expectancy that engages us here.

Such expectations arise from standards that express a generally accepted desire of mental origin, such as might reflect a moral judgment. Implied in such a desire is the hope that impulses or appetites arising from the will-forces and the ego, which if given free rein would discommode, give pain to, or even injure others, will be restrained. A consensus of condemnation may be reached from much interchange of experience, headshaking, and common expressions of disgust. An implicit "thou shall not" arises from the consensus of condemnation. The mere conventions and amenities of good breeding also exert great influence on behavior. Indeed "social standing" may be judged by the conformity of individual "manners" and usages to accepted forms. The concept of "ought," however, implies a moral tone.

The "ought" applied to conduct is therefore a product of the *human* estate, and, as we have seen, arose from the effect of individual human behavior on associates, large, medium, and small; children, adolescents, and adults; men and women; the bright, mediocre, and opaque.

By a process of slow accretion, the reality of social sanction thus dawned on the company of man. The possibility of restraining pernicious behavior had been born when the intelligence of the relatively weak found means of avenging the atrocities of the strong. Otherwise the strong would hardly have found means within themselves to restrain the primary will-forces or primitive ego. There would have been no one to say to them nay, except the few equally strong ones and these too had no concern beyond themselves. What was put in them by the cooperation of the weaker among themselves was conscience, which has already had our attention, or, more accurately, a "social conscience."

Nietzsche, as already observed, deplored the power of the weaker over the strong and therefore abhorred the political institutions, such as democracy, that took their cue from the interests of the physically weaker elements. He despised the teachings of Christianity. In his lexicon, kindness, except as exhibited among the elite toward each other, was a curse that held back the strong from their high destiny, which was superman. There was a tendency to mistake physical strength for mental or moral force.

Marxian communism entered at the other extreme. The powerful elements, Marx averred, contrived laws and institutions that were designed to perpetuate their powers and privileges over the weak and dispossessed. To dismantle this overtowering predacious structure, the system of morality on which it was based must itself be dismantled.

Thus was joined an issue that has pitted the weak against the strong and the strong against the weak in an atmosphere not of understanding and of mutual efforts to overcome the scarcities decreed by nature but of ill-will and hatred. Man thus was prodded to fight against himself instead of pooling his talents and capabilities toward a common end.

In the animal world, deception represents a means of survival, both positive and negative. On the positive side is the concealed crouch, the inaudible footfall, the treacherous habiliment that copies innocence; on the negative side is the protective coloration that helps to conceal the body against predatory detection, the feigning of lifelessness, and other devices for escape from destruction.

Man's animal heritage incorporated similar devices of deception, and his intelligence, prodded by his primitive endowments, refined and elaborated them beyond anything mere animal could achieve. The object of deception is really to frustrate or upset the expectations of others that guide many actions.

In his forward movement, man has indeed come to despise these inherited devices of behavior as being too animal-like, and has tried and tries to escape them, but they persist even as do the less admirable tendencies of the primitive appetites and impulses. Man inevitably brings the animal world, the world of outer nature, with him wherever he goes. It is something he seeks to overcome, while still being dependent on it, and he is fated to see the heritage renewed in each new birth. Thus is parenthood assured a perpetual task.

Intelligence indeed enhances the ingenuity of deceptive devices and maneuvers; but it is also man's reliance on intelligence, or rather the data of intelligence as the basis of judgments, that has brought him to regard deception as a subversive force. (Thus is the duplicity of intelligence demonstrated once more.) As he proceeds in selection of his options among many alternatives that confront him, he knows that his expectations and judgment will be misled by deception. Both his will-force and ego interests will suffer the consequences. When judgment expends its precious powers on false premises and expectations, it will be led to foolish if not destructive ends. The ego, above all, does not relish seeing itself occupying the dunce's stool.

Yet, of course, the raw ego is itself not above using deception in one or more of its infinite forms, to mislead a rival, enemy, or competitor. Quite the contrary. It indulges in a veritable bath of glee, exulting the more, the more devilishly clever or cunning the deceptive stratagem had been.

To classify deception as an animal heritage and therefore a device of the primary will-forces and the primitive ego, we have but to advert to the practice of deception in war. Stratagems and devices that are beyond the legal pale in peaceful society are still commonly employed against the enemy. War has not advanced far beyond the limits of the animal heritage of man. The primitive impulses can be indulged against the enemy with impunity. Deception is not only not frowned upon in war but is highly prized. Clever deceptive devices of the enemy are eagerly copied when the occasion permits. While the enemy may be cursed bitterly and hated for his outrages, he is admired for his cleverness at deception.

Diplomacy itself is hardly a stranger to deception. The lack of trust among nations arises from the very knowledge that deception is practiced universally in the prosecution of international relations. Statesmen have confessed that in the name of the state they engage in practices *vis-a-vis* their foreign counterparts that in their estate as private citizens would soon lead to their ostracism or imprisonment.

Distrust among men lies in the very readiness of man to deceive under a variety of circumstances. Distrust merely represents a suspicion that another person might do what oneself might be tempted to do. The temptation is of course usually resisted in common practice. Indeed fraud and deception are not only frowned upon in civil affairs or the everyday world; fraud is an actionable offense at law. Heavy penalties may be assessed against an offender who is convicted. The many devices designed to offer protection against deception give evidence both of how prevalent it might be were it not discouraged, and how abominable it is held to be.

However, the arm of the law does not reach across national boundaries with the same determination and power as is its wont within national boundaries. International law is virtually a permissive form of sanction. National sovereignty provides the consent decree, so to speak. A statesman or national delegate is therefore not seized outside his own borders if he is on an official mission. He operates under the egis of the comity of nations, and is guaranteed safety of conduct. While he may be detained if he violates local law, he can plead diplomatic immunity. Such amelioration of savagery in diplomatic interchange, small as the circle is, does demonstrate that the primary impulses *can* be restrained if reason endorses and indeed demands it. The expectations of safe conduct are seldom violated.

The diplomat's freedom to deceive is not recognized in the commercial sense. In that respect he is not above the law. His own country will answer for misdeeds of this character. It is in the field of national security and national interests that he is given a release from the moral standards that bind him in his own country. He may carry on duplicitous schemes with impunity. Therefore he reverts to a more primitive state; for despite patient efforts to extend the rule of law across national boundaries, progress is slow. Man awaits internationally more experience of the kind that established morality and law in the more restricted areas. The reach of such law was usually coextensive with the power to impose and enforce penalties; for beyond that limit there need be no fear of penalty.

Man's problem is that of finding his real enemy, which is within, rather than dissipating his energies battling among his own kind. However, since he brought his animal heritage with him into his special world as man, he faces an enemy within that is yet not totally enemy or destructive but even necessary as an asset, namely, the many times mentioned primary will-forces and the raw ego. Thus is the problem aggravated. Man cannot do without the forces that give rise to envy, deceit, greed, and others of the less inspiring motives. The problem is how to bring them under rational control.

Man was able through the past millennia and slow-footed centuries to live with the rude forces that guided him through a rough world. In retrospect his task of subduing outer nature was not as difficult as his conquest of the wild inner forces. This is a continuing stubborn contest, and hope feeds on the reflection that it has persisted despite setbacks. Essentially it is the battle for freedom against dominancies that have characteristically taken their defensive guidance from the primitive impulses; and these have predictably acquitted themselves as stubborn masters and defenders of their own premises.

As we have endeavored to delineate, there came to be recognized a community of interest among those who suffered torment from the strong, no less than from the wayward and lawless ones; and a common aversion, often long endured, was led by the available intelligence and covert modes of communication to await the opportune moment for redress. The setbacks were surely numerous, cruel, bloody and bitter, as history records, but the spirit was indomitable and ever rose again.

Even if bitter memory of harsh experience, including the whiplash, the wrack and torture, or deprivation and loss, subdued those who had felt them, there followed new generations in whom the memory was not actual but hearsay. Under the same oppressive, cruel, or deceptive usage, the replacements in the form of progeny would in turn and on appropriate occasion also revolt and seek to put the halter on the offenders. Therefore the spirit of resistance to either oppression or fraud, robbery, and the like did not die even though in its name and in standing true to it many did indeed die. The spirit was inherent in the human composition. It could not die among human beings because it was reborn, ready-made, in each new generation.

Unfortunately, as will appear later, the oppressed or mistreated are subject to the same unruly inner forces as the oppressors and misfeasors; in other words, if they prevail they in turn will come under domination of the common enemy within unless they take great care to guard against the natural animal inclinations of their own. The animal in man, as observed just now, cannot be extirpated because it is reborn in every cradle.

Man's sensibilities explain his objection to and resistance against intentional abrasions, jostlings, the harsh and offensive usages of domination, and the deprivations of robbery or deception. These sensibilities have a tenderness unknown to the lower animals because the nervous system of the latter is developed to a lesser degree; but are present among the oppressors and the oppressed alike. The resistors resist because of these sensibilities, and the defenders defend because of the same sensibilities.

This fact is also wholly disregarded by either attacker or defender. The opponent, rather, is immediately cast in the role of an enemy reciprocally, and the primitive impulses are unleashed to do their worst.

Progress, therefore, was and continues to be difficult; man is tried and re-tried in the process, often beset and beseiged by the adversities and doubts and cynical reflections to which he is host; often wondering if there is any purpose, any rational goal, any possible noble achievement. He is not aware that he is always centered on himself, thinking about *his* particular interests, those of *his* group, of *his* calling, of *his* nation, of *his* race. This is his natural inclination; but if he is to cast off the guiding impulses that lead him into misunderstanding, lack of sympathy, and hatred, it must be otherwise. He must promote his better, if rarer, inclinations—those that reflect his tutored ego and his higher aspirations, represented by his secondary will-forces.

The interplay between rising and ebbing fortunes, expressing, as it seems, the turn of probabilities or cycles, maintains for man a suspense that tries his faith, fortitude, level-headedness, and purpose. He interprets all in terms of his own fortunes and those of his various allies. So long as he remains thus provincial—a likelihood of possibly long-term duration—he will continue to collide with the corresponding and possibly antagonistic interests of others who are equally firmly provincial.

Because of the vastness of the forces and relations impinging on man, he often wearies of reflecting on what he cannot understand, and buries himself in his work or has resort to bitter cynicism if not nihilism, seemingly, from its literature, a Russian specialty, a product of oppression of a sensitive people. We have reason to conclude that living is indeed partly process, much of it, indeed, absorbed and expended in process, which is to say, in the doing. The process then, in this sense, needs no purpose and has little occasion for reflection. It is self-sufficient and speaks for itself. Dedication to a task, a career, or a great endeavor uses up and consumes life, even as a fire consumes wood, and accounts for purpose by using it on the way. A man who thus dedicates himself through the course of many years lives his life, accounting for it day by day; and when his life span has run its course, he has no regrets, his impulses have receded, his wants of youth are forgotten, and he is ready to close his eyes and vanish, having expended himself in the course of his devotion.

Numerous such specimens seem to exist, but reflection is not wholly absent: a time to ask how far the road has been traveled, how much distance lies ahead, and how it is to be interpreted.

Process does indeed occupy much of life's activities and returns many satisfactions. The composer awaits the time when his notes will be turned into actual music, brought to life in harmony and rhythm, and heard by human ears other than his own. The painter, even as he becomes a part of his process of painting, deeply absorbed in color, lines, shapes, and perspective, is immersed in a veritable ambient of expectation, awaiting the time, even in the midst of the process, when he can step back and behold his finished work and then bring it to the eyes of others for admiration or criticism—but mostly admiration, he hopes. All creators of rare artifacts, all inventors, discoverers, fond researchers, writers, and others who are greatly attached to their work, aspirations, and endeavor, look to the final product and expect from it evidence of having done well or excellently or even superlatively, or at worst, passably; so also life is not all consumed in the processes by which it is so greatly taken up.

Man wishes to contemplate what he has achieved, if anything, or what he has wrought. He may then take heart and apply himself more assiduously to his work; or he may gain little but discouragement and lose heart; or he may gain some satisfaction, quite short of ecstasy, and some discouragement, quite short of despair, and this is the lot of the many. In whatever category he finds himself, much of his inner feeling will be determined by what others think of his accomplishments or lack of them.

The many will plod on, walking a course in which the light of reality neither dazzles the heart nor invites the pall of gloom.

This great host constitutes the admirers, the envy-ridden, the encomium singers and the scorners, the copiers and the pretenders—all for whom in a sense, the genius, the inventor, the great artist and composer, the rare ones, labor and expend themselves. They, the many, are the consumers, those who have expectations, so to speak, of the arts of civilization. It is they who erect the monuments, place statues on pedestals, and supply the hero worship. Among them are also good critics no less than the detractors and the cynics whose tongues and pens are guided by their beleaguered and sometimes wounded egos.

This great host also constitutes the spectators, the audiences and the readers and viewers, as enjoyers of or groaners over what is played before them, set before them for their edification, or enacted for their entertainment. Among the spectators may indeed be found some of the rare specimens of genius who wish to sample the works of others in their own field and also perhaps to enjoy the fare offered by the elite in the fields in which the genius may himself be one of the mediocre multitude, perhaps even a Philistine.

There is enjoyment, we may conclude, in process as well as in contemplation, consumption, or reflection. Likewise pain, discouragement, and gloom may attend both the process and the contemplation or use of the product. Man is much bent on seeking the best; but both in doing and in consumption, the best is rare, which is to say, scarce, and there is much trial and tribulation in bringing forth the best and also in coming into position to enjoy it. The endeavor to meet expectations may be quite compelling.

It is often in the processes that human beings experience their most intimate and remembered experiences outside of the matings. The hunter is in process as he stalks and trails his game. The plowman is in process as he cuts furrow after furrow, inhaling the smell of fresh earth while hearing the rooks caw and the dove intoning the arrival of spring. The modern worker is in process as he oversees the humming machines that have displaced the craftsmen who were also in process as they shaped, cut, turned, etched, polished, and refined the materials of nature; the physician is in process when he heals, the clergyman when he ministers to the spirit, the songster when he gives inspiring vocal turns to sentiment.

The customs and usages that center about and guide behavior in the processes form a world of their own within man's world. It is usually the public world, and is quite distinct from the private world, the home world, the family world.

The two, the world of process and the private world, do often intermix but are divided to such an extent that those who work together in the processes are often virtual strangers after the day is done. If they do come together in the private world, they often become aware of the difference in climate, concerns, considerations, and attitudes that separate the two worlds.

The private world has its own environment, its own aspirations, expectations, and disappointments. It has its own style of relations, forms of address, manners; its own outlooks, attitudes, and values of regard, leading either to esteem or disapprobation of others. To the family, the public world is framed as something external, a species of stage on which this one or that one of the family makes his way, judged impersonally and without the understanding that may be and often is commonplace in the kitchen, at the dinner table, in the living room, upstairs, downstairs, or in the yard, despite outbreaks of will-force and ego animosities and pique.

No one knows how the mediation between the immediate family and the other world of people was performed long ago, but the relations were limited simply because there were few human beings. In the home, whatever it was, the parents took the first hand at molding the tender new life. Here it was and is that the expectations of life are most vividly exemplified, both in the sense of how the individual should acquit himself and what is hoped life may bring forth. In both senses, reality usually falls short of the bright hopes. In some instances, indeed, tyranny and oppression may suppress innocent freedom just as excessive permissiveness may sap freedom of its appreciation.

Here it is necessary to step back once more to beginnings and to trace further hypothetical origins.

The primary will-forces and the raw ego had their play in the home and then met the outer world. Relationships had to be guided; but the question comes, who or what guided the first child that could be called man, the first one that was sufficiently liberated from instinct to become aware of the options or choice that called for judgment rather than instinct? How sudden was the onset of the distinction? At one time it was absent; then it was present.

How minute was the first distinction? Did it appear as a "mutation" so that the one in whom it appeared was in that respect different from all others and all alone in the world? If so, how far did the difference extend? How could the new one inform the uncomprehending ones about the new world?

It must be assumed that the one who had the new capability reproduced himself and that he or she had several offspring, and that one or more of them inherited the new capacity or additional brain cells and then, in turn, survived and transmitted the same new power to yet additional offspring. Communication was then possible on the new level.

If the first one in what might have been a chain and the origin of a new race died without issue, the "mutation" was lost. Then an independent new start toward manhood would have been necessary. Should this one also have perished without procreation, or having procreated, had not passed on the new organic development, as might indeed have occurred, it would once more have been lost; and a third start would have been needed. Thus it is possible that man may have lost his first possible ancestors, and also that man appeared in more places than one, differentiated from the outset.

The question would then arise how many seeds of mutation existed, and what was their source. It must be said that man cannot answer the question of his own origin. No skeletal and no missing link can speak. It is safe to say nevertheless that man was somehow launched; otherwise he would not be here. This fact indicates that the existence of a fact does not depend on *proof* of its existence. We need only to say, "We are here; therefore we must have had an origin." Descartes put it differently. He said, "I think. Therefore I am." He could have omitted the thinking and simply said "I am here. Therefore I am."

Mutations have been considered as of a physical nature, but some mutations might be outwardly invisible. Self-awareness or mental originality would be of this character. Moreover, the origin of the secondary will-forces might be attributed to forms of originality that might be expressed in thought. The potential to which earlier reference was made could be explained by a mutation. From the appearance of the mutation, a potential that was previously absent simultaneously came into existence, borne in the mutation.

Nevertheless, as previously observed, the presence of a potential merely makes possible a new development; it does not assure it. Yet the potential would probably be accompanied by a desire or impulse to express it.

Claws on the feet of bird or beast are not mere ornaments as they are when they are worn as adornments by primitive people to impress one another. The claws having appeared on the feet of an animal as the result of evolution or otherwise, the instinct that guided the use of them also miraculously appeared. Such a correlation between physical equipment and instinctual ability to use it does indeed represent a simultaneous development of necessary brain cells capable of making use of the new equipment; otherwise the new equipment might not only be a hindrance but perhaps a fatal liability. Such noncorrelative mutations have possibly appeared from time to time, with predictable consequences.

Two-headedness in monocephalous creatures, for example, is not an advantage and the specimen usually dies.

That there must be a correlation between physical equipment, such as limbs, tentacles, or claws, that is suitable for new use of that which is present in the environment in the form of objects and properties in outer nature, or new possibilities of discovery by enhancement of one or more of the senses, or better possibility of escape from enemies, or other physical assets, on the one hand, and brain and nervous development, on the other, seems inescapable as an hypothesis of advancement or progress.

We may assume then that man came on the scene at the point in time when he became fitted simultaneously with mental ability to cope with new physical equipment that was sufficiently adaptable, pliable, and flexible to require the quality of mental equipment that indeed was capable of coping with it. The many new possibilities of interchange between man and outer nature needed capabilities beyond the reach of the lower animals.

When his hands came forward with an opposable thumb, man had the potential capacity to become a user of tools. Had he not been endowed simultaneously with the mental capacity to make use of his new equipment, the latter would have been excess baggage. Had he not also been given insight into the properties of matter and certain physical laws, the physical ability to use tools would have been useless or would not have carried very far. Had he not had the potential capacity to appreciate how existing objects might serve him, such as a stick or stone, his opposable thumb would have been of little or no value. Had he, further, not also been provided with a potential capacity to fashion new tools beyond the existing ones lying about in outer nature, such as sticks or stones, man would still be a stick-and-stone race of beings. Some indeed have not advanced far beyond that stage. He needed capacity to observe and to infer, to perceive relationships and combinations. There were the capabilities that distinguished him from mere animal and led him forward.

Therefore, the mental and nervous equipment necessary to advancement called for as radical a departure from the existing mental equipment as was exhibited by the physical departures.

It does not follow, however, that the reverse is true; namely, that brain development is accompanied by new physical equipment. Knowing how to fly did not bring man a set of wings. It was not necessary that he have them. The need was overcome by the possibility of extending sense penetrations and perceptions by instruments devised by the brain's visions. Man very early had the necessary physical equipment, for example, to produce a microscope that vastly increased the power of the eye if his brains could have envisioned the mechanical means of contriving the instrument. The same was true of many other devices and contrivances that helped man to ever greater dominion over nature. The potential was present long before the device was actually brought into being. No further development of man's limbs and senses was necessary to keep pace with what his brains envisioned. Physically man is perhaps as well turned out as he need be to carry out his conquest of nature. It might help him to have eyes in the back of his head, but such additional arrangement does not appear necessary. He already has the rear-view mirror in his mechanical locomotor contrivances, and what else he needs he has the physical capability of bringing to pass if his brains show the way.

Therefore his progress depends on mental and moral development rather than further physical mutation. He needs to go farther, as he has already gone some distance, and, as has already been said, in the development of his secondary will-forces and in the civilization of his ego.

We may now say that the secondary will-forces have the same propelling function as the primary ones, but ordinarily the secondaries, as already observed, lack the peremptory demand of the former.

The secondary will-forces, as also previously described, represent certain interests and values that are unknown to the primaries. They arose, no doubt, much as the physical capabilities arose. This is to say they came forward as potentials, but were spread by individuals in whom particular capabilities appeared.

Once man had the opposable thumb in addition to his other physical equipment advantages such as highly developed senses, his physical equipment was ready to rest on its oars for such a number of millennia of time as might be needed to exploit the full potential. Some new departure, not now even conceivable to man, might after that time appear on the scene. It was and is different with his mental equipment and particularly his moral attributes. These depend on the development and refinement of the secondary will-forces and the ego, by a variety of instrumentalities, including parents, family, school, church, and the state.

We have previously mentioned man's liberation from the need of virtually complete devotion of his time to warding off the ever-present phenomenon of scarcity of need-satisfying means. Progress in that direction depended on the birth of rare insights in particular individuals—after the manner of a mutation in the minute areas of the mental equipment. Here there might be small jumps as well as medium or long jumps, as indeed is reputed also to be characteristic of the evolutionary process in the physical field.

The secondary will-forces came into play as interest beyond those attached to the provision of the bare necessities began to assert themselves. The question arises how man came to feel an interest in anything other than the necessities. If needs were his concern and if these needs were met, what else should attract his senses?

We can only say that man was destined for more, for reasons that he cannot fathom. If he did not have these interests, he would be unable to conceive of their nature, even as a congenitally blind person has no conception of color.

Since he was destined to have them, they had to be provided for in his seed somewhere on earth in one or more individuals. We have to proceed on the assumption that at some moment in time at least the potential appeared in an individual, and we are back again to the question of its development.

In the rude world of primitive man, perhaps the first item of relation between one member of the company and another was who was entitled to a given item of food, drink of water, or standing or sitting place or bed, as previously noted. We have remarked that strength, size, agility, and intelligence were the initial arbiters, with the exception of the young who needed protection and provision by their elders. Might and agility made right, including that of oppression. Selfishness and lack of consideration for the nonself was a natural sequence.

What is called justice would therefore appear to be among the first items of human relations that received conscious attention, since disputes must be settled and there must be some basis of settlement. In the animal world, the "pecking order" or hierarchy of domination resolved such questions.

In the human race, this simple system became deficient at some point. Where that point was and when it appeared is utterly lost in nonhistory. If we are to pursue the subject, we are reduced to inferences and conjecture.

Justice, even if entertained as a concept, remains sterile until it can be enforced. First, however, there has to be a need for justice. This was found in disputes over possession. Someone "saw" that if strength and agility alone determined title, things did not always turn out for the best. Such a one was an unusual observer. He noticed in the consequences that some few were always deprived while others gorged themselves, feeding their own hunger and no other. Perhaps the observer was himself among those who were often deprived. He could feel sympathy for them. Sympathy was the echo from his own ego projected to the other victims of deprivation.

He took mental notes and in good time tried to communicate his conclusions to his chief, who had no doubt reached his own post of eminence by grasping for himself whatever he desired—although other and more endearing qualities might have accounted for his ascendance. In any event, communication being still in its primitive stages, well antedating the smoke signals, the promotor of justice encountered difficulty in explaining his mission. The game of charades having not yet gained the prominence conferred on it by the British very much later, if it had indeed been thought of, it stretches the imagination to come up with an idea of how the first proponent of jurisprudence could have argued his case.

We have to be satisfied with the thought that he must have accomplished it in some fashion or the system could not have gotten started.

The point of importance is, quite aside from questions of origin, that justice or the notion of justice interfered or was designed to interfere with the ordinary course of the primary will-forces and the crude ego. An external consideration was injected into what were thoroughly natural relations. Might must be made to bow to the right, and this concept, perhaps not formed until much later, was the only road to freedom.

If this style of interference went on and should spread, the privileged bruisers grunted to each other, however, the world would be ruined. There would be no point in being stronger. The world would soon be run by the women of either sex and their children. A man could no longer be a man. Who was it that fomented these ideas anyhow? Whoever he was, he should be waylaid, perhaps in some coconut grove, and put out of circulation.

Our bright observer who hungered after justice was too clever for the lowbrows and kept his rendezvous with the chief concealed from them. It happened one day that two adolescents were locked in a struggling brawl. The fight was over the possession of a clam or a coconut, a big clam if it was a clam, a small coconut if it was a coconut. The struggle came into the chief's line of vision, and while so small a matter would ordinarily have been beneath his dignity, he had the youths brought before him. Then he called the man of justice, who had already become known, to come forward, to present him with a case that would no doubt try his judgment and expose him to laughter.

The youngsters stood subdued before the august chieftain who in his own manner of gesture and sign language established the fact that there was a dispute between the two. He glanced askew at his honor, the would-be judge, and sought an answer from him. What disposition should be made of the case?

This was indeed a new experience for our first jurist, and he gulped as the meaning of the chief's question entered his understanding like a cunning messenger. His thoughts ground slowly. After all, this was something really new. Earthlings had never witnessed it before. Blackstone's *Commentaries* had not yet been written.

Rather than answer, which he really did not know how to do, he made a turning motion, hoping to walk away, but a split

glance at the chief halted his idea of evasion. Blood was beginning
to pound in his temples and he wondered why he had been so
foolish as to bring his ideas to the chief; but he saw that it was
too late. Yet, no ideas came to his mind; rather it emptied out
like a cavernous pit.

The chief grunted menacingly and nodded to two men to seize
him as a silent defier or a dunce, as the case might be. The two
jumped to his side but he waved them away. The chief's eyes
opened wide and blinked in amazement. Before he was able to
move, our first jurist shot past him to the two youths, one of
whom still held the coconut or clam. Our Solomon seized it,
turned about and handed it to the chief, who held it in his hand
as a little child might hold an object placed in its hands, not
comprehending the least aspect of it.

Groping for self-mastery, the chief made no sound, but looked
inquiringly at the object in his hands and then at the primeval
judge. The latter waved the boys away in a gesture meaning departure. They turned, looked at the chief who was still without
grunt or other sound, trying to encompass the meaning of what he
had beheld; then they walked away slowly, heads hanging forward,
also sundered in the incomprehensibility that afflicted the chief.

Thus had man paid his first fine.

The chief looked once more at the object, placed it under his
arm, and also walked away without reprimanding the judge or
showing him his face. He was deep in a species of thought and
wished to have time to ruminate over the incident.

The onlookers were mystified. Why had not the chief laid a
hand on the brash interferer? Why had he allowed him to dismiss
the boys?

They glanced at each other among themselves and were
incredulous if not stunned. Never had they seen such an incident.
Without knowing it, they were attending the birth of the administration of justice but were sublimely ignorant of their high
fortune.

Knowledge of the strange incident circulated among the
members of the tribe or group; and the strong ones were not
happy over what they had seen or heard. The chief was highly
regarded, but this incident was the occasion for questions and

indeed, of alarm. If one of the weak ones could be so bold, as this one had been, and could escape and walk away with impunity, the world verily had come to a pretty pass!

To attack the chief would be a risk no one was willing to take, but the intruder, the one who had been so bold, he had no strength and it would be easy to find him alone in good time. Then he could be seized and confiscated, as it were. After all, the intruder must be mad. He would upset all that made life worth living. Left to his devices, there was no telling what sort of spell he might weave over the chief.

The more they thought of the protojudicial specimen, the more they despised him. Grimaces came on their rude and heavy faces as his identity was grunted. They feared him, afraid of what he might do next. Fear moved into hatred. Their primary will-forces, counseled by their intelligence, sensed deprivation if this man should establish himself. For the will-forces, this was an unsavory prospect. Intelligence said in effect: "You know what to do. Do it! Otherwise you will go hungry like the thin ones, the weaklings, the timid ones."

The raw ego joined the clamor. "Who is he compared to us? Why should he be able to come before the chief and take over, yes, you might say, take over the place of the chief himself? Who is he indeed? He is a weak, thin one, and he cannot fight very hard."

They felt debased. If one of them should try what this weakling did the chief would have him stoned or run through! The very thought of the boldness of this wretch, when he had nothing to back up his bravado, was galling. Why, why, did the chief retreat, when anyone, even one of the boys, could have driven the interloper away and trounced him?

The procrustean judge was, however, wily and was not easily caught away from refuge. Not only was this a frustrating and unwelcome fact, but the chief had only a kindly face for the insufferable imposter!

Perhaps they could entice him or delude him by showing him signs of friendliness. Perhaps they could contrive another fight within his sight and draw him into their circle, far enough away from the chief to go undiscovered. They could fall on him then and there or lead him away to some more distant spot and

allow him to lose himself; or at least make plausible to the chief
the report that he was lost.

Their primary will-forces and their offended primitive egos
could go only as far as their intelligence could lead them. They
shrank from the deprivation of privilege and therefore of food
that might ensue, and they beat on their breasts over the insult
to their standing implied in the attitude of the chief.

With all their wiles they were unable to lure the judicial
prototype to his doom. He too had intelligence and shrewdness,
and he acted on the behest of his fear of what would be done to
him should he fall into their hands. This fear drew on his intelligence, and this strange power provided him freely and cheerfully with foresight and the notion of gaining the friendship of
the other weak ones—those who had so long been deprived and
kept hungry by the strong ones. They would be of little help
if an onslaught were made against him or should he be ambushed,
but they could help him by watching covertly and not exposing
themselves in the process. He could then keep out of the reach
of his enemies.

Thus were his wits matched with those of his enemies and
he remained out of their clutches until one day he himself erred.
His intelligence failed him, not because of its dullness, but because
his senses, his eyes and ears, misinformed him. He was deceived,
but by himself alone. He mistook an enemy for a friend—they
looked so much alike and his acquaintance had not been of
long-standing.

He walked with the enemy and was soon delivered into the
hands of those who thirsted for his blood. He was quickly aware
that his outlook was bleak, but his ego made him determined to
show no fear, no matter what his primary will-force expressed,
which, naturally, was fear. His ego was ranged against his instinctual will-force which would have him twist and pull and twist
in an attempt to pull loose and escape. His ego had intelligence on
its side. His wit told him that he could not in any case escape.
Therefore it was better to put on a brave front. The impression
he would make on his captors might give them pause.

He was engaged in these thoughts when a shout caused an
involuntary side-turn of his head. Into his view came three or

four of his gaunt friends over the brow of a low hill not far away. He was not sure that they had seen him since they had paused only momentarily before they turned and ran, jumping angularly over obstacles, fleeing as rapidly as their thin legs would carry them. They were making all speed toward the lair or abode of the chief, which was some fair distance away.

A small number from the band of kidnapers who held our judge sped after the fleeing thin ones and were soon close on their heels when one of the leaders who had stayed behind holding the judge shouted for their return. He was haunted by fear that the pursuers might be detected and the whole plot might be exposed. Fear of the chief was not without foundation, as he had taken pains to establish it early in his ascendency. More than one recalcitrant had tasted his prowess and gone down before him.

The pursuers at first gave no heed, possessed with the desire to catch the detectors of their perfidy. If they should make their getaway, the chief would surely learn of the plot. Nevertheless, when they heard the shout, the idea of obedience took hold, and they returned, protesting. But the rudiments of conscience had pricked the fortress of the primary will-forces and the raw ego of those who held the captive. It was not certain that the thin ones had seen the captive. If they had not seen him, there was danger in capturing them or pursuing them too close to the chief's vicinity. Conscience resided in the uncertainty—a lurking fear of being discovered.

If the thin ones had seen the captive, they might still report what they had seen, but uncertainty might cloud their report. Better under the circumstances—oh, how conscience was concerned over evil doing!—better, perhaps, to liberate the captive. They had not yet done anything against him, and he might be grateful for escaping what he surely knew would be no feast of friendship.

A division erupted among the captors. In some the will-forces pulsed strongly, to the exclusion of all else; others were silent, bothered, and troubled. In them, no clear ascendancy of conscience or rational fear, only an amorphic fear, pressing, but not distinct, declared itself. Two of the group, not the strongest physically but the most listened to for their wit, moved resolutely for freeing the captive, led by relative strength of reason that was dominant over their own will-forces and pestered by the vague fear of consequences that spoke for conscience.

The judge was freed and he went his way. He returned to his own bailiwick and we lose sight of him, but what he had done was not forgotten. The chief had seen something he had not witnessed before, and having witnessed the original act of crude justice, he was able to vary it a bit. He did not confine the forfeiture to youngsters but applied it subsequently to the older ones in his fold. He did not often hold court since there was danger of defiance or even resistance. By being judicious he avoided withering the tender bud of justice. It could grow and blossom into a full bloom in time.

He was aware that interference with the rude and violent passions of his followers must be tempered with restraint. The halter must be slipped on gently but firmly. Onlookers must understand that it was not merely for the comfort and tranquility of the chief himself that he applied the curbs, but for their own better repose and safety. A community of interest could thus become recognized. It was the peaceful ones against the few troublemakers. The community attitude, supported by the power to punish, paved the way for justice and a degree of freedom. It also sowed the seed of social conscience in the form of community *expectations*.

That restraints that could later be turned inward, as already discussed, must first come from external sources lay in what appears to be a law of the will-forces and the raw ego, namely, that it is impossible to feel actual regret over an act committed in gratification of a primary will-force or the raw ego if the attendant sense responses and emotions were pleasing. This would be unnatural and would contradict the purpose of these impulses and appetites. Regret can only come from the secondary level, from mental sources. A primary will-force cannot wish above all to eat and then regret having eaten, so long as no unpleasant result ensued, as remarked in a previous chapter.

If the food should not have been touched because it belonged to someone else, the regret over having eaten it in any case must be referred to another department. It would be useless to ask the stomach to be sorry and to repent. The same may be said of all normal appetites of the flesh. One may *regret* (mentally) an illicit act of sex, but it would be hypocritical to say that one is biologically sorry. The regret or repentance must proceed, to repeat, from another department. It is impossible that an appetite should regret its gratification. *Repentance of an act that was biologically pleasant can come only from the mind and moral or religious considerations.*

Therefore, it seems clear, as previously observed, that the arresting hand must first come from the outside; and the first clutch of the arresting hand had of necessity initially to be instructed to do so by an impulse or reaction in one person to the act of another. There must have been an interest in the cessation of the offending act from the outside.

Next, for such an arresting motion or act to be based on anything more than a reacting primary will-force or raw ego in the person exerting the restraint, i.e., if justice was to be done, there had to be present a consideration external even to the two immediate parties; for it is not justice if a superior force arrests a lesser one merely for the sake of the comfort or convenience of the one applying the superior force. It *might* not violate justice, but it would not constitute justice on the face of it. The lesser force might have had good reason to annoy or disturb the superior force. Thus we come back again to the referee of a previous page.

Justice, to repeat, is more a concern of the ego, the secondary or refined ego, than of the primary will-forces. The interest of the latter lies in the deprivation attendant on an injustice—deprivation of property or goods or of the means of coming into possession of goods or property. This represents an extensive scope, to be sure, but the ego as the mirror of man's relation to others of his community and of his species, reflecting how he stands in their eyes and how his acts impinge on them, including, in turn, their standing in the eyes of their neighbors or before the public generally, has less tangible but not less significant ramifications.

It seems impossible to avoid the conclusion that the rudiments of justice first had to be privately established as an act of intervention in conduct before it could be established as a third force or as an arbiter. One individual must initially have intervened between two others, throwing his weight to the one whose interest he shared; but we have just now said that justice could not be asserted by an act of self-help. Yet that is not the same as saying that justice could not have *arisen* from such a source. It seems most likely that it did indeed so arise, since no one, with the exceptions previously noted (referring to the protective shield of parents over children or of men over women), would know, save through self-experience, that any particular act of behavior was or was not objectionable, except in extreme cases. Only first-hand knowledge would supply the appropriate familiarity. Therefore, self-interest was virtually a *sine qua non* for intervention.

In any event, whether the intervention was in behalf of another or in behalf of the self, it was private. Initially, there was no referee. A referee had to be agreed upon or he was no true referee. A private person, if he had the means and the wit to seize power, could indeed become an adjudicator, but this would not convert him into a referee. A tyrant could establish courts for civil and criminal cases, and justice could be dispensed—often, no doubt, quite impartially—but justice would always stop at the tyrant's own interests. These he would not allow to be adjudicated; or if he allowed it, he would or would not comply, according to his own pleasure, or he would control the judge or judges and thus assure his own "freedom" while denying freedom to others.

Such a caricature of justice might yet in time be converted into real justice, so far as this is attainable in the hands of men.

All human institutions have rude beginnings, and the dispensing of justice is no exception. We are concerned here about the origin of justice in man's character and his relationship with others of his kind, and not, at the moment, in the quality of justice. Justice represented the first step toward other regard, and paved the way for the first halting steps of freedom and away from oppression of the weak by the strong or the parasitic.

The war crime trials after World War II were widely condemned as being no more than the imposition of penalties by the victors on the vanquished, and not an act of justice. The charge cannot be denied successfully. It was virtually an *ex parte* proceeding. There was no impartial referee.

As human beings, however, we should not register high surprise. To repeat, all human institutions have rude beginnings. Man is a blundering, groping creature by nature because he is prodded unmercifully by his primitive impulses and at the same time very prone to error; so that even when he dedicates himself sincerely to a new enterprise or a new and complicated endeavor, he does poorly, even if it is his best.

We have but to turn to the progress of mechanical inventions and improvements to appreciate the crudity of the first endeavors in a new field. Compare the modern airplane with the one flown at Kitty Hawk only two or three generations in the past! Compare the modern automobile with what now seem the pathetic contraptions of only fifty years ago! Why should we expect international justice to spring fully perfected over night? It is much more difficult to perfect justice than to perfect mechanical devices.

Therefore the war crime trials after World War II can at least be regarded as a beginning. They may properly be criticized for their deficiency in point of justice, and should be analyzed without bias and their defects pitilessly exposed. In the future, man may do better if he is aware of the previous deficiencies. Nevertheless, progress will be very slow because of the fiery primitive passions to be overcome—the demands of the ego, the national ego, and that of those allied in purpose in league against the enemy.

Were the passions of hatred and revenge not so greatly stirred, the proceedings of international justice in the wake of war would still offer a sufficiency of difficulties because of the coming together of divergent national systems of justice, wholly different approaches to the establishment of the facts and guarding against prejudice. With passions at high heat, it is quite clear that in the present state of international division into separate sovereignties, none yet subject ultimately to external restraint (with minor exceptions), it would be impossible to constitute an impartial tribunal—one before which the conquered would enjoy the same rights as the victor. Yet in the absence of such equality of rights, justice cannot be administered. It would at best be one-sided justice, and that is a contradiction in terms.

In spite of these objections, it was nevertheless well to make a beginning: a step toward the creation of a new set of international expectations. No undertaking of such fantastic proportions could ever be launched should we await its perfections before starting. So long as man is bent on perfecting or at least improving, so far as he is able, the means to a desirable end, he should be encouraged to do so, but yet not shielded from criticism; for it is criticism that builds his determination to do better. Criticism represents the opinion of outraged or contrary-thinking observers and onlookers, and man's ego is sensitive to the opinion of others, no matter how much he may sputter and rebel at what to him seems unjustified attacks. They will take effect in time if they are well grounded, and his efforts at refutation are a part of the refinement process.

The recent effort launched by Lord Bertrand Russell represents what might be a typical excrescence as an offshoot from the first major endeavor, an aberration perhaps. The big event is often followed by minor ones, such as was the great charter of England of 1215. Subsequently, a succession of kings and pretenders offered charters until the fashion ran out.

Russell's effort should nevertheless not be denigrated, assuming its sincerity. The time to take a step in the process of progress is when the occasion arises. The eminent philosopher can, however, be criticized for proposing another *ex parte* proceeding. He would try only the leading statesmen of one country, as if the others were *ipso facto* innocent, and this would represent a prejudgment in itself. To be an instrument of justice, such a tribunal must be vested with power to bring all parties before it.

It is not enough to brand one nation as an aggressor and then undertake to try its leaders. Again, the case would be prejudged. In the world as it is constituted, and the nations as they act and interact, having ambitions and objectives of their own, it would be surprising indeed if all the virtues were ranged on one side and all the crimes and evil on the other.

A tribunal would cite all the nations that had a stake in the controversy. After a thorough investigation, including the questioning of witnesses under agreed rules, indictments might be drawn; but an indictment must not be mistaken for a conviction.

Again the pertinent witnesses must be called in the ensuing trial and all the pertinent facts examined. Only then could a judgment be made.

And who, in the present state of the world, would enforce the decision? To contemplate this question would quickly show how far the nations of the world today are from an international order in which justice would hope to be instituted; but, to repeat, the mathematician philosopher, assuming his sincerity, should not be condemned for seeking to help the establishment of a world rule of law. His method and timing fell far short of perfection, but such is the lot of mortals.

A little reflection will reveal to us the ordinary fact that the law or rules of the game *initially depended for their invocation on the person or persons who were injured or placed at a disadvantage by an infraction or violation.* Even today those who are beneficiaries of a breach of rule or law are highly tempted to wink or to be blind and let the incident pass; and if ordinary observation in the form of mere empiricism is to be trusted, they readily in many instances succumb to the temptation.

If, indeed, a referee has been established, invested with power to make awards or at least to hold for trial, he becomes the initiator of an endeavor to redress the infraction.

Rules and laws are made to redress injustices and inequities. They represent the restraints on wayward impulses that lead to excesses and damage. Therefore they are in behalf of the innocent and the violated.

Referees or even guardians of the law, however, are not ubiquitous; in fact, they are apparently more often absent than present when an infraction occurs. If the injured or offended party (in the legal sense) did not complain or denounce the offender, justice would be left unattended in numerous instances.

Going back now to early man, it seems safe to say that the primitive *Homo* did not volunteer to say or otherwise make it known that he had hurt someone or wrested a shank of venison from a smaller companion and then declare: "I should be punished." Quite the contrary. If he was accused of such a despicable act, he was probably quick to deny it and to indicate that his accuser was falsely accusing him. The "ought" of the case depended for its invocation on the injured one. He was habituated by the inculcated expectations to call the violator to account.

To be punished means to be inflicted with pain. The organism by nature seeks to avoid pain. Avoidance of pain or other unpleasant consequences is represented by a primary will-force. Punishment is therefore automatically an object of avoidance. The will-force will look to intelligence to act accordingly. In the absence of a contrary mandate from conscience, the avoidance will unquestionably be sought.

Where referees and police are established, they are regarded as unbiased substitutes or agents for the injured or offended ones. Even then, as just noted, the victim must himself often carry his message of woe to the guardian of the law and make appropriate representations of the incident. Such a choice represents the very heart of freedom, no less so than being left undisturbed in the peaceful pursuit of legitimate goals.

In the field of sports, the referees are usually the first and last resort for the detection of infractions. Even under these circumstances, the offender does not report voluntarily. If a violator of a rule has ever halted action or "blown the whistle" on himself when he committed a foul, the incident has not been publicized sufficiently to become commonly known.

To recognize the absurdity of any notion that players would report their own infractions, one has but to imagine a professional player in a game of American football suddenly throwing up his hand and shouting "Referee, in that play I committed a personal foul. I think my team should be penalized fifteen yards!"

Yet, in much of our thought about public, civic, and international affairs, we seem to expect conduct of this order.

Shakespeare's Falstaff, in his droll irresponsibility, called to Slender:

"Slender," he rasped, "I broke thy head! What matter has thou against me?"

Falstaff was free to be so bold, knowing the Slender was hardly a threat. Should Slender indeed have remonstrated, Falstaff could have broken his head a second time with impunity. In a guffaw he could then have repeated his question: "Slender, I broke your head this second time. Hast thou not yet any matter against me?"

In the absence of a referee, Slender was helpless and oppressed, and Falstaff did not fear that Slender would go to the guardian of the law, for he would surely see Slender again. He might then break his head a third time, and for good.

Had there been an onlooker who was equal in physical powers if not in girth to the obese buffoon and who for reasons of his own bore him hatred and malice, Falstaff might have fared differently. He might indeed have refrained from addressing Slender as he did and would not have confessed to breaking his head. He would have had a conscience. It weighed about two hundred and fifty pounds!

To impress the primary will-forces or the ego sufficiently to beget restraint, the outside force must be in the form of a physical presence in the immediate environment. The farther away or remote the source of punishment and the greater the chance of escape, the less powerful will be the incentive to practice self-restraint.

The first instance of self-restraint, already reflected upon in these pages, was no doubt a matter of experience and memory of consequences that were not pleasant (leaving out again special biological relationships, such as parent and child). Had Falstaff repeated his headbreaking offense on Slender while, unknown to him, his puissant adversary was close by and witnessed the act, but only later made known to a Falstaff, Falstaff's future behavior, we may be sure, would have undergone a modification.

The primitive bases of freedom may be discerned quite readily in the restraints placed on the primary impulses. We saw earlier that the internal freedom within the individual arose not from free expression of the primary will-forces and the raw ego but by establishing mental dominion over them and then exercising free choice among alternative courses of action or conduct.

In relations with others, two types of freedom may be distinguished. One is the freedom of the individual from oppression by the ruling power. The other is freedom from interference by unruly, freebooting, and lawless elements in the peaceful pursuit of life. In this instance, the ruling power becomes the repository of freedom by exercising the police power and dispensing justice.

In the first of these varieties of freedom, oppression by the ruling power is analogous to the tyranny of the primary will-forces or the raw ego, or both, within the individual. The result is slavery to the appetites, impulses, untamed ambition, and untempered selfishness of the tyrant.

The subject of a tyrannical ruler, be the latter a tribal chief, king, or dictator, is not free because he is at the mercy of the ruling one's impulses, whims, and desires, without recourse. Until the ruler is brought under the restraint of law, which is to say the product of mental reflection guided by wisdom, his subjects will not be free. A ruler who is not answerable to a referee is not a true dispenser or guarantor of freedom. If he cannot be made accountable to law, he is a potential tyrant.

We now have the paradox before us in full splendor: Freedom is the child of rational *restraint*.

The individual can only be free if he is ruled by his mind, steeped in wisdom. The citizen is free only when his society is free of the depredations of wrongdoers, and the society is free only if it controls the ruling powers.

7.

Leaving the
Animal Behind

It is indeed not improbable that some human beings are innately drawn toward the good as they comprehend it. To say this is not to deny the wayward inclinations of the primary will-forces or the raw ego. Human traits and characteristics are indeed diverse and variable, both physical, mental, and moral. The law of probability in the assignment of genes seems to ordain that there will be few beautiful specimens, few who meet the widely recognized canons of comely features, coloring, shape, and posture. In the mental field, the law seems equally bent on bestowing the highest intelligence on only a few while it distributes ordinary intelligence on the many. It is kind, however, in maintaining at a low level the number who are mentally deficient. In the same manner, some human specimens seem to be born naturally good, or born with an inclination toward the good and an aversion for evil.

Indeed, but for these seeds that grow into good examples, the course of civilization might have faltered even more than its history has shown it capable of doing so well.

Since the primary will-forces and the raw ego are not given to reflection, some additional force had of necessity to appear on the scene if things were not to go on forever as they were. This is to say the human race would not have occurred.

The fact that the human race is here is sufficient evidence that the other force did appear, and we have endeavored to show how it may have manifested itself originally and made a beginning.

143

This force, we may repeat, was the origin of the secondary will-forces and the ameliorative or civilized ego.

We have mentioned justice as possibly the first need of man if he was to live in at least a tolerable degree of harmony with his fellow-beings as his numbers increased. Yet justice is only a condition of life, not an end in itself. It makes the living of life with others in society possible. It does not supply the content of life. This is a function of a variety of interests and aspirations. Justice, we saw, was principally a concern of the ego, although the primary will-forces also had an interest in it.

Man also was endowed with a desire for knowledge, a penchant for inquiry and exploration that went beyond mere curiosity. He aspired to know more than it was necessary to know in order to catch a rabbit or a fish or snare a bird. His rudimentary mind ranged beyond these simple devices. For a reason for which itself no reason can be found, he was not satisfied with what he already knew, nor content with doing all things always the same way. The novel attracted him; the ingenious fascinated him. He wished to know the reason for the phenomena he beheld, and was much given to looking below the surface, above, inside, and around. Great wonders were often hidden in unsuspected places, and man was captivated by wonders.

His desire for knowledge, for truth, and for explanation was in the form of a compelling force that drove him, urged him, or drew him into paths and endeavors that he expected would yield what he sought. But for the existence of this secondary will-force, man might be fond of such truths as were laid before him and grateful for knowledge that came to him on the wings of doves, but he would be a passive receptacle. He would feel no inclination to exert himself. He would not be driven to delving, exploring, reading, experimenting. He would stand flabby and apathetic before the stream of events. He might fold his arms and contemplate, but if he had never for a prolonged period dedicated himself to learning, he would understand little of what passed before him. His stance and act of beholding would be little more than a vacant stare. The meaning of a thousand details and facets of reality would pass him by.

Desire for knowledge sustains the process of learning. Yet

this desire is neither uniform as an impellent nor undifferentiated as to predilection. Some incline, as noted earlier, toward mathematical knowledge, some toward legal knowledge, or medical or philosophical or scientific knowledge.

It can, of course, be said that the will-force that drives the motor for learning is sometimes of a fractional horsepower, and in some instances turned in reverse, but any positive activity depends on the driving power of a will-force or the ego.

Man does not simply "will" to do something. The desire to do something is specific and it arises in him. It carries its own force; the desire *is* the force, and it is differentiated from other desires by a qualitative distinction. The desire to know is also directed to specific ends. To be sure, some knowledge is foundational and therefore not substantive; it is instrumental, such as arithmetic or spelling, grammar, or logic. We use it toward other ends, such as determining quantities, constructing words, or making sense out of them.

The desire to know in the more fruitful sense lies beyond the instruments. It lies in the substantive areas. The biologist seeks knowledge of plants and animals, their structure, behavior, habits, usefulness to man, or their noxious characteristics. The sociologist seeks knowledge about human society, manner of living, means of livelihood, welfare of people in communities, and similar data that will be useful to him in his work.

If he has but little attraction to the field, his will-force impelling him will be weak. Knowledge must be sought, pursued, organized, and applied if it is to have significance.

Yet knowledge for all its value does not direct itself. It is directed by him who possesses it. What he does with his knowledge depends on his character. To be sure, his character may be modified by knowledge gathered on the way, in school or from reading, listening, and observing, and from experience and cogitation upon it.

Knowledge may be of use to intelligence, in the sense that it supplies data or raw materials for the exercise of judgment. The latter may be ever so good, but if it expends itself on misinformation or lack of information, it is greatly handicapped. Ignorance may consist both of lack of information and misinformation

Often the ignorant person is misinformed because of indolence and disinclination to verify what he has read, heard, or observed. His secondary will-force constituted of the desire to learn is relatively weak, as any secondary will-force may be!

Knowledge of itself is neutral in the moral sense. It may be used for one or another purpose by this person or that, indiscriminately. It asks no questions.

How much knowledge is gathered by a variety of individuals depends not only on the strength of their secondary will-force dedicated to learning but also on innate capacity, competence of instruction, and on the order of inspiration.

In essence, knowledge is an instrumentality and as such may be useful or perhaps even a handicap. Wrong knowledge or deficient knowledge may be compared with a wrong instrument; and deficient knowledge with a second-rate instrument or one that is not in good condition, such as a dull saw or worn motor.

Because of the great variety of subjects to which modern man is exposed, any individual's knowledge will be found deficient in so many departments in which he is called upon for intelligent responses that he may be justified in regarding himself as an ignoramus in most departments. He cannot hope to be more than a sciolist in the great majority of fields to which he is exposed and in which he has a stake. Even the specialist is usually aware of the deficiency of his knowledge in his own field. If nothing else limits him, the current state of the art or discipline or science limits him. Man is inadequate before nearly all possibilities, and it is his realization of this fact that continues to drive him in search of more knowledge. Even though man moves and operates in a finite medium, to him the possibilities seem infinite in nearly all directions.

H. G. Wells called for a "world brain"; true, a synthesis of existing knowledge in all the vital fields is desirable; but what mortal man will have the capacity or the time to absorb it all? We do have encyclopedias, and they are useful as books of reference.

When all is said and done, knowledge will not and cannot satisfy man because it represents a means to an end. Therefore it is the ends that contain the values. This is not to say that the means are to be deprecated or reduced to insignificance. On the contrary, the means may determine whether we reach the end, as anyone may verify who begins a long overland tour in a dubious conveyance. Nevertheless, the conveyance is still a conveyance, even if it has a value of its own or is devoid of value.

It is a characteristic of knowledge that its pursuit is zestful if it is in a field to which the individual is drawn by his mental constitution. It is zestful just as the pursuit of a primary will-force is absorbing and possibly full of gusto. It can also be considerably less than zestful if it lies in a field in which one is devoid of interest. The lack of interest is not the fault of the field. To someone else it may represent the summit of dedication of attention, accompanied by joy and self-immersion. Lack of interest represents a deficiency in the sensibilities of the person, and such lack resides in everyone. Who, for example, would be expected to find a deep interest in so various a group of fields as painting, musical composition, banking, taxation, numismatics, insurance, theology, botany—to mention only a small number?

To pursue knowledge in a field that is not congenial may be an irksome exercise, or be felt as an imposition. The mind is not hospitable to learning what it apprehends with difficulty. Any schoolboy will testify to the natural revulsion he feels when he must study a subject that is not to his liking. One may find literature "dry"; in another it may be arithmetic. Yet another may find history boring while chemistry attracts him and makes a joy of its pursuit.

The feeling of revulsion or joy is not itself mental. The mind does not feel, but its efforts are accompanied by feeling. It also arouses feeling at times; and the state of feeling in turn affects the mental process, sometimes indeed disturbing the process and hindering its orderly progress.

The relation between the secondary will-forces and the mind may be observed as we contemplate a repetition of effort in an anticlimactic sequence. The effect is not unlike that observable when a primary will-force is confronted with repetition of an act that represented full gratification of an appetite. If a table d'hote dinner is set before a gourmet who has only an hour previously assuaged his hunger with a full meal, he will be repelled by the very idea of eating again so soon. The food may be of a kind that would arouse a sharp appetite in one who had gone five or six hours without a meal, but in the sated gourmet it arouses no temptation. He can think of nothing more cloying than food at the moment. Were he compelled to eat in any event, he would find that what was ordinarily and so often a great pleasure was suddenly converted into an ordeal.

If we substitute a mental exercise or an exercise entailing mental exertion for the experience of the gourmet, we may detect a similarity. Assume that a writer has written a dramatic presentation after much effort, loses his manuscript, and is left without a copy. If he now undertakes recreation of his work, his elan will have suffered a declination. His secondary will-force now feels the friction of reluctance. Left to itself this force might be too weak to carry him through the whole process of reconstruction and rewriting. He would be inclined to lay the undertaking aside, and might indeed make slow progress. He would much rather write something new. To come back to the beginning for a new start would be much like sitting down to a warmed-over meal. He might indeed write only intermittently for lack of zest and feel a temptation to give up his effort.

At this point, however, his ego might step into the breach and call for completion. It might be a matter of pride or of reluctance to disappoint those who, having confidence in his work or having seen the manuscript and thinking highly of it, might urge him not to desert it. Again, even the primary will-force might show an interest. If the author were rather impecunious, he might be in need of replenishing his coffers. The will-force representing the basic appetites or needs would then call for return to the original endeavor, assuming that the author's judgment indicated to him that he could, if he had the inclination, redo the last play in much less time than he would require to write a new one.

It would be a question of the relative strength of the opposing forces. Under certain circumstances, the balance of force would indeed decide the issue, assuming that no moral question were involved. The decision would once more, then, be of the order pictured by the determinists who deny the existence of freedom of will. If the relative strength of the opposing and allied forces could be measured after the manner of a flow of water or electricity, it would be possible to determine the outcome. Either the combination of the desire of the ego for completion of the task by rewriting plus the positive contribution of the primary will-force would be sufficient to overcome the mental reluctance to retrace the original steps, or it would not. If it were of sufficient strength, the mental reluctances would be overruled. If the combination were of less strength, the mental opposition would prevail, and the author would not rewrite the lost manuscript.

Of course, an overt final decision might not be reached at a particular moment. The question might be left undecided and might become a nagging and taunting ghost in the background of feeling, never quite absent but also not insistent enough to demand a final resolution of the question.

We may say that the secondary will-force that represents the desire for knowledge is indeed a variable force, one that is often not only weak but at times negative, while in other instances (meaning in individuals) it may be quite strong or even indefatigable in some departments. We may be quite sure that in no individual is the desire for knowledge equal in all departments, as we have already observed. Again, even in a department in which interest is strong, circumstances may intervene in a manner that will drain the interest of its vigor or even convert it into revulsion, as we have only now tried to exemplify.

However, whatever may be the variable voltage, so to speak, of the will-force that drives or attracts man to a pursuit of knowledge, it is evident that despite its variation from individual to individual and from one interest in the same individual to another, including reluctance to engage in effort and sometimes a veritable resistance to learning, the pursuit of knowledge by man continues despite all obstacles, all hindrances, such as those reflecting reluctance, and despite all tendencies to apathy and resistance.

The net positive force has had a greater magnitude than the negative and inhibitory. The rising educational level of the world and the clamor for more higher education reflect the high potency of this secondary will-force. We must, however, be careful to note that the force derived from the primary will-forces and the ego

often sustain the secondary will-force, and may be credited with
a forward surge when the secondary force would flag, as we have
just seen. While on numerous other occasions the primary will-
forces and the ego are at dagger-points with the desire to study or
to learn, they do upon occasion come to the rescue. The ego may
be greatly concerned about the status or lack of status that centers
about education or the lack of it. It may drive the individual to
learning and to an educational regimen against the natural inclination of his secondary will-force.

The ego then gains the support of intelligence and this power
helps to shape affairs in a manner that will make possible study and
education, either through formal schooling or by other endeavor.

Of course, the ego may ally itself with an already strong inclination to study and learn. In that event, the result may be a
scholar or a degree of erudition far beyond the ordinary.

Much as the secondary will-forces plus the occasional help
from the primary will-force and the frequent help of the ego combine to promote the interests of learning or the acquisition of
knowledge, other forces, conditions, and circumstances may produce a countervailing effect.

The need to spend a great amount of time and effort to gain
a livelihood has not yet been overcome in many parts of the world.
Therefore study and learning are retarded by the need of meeting
the primary necessities. In many parts of the world, this low state
of productivity per man has promoted illiteracy and ignorance.

Other inhibitions have also frustrated the desire expressed by
this secondary will-force. One of these has been the external restraint exerted by dominant elements of society that had an
economic stake in the suppression of education of the masses.
Ignorant serfs and peasants were more docile and more easily held
in subjugation than enlightened ones. Education would have
produced two effects that were not desired. It would have created
discontent and dissatisfaction with the existing order, and it would
have provided greater competence toward preparation of a rebellion and its prosecution. Therefore schools were not provided,
and no provision was made for general private education.

The question foremost in the minds of the dominant stratum
of such a society was: why provide education to those who are

most useful to us in a state of ignorance? On this there was little disagreement and the position was solidly supported by the primary will-forces and the ego of the dominant group.

It is once more a question how such a condition could be changed wherever it existed. Who would offer resistance? Who would be so bold as to defy the ruling order? Who would expose himself to the disciplinary harshness that lay in store for any dissident or revolutionary individual or coterie?

Surely it is a measure of the power of the will-force speaking for the desire for knowledge that someone did appear on such a scene from time to time to challenge the existing order. How many became martyrs and how many succeeded at least in part is a matter of history, and it is imperfectly recorded; for in many instances other grievances, some of them more vociferously expressed, were also present.

The history of culture, however, is not simply a history of revolt of the deprived, decisive as this element may have been in many instances. Much culture was developed within the upper strata, and in various degrees this was absorbed by the underlying strata, both as a natural inclination to learn and as prodded by the ego to imitate and emulate.

It would be expected that those whose intellect and sensibilities more nearly approached those of the higher strata had the incentive to challenge the superstructure. This would explain the irony that is the affliction of liberalism that soon finds itself challenged and often overthrown by the next lower levels for being too conservative.

In any event, man has on occasion been willing to battle for the privilege of education. This has been true of individuals, in a milder sense, who in behalf of themselves have overcome many obstacles in their way toward education.

Once achieved, an extensive range of knowledge and opinions based on it may be regarded as a personal preserve, and defended as such.

There is indeed a species of vested mental interest in a store or system of knowledge once it has been organized and published to the world. Pride in it may lead to a defense of it that may be and usually is both tenacious and belligerent. Academic econo-

mists, for example, who may be given to citing vested economic
interests as the dark selfish forces moving in the background of
legislative chicanery, may regard themselves as objective viewers
of the scene, resting self-satisfiedly arm in arm with the noblest
virtues; but they may soon be found to entertain vested mental
interests and to be mere mortals with ordinary blood in their
veins.

Question the logic, force, or soundness of their elaborated
theory that underlies their stand on some issue, and their objectivity may quickly vanish. The ego has been wounded and the
response may be a wonder to behold! No vested economic interest
will battle so ferociously! The secondary will-force associated with
learning, which has been the subject of our attention, will not
be as vehement as the ego, but it may be outraged under the
attack sufficiently to drive the host, murmuring, to the library and
reference books to sustain his thesis.

The ego on its part will go the usual route under the circumstances and may easily outdo in vehemence the will to research. It will slide into the *ad hominem* gambit while disavowing
most piously any such crude motive. Nevertheless, it will suggest
that so and so, who happens to be the very one who mounted the
most telling criticism against our host, is guilty of what really is
shabby logic. This lapse of logic is surprising, his ego suggests, in
one who is usually so careful or at least prides himself on being
scrupulous. Recall that he, the critic, makes a great to-do over
intellectual dishonesty!

"It is a funny thing," the ego further suggests, "having
nothing to do with the criticism, but he (the critic) is so intellectual he forgets to clean his teeth—have you noticed?—and to
have his shoes shined. He is obviously above these mundane little
things.

"All in all he is an admirable person and I wouldn't say
anything against him. They say he is rather fractious and hard to
get along with—but then that is true of a great many people. He
shows some absentmindedness but I wouldn't say that he verges on
senility. Anybody can forget things at times, even so small a thing
as buying toothpaste. Everybody, of course, has his faults but we
should forgive them considering one's own faults. Brilliant people

—have you ever noticed?—sometimes have remarkably poor judgment in some things, through no fault of their own. They don't know any better. It could be a genetic deficiency, and who can do anything about that? It begins to show especially, I have read, at the onset of senility. Before that it often succeeds in concealing itself by instant corrective measures, and a man may get a high reputation, but then soon go to pieces. But we shouldn't criticize and I would be the last to do so. What ails him could happen to anyone!

"I don't mind what he says about my argument and supporting data. They speak for themselves. He couldn't hurt anyone anyway. I doubt that many people would pay any attention to him. He has never really done anything to be taken very seriously. I hate to say this, but he made an awful—well, no! No use to go into that. I give him credit for meaning well and let it go at that. If only he wouldn't set himself up as some great authority in a field in which he is really second-rate! That's what amuses me. He takes himself so seriously! I guess he's afraid that if he didn't, no one would.

"Just the same, I like him and wouldn't do anything in the world to hurt him."

The difference between the secondary will-force that has had our attention and the ego lies in the character of reaction to frustration or hindrance. The desire for knowledge is not itself concerned with the ego's affairs. The ego comes on the scene when the integrity of the knowledge already gained is questioned, or when the path to further pursuit of knowledge may be impeded.

When the desire for knowledge is frustrated, backbiting becomes the ego's specialty. Resistance of the secondary will-force to barriers that lie in the path of learning and gaining knowledge will call on intelligence to find means of removing the obstacle. The resistance will be great or small as the thirst for knowledge is great or small. A highly active mind feels the deprivation keenly, or rather, the person feels the hindrance more acutely than does one whose mind is otiose or sterile. In either case, the typical ego reaction to frustration is not duplicated—unless, of course, the personal interest of the ego is aroused, as it may be, since the ambition of the person to achieve a higher status may be obstructed. The ego will then become involved simultaneously with the secondary will-force. Moreover, as already observed, a primary will-force may also show its face, interested, by way of the intelligence, in the larder.

The great influence exerted by this secondary will-force on civilization needs no further emphasis—not only in causing discontent and uprising, but in impelling individuals to make extraordinary effort to achieve more knowledge, and to defend acquired knowledge.

We have now given brief attention to the desire for justice and the inclination to learning and knowledge, as representing both the secondary will-forces and the ego.

We have mentioned also the direct aspiration to a greater beauty, lodged in the esthetic sense. There is a fourth secondary will-force that is secondary in one aspect but rests on a primary will-force as its point of departure. This is romantic love.

The primary aspect is clearly the continuation of the species; but its elaboration into a thousand paths of romance, given to the world in song and music and literature, is a far cry from the primary function.

The manifestation of sex in man is a prime example of the partial release of man from complete instinctive guidance. The remainder of his activity in the field may then have a meaning beyond the primary function of the instinct. The conduct of man in this area is relatively free, and the quality of his conduct depends on reason, or, as used in these pages, on man's mind. The release of sex in man from instinct includes the liberation from seasonality or periodicity of the sexual appetite, and the substitution of reason for instinct in the regulation of sexual activity and its results.

One of man's great sources of motivation is indeed found in the secondary level of the mating instinct. Personal ambition of the male is often centered around the attachment and lure of romance that in turn springs from the division of the sexes. The so-called love motive has filled library shelves with poetry, drama, and novels. It has lent its hand to operas, cinematic creations, and folksong. It has gone beyond these cultural expressions into dance and into personal adornment, in the form of dress, jewelry, and coloration, and has practiced a variety of accentuations and concealments.

It is not necessary to award to sex the all-pervasive influence awarded to it by Freud to recognize the influence it has exerted and continues to exert on human existence and civilization.

Some of the great struggles with conscience have raged around the devastating influence of this secondary will-force. Its great power is, of course, rooted in its basic function.

It seems to be a practice of nature that all needs and avoidances are attended by great potentials of sense gratification or great pain upon frustration. This potential rises to the secondary level in romantic love where the initial purpose is all but lost. Who, when he sits down to a meal that has been exquisitely prepared and served under circumstances in which elaborate and artistic settings and placings abound, feels that what he is about to enjoy is dedicated to the purpose of remaining alive? Yet the purpose of taking food is precisely that.

Our secondary will-forces overlay the primary needs with a great variety of esthetic contrivances and elusive concealments that to man enhance his interest and cater to his ego.

Romantic love goes so far afield in some of its fanciful flights that its primary motivation is not only concealed but made to seem a barbarism. The elaboration of the instinctual into secondary pursuits is not altogether confined to the human species, as may be learned from observation of the so-called nuptial dances and flights of birds, and similar odd behavior in others of the higher animals.

Nevertheless, man carries the secondary activities and circumlocutions far beyond any similar behavior of the lower animals. This much to-do about something provides an example of how process can be converted into what seems to be an end in itself. The process of feeding the body becomes a part of the process of living—in many instances an enjoyable part that pays its own way, so to speak.

The same may be said of romantic love. Although it is part of the process of achieving continuity of the species, it stands on its own feet as if it were an end in itself. The joy and rapture and deep sentiment, the ineffable yearning for mutual companionship, all seem fully sufficient unto themselves without being mere means to an end.

The question here is not why nature should lure man in this fashion, set the "tender trap" so to speak, but how much of life is devoted to and motivated by the secondary will-forces.

The power of romantic attachment has been demonstrated on occasions without number, but the agony that may accompany a decision to frustrate it is seldom more sharply drawn than when the sacrifice is made in behalf of duty, faith, or moral principle. Frustration, of course, permits the whole potential of emotion to pour out its contents.

The debate may develop into a bitter internal battle, as when a priest finds himself enmeshed in the web of this sublime emotion. In such an instance the battle between faith and the secondary will-force may bring into action the various battalions that will naturally be ranged on the two sides. On the one side will be the mating instinct and its superlative emotional companion, romantic love, which had been foresworn in solemn vows. On the other side will be the faith for the propagation of which obedience was accepted as a precondition. Between the two, intelligence will act as the middleman.

The ego surrounds the whole scene both as a participant and respondent. Conscience comes into the contest as it rages between mind and the will-forces, faith and the ego.

The place of the heart is honest. No one need ask the position it will take nor ask how it will make its influence felt. The emotion of romantic love is capable of shaking the being to its foundation, and has been known to do so. Its manifestation may be exaggerated as a means of assuring continuation of the species. The latter might be accomplished with a lesser lure than romantic love evokes at times. Nevertheless, its persuasive power need not be questioned. It has power, upon frustration or danger of defeat, to drain the vision of future of all attraction and replacing it with a void so great it could swallow a universe. It can make all things stand silhouetted against reality and give it all a face of mockery and utter futility.

On the defensive side, the will-force will mount a battle of its own and will enlist intelligence. The natural point of attack will be the law or the institution that exacts so inhuman a sacrifice as forfeiture of happiness, such a cruel imprisonment of the human spirit.

In a recent instance of this kind, the victim, a priest, complained of "the perpetual dominance of the system over the person." Even the finest people in the ruling position were victims of the system and ceased to act toward others in a normal manner, according to the apologia. Too many in authority, the defense continued, were kept immature or were frustrated, and became "eccentric or neurotic."

The battalions of self-justification were, of course, commanded by the ego; and the typical defense was the strong offensive which consisted of denigrating the enemy forces and dissolving their integrity.

One of the conclusions in this instance was that when the victim saw the institution (which was the church) "in its structure and activity as destructive of genuine human relationships," he could "no longer accept it as the embodiment of grace."

He broke his vows and was married. Thus was his anguish resolved.

The combined primary and secondary will-force had gained the support of intelligence and with its help ousted faith—or at least the faith which had at one time burned with sufficient light to claim the priest's allegiance.

The intrusion of the mating instinct and its fixation on an individual, illuminated by the light of romantic love, assured a collision. A test of strength was inevitable.

The priest might simply have turned in his robes of ministry and gone on his way, but the ego would have suffered great anguish without an act of justification. The opinion of those he left behind and that of his future associates meant too much to be treated with contempt. Therefore it was necessary to invoke certain principles to justify the action decided upon.

The former priest expressed the opinion that if he had not followed the course he did follow, he would probably have suffered a mental breakdown within a few years. In saying so he was attesting more to the power of romantic love to cause havoc on the occasion of its frustration than he testified to the mental oppres-

sion caused by his disagreement with the institution of which he
had been a loyal supporter. Frustrated romantic love has wreaked
havoc outside the walls of an institution. It is not necessary to be
bound to a frustrating vow to experience the subversive power of
a frustrated will-force. A clear negative from the object of affection
can accomplish the same result in open-ended life. In such an
instance, the ego makes things worse because it can find no institution, system, establishment, or anything else to blame but the
deficiency of the first person singular as a suitor. That is why in
such instances suicide is sometimes shown as the most attractive
exit.

The purpose in citing this case was not to enter the list of
defenders or detractors of the priest, but to illustrate the power
of the secondary will-force that represents romantic love. It is
not necessary to say that if the priest had not made the attachment
that attracted him so powerfully, he would not have quarreled
with the institution to which he had submitted his future. It is
enough to say that the attachment accentuated the differences he
expressed, if it did not manufacture them. It made a "federal case"
out of them. It not only accentuated them, it drove the ego into a
battle that otherwise might have been passed over without a
nervous breakdown.

The frustration of romantic love as a source of mental activity
in search of justification and in efforts to destroy the barrier is not
matched in its fury by economic frustration; but the latter may
arouse diverse furies of its own when it is prolonged and darkens
the future. Economic depression is not backward at finding and
flagellating a variety of scapegoats.

A mental conviction is never stronger than when it is supported by a strong, if concealed, will-force or ego interest.

Actually a conviction without the support of such an interest
or some other will never raise a pulse nor do battle on any front.
It would be a passionless posture of mind, a disembodied opinion
uttered without emphasis, inflection, or effective turn of phrase.
It could be likened to the opening of a container and letting issue
from it a scarcely visible vapor embodying a possible or probable
truth, take it or leave it.

Flesh and blood does not customarily express itself in that fashion. Even the presumably passionless philosopher will betray his human heritage if a rival philosopher questions the altitude of the thought fathered by the former. He will not be slow in revealing the existence within him of an ego that does not relish depreciation of its own host.

8.

Amelioration of
the Raw Ego

IT IS VIRTUALLY IF NOT ACTUALLY IMPOSSIBLE to speak of progress or happiness without assuming a purpose or final end. Progress cannot be measured without assumption of a destination or objective.

True, happiness has been defined as an absence of pain. Schopenhauer so described happiness; but this view represents a purely negative assessment. Happiness is not only negative; it is also positive. It is experienced when the action of the organism is in rapport with its situation *vis a vis* the outer world. The earthworm is happy in moist earth containing an adequate supply of the variety of organic matter that fits the needs of the worm, assuming that the oligochaetous creature was born in full possession of its parts, not deformed or deficient, and is free of a variety of enemies, such as the ever-alert robin. The worm's organs and tissues may then feed and be fed, and the organism will be able to fulfill its destiny.

Earthworm happiness is, of course, a figure of speech, but the simplicity of the creature's concern compared with that of man offers a tempting example of rapport or concordance such as man is not so likely to find. To say this is not to suggest that the earthworm is simple. It is not simple; only relatively so in relation to man.

Man is happy when he is not only in rapport with his physical environment but when in addition he is in harmony with his fellow beings and is able to develop and exercise his capabilities

160

and special talents. He cannot in fact be happy unless he is in rapport with his human relations. How to achieve the double rapport and harmony is itself a question that is a challenge to man's intelligence and to his mind and moral pretensions.

That man should even aspire to happiness so defined indicates that he is endowed with the necessary seed. Man would not reach for anything if he lacked the inclination. Also, when he reaches he must reach for something. This something as a destination is also implied in progress. Man either moves in the direction of his destination or he stands still; or he may move away from it, thus increasing the distance between his attained state and his presumed destination. If he has no destination, as some are inclined to believe, there is no proximation or deviation to be measured. Man then merely exists. He can make no measurable progress in any direction since he is not going anywhere. If he is not on his way to any destination, all his concern about learning, refinement, seeking, and exploration are to no purpose.

The pain of the world is not only not justified: it is an imposition by an unresponsive fate that cannot even be blamed. Little wonder that some modern philosophers find life not only empty but an exercise in anguish and despair.

According to these philosophers, man should be satisfied or not satisfied with his present status and locus for that is all there is. Primitive man according to that view was then no different from civilized man. Whatever man is now, he did not, in that view, *develop* to his present state. He made no progress in any direction even if it were only a change toward which development was pointed.

Yet it would be difficult to find a civilized person who would be willing to substitute the situation of the savage for his own. His reason for declining such an invitation would be found in the changes that occurred over the many centuries that separated his period from that of the savage. These changes were not abrupt or did not represent great leaps overnight, but were in the nature of accretions. If the state of the civilized man is preferable to that of the savage, the cumulative changes that wrought the transformation for the better represented nothing other than what we are pleased to call progress. If we can identify the changes between the savage and the civilized state that combined to make the latter state preferable, we can isolate the elements of progress.

We have already marked justice and the aspiration to beauty as elements of this order. These aspirations we have identified as secondary will-forces and in part as ego interests. We now come to that special sphere of the ego which lies above the level of the raw ego. The development of the secondary will-forces and the amelioration and refinement of the ego probably proceeded hand in hand.

As human beings multiplied and therefore lived together in greater numbers, they wore against each other with greater frequency and intensity. Finally elbow-rubbing became more commonplace than rare, as it was in the early dawn of man.

As man was no longer satisfied with the crude fare provided by nature with little elaboration, and as refinements were worked on the raw materials wrested from nature, yet other questions loomed, and as more occasion for closer relations among individuals arose, the need for refining these relations also became more insistent. As the cruder fare no longer satisfied, so also the rude relations that sprang from the primary will-forces and the raw ego no longer satisfied the more refined sensibilities. Rather, the crude expressions offended the latter.

Amelioration of the rude exchanges, of the harsh resort to force and the raw usages of dominance, became an increasingly conscious element of relations. We have already indicated a probable origin of the ameliorative force. Like all else concerning human behavior, there must have appeared at some instant in some individual a desire for what had not previously been present. In the case of amelioration, this desire, once more, was no doubt a desire that others behave more gently toward the person who felt the need. This desire also had to reach a state of consciousness before it could be reflected upon and, so to speak, recommended as a guide to behavior.

One of the elements of great importance to the greater harmony of relations in a community was kindness. The development of kindness, which is an element of charity, is, of course, lost to history. We can only guess, but the guesswork may at least provide a reasonable assessment of the possibilities. First, kindness and tenderness was provided by instinct, as already noted. It extended from parent to offspring and quite surely at times and possibly in some instances for long periods from mate to mate. Therefore the feeling already had a lodging in the human breast. It came to man as a Christmas present, he knew not whence; and before he had turned to reflection as a habit he was no doubt totally unaware of its existence. Kindness and tenderness toward offspring and protection during the period of helplessness is, of course, a commonly observed disposition in the lower animals. It needs no exemplification.

As previously remarked, the first extension of kindness beyond the limits of the young family and mates was, it stands to reason, toward those favored for one or another reason. Probably the first reason was that of affinity and the natural liking of a person for someone else. Mutual affection outside of romantic love between sexes would be expected to beget a kindly regard of the other and a tendency to treat differences of opinion with understanding. Also there was a natural inclination to confederate with each other in the face of a common danger or difficulty.

A feeling of kindness toward another was rewarded by a bright and appreciative countenance from the receiver whose response was natural and uninhibited. A special link was thus forged as a beginning of friendship. The one bestowing the kindness felt assured that the sentiment would be reciprocated. If it was not reciprocated, the ego of the bestower recoiled, and the warmth might change to ice if the overture were repeated and were again rejected.

Some advances might indeed be and often were tentative, where acquaintance was new or where the possibility of a mutually helpful alliance was perceived by the one or the other or both. An overture was then natural if there was promise of reciprocity. After a period of interplay, the alliance might become more tightly cemented and much pleasure and mutual satisfaction might ensue.

What were the fruits of kindness? How did an act of kindness differ from any other normal form of address? What came from the kind man in terms of behavior that did not come from anyone else?

The answer to these questions goes to the very root of the nature of kindness. That it arises from a special disposition seems obvious enough or it would not be recognized as being out of the ordinary. First, there must be sympathy, and this may be followed by empathy. Understanding, explicit or implicit, of another's problem, perplexity, or pain may open the way to an act of kindness. By projecting his own feeling into another, an observer may be moved to sympathy and then to an act of kindness.

Such an act is different from the ordinary address. It avoids harshness of tone or facial composure and substitutes gentleness of address and agreeable countenance. It proffers warmth or regard instead of a cool assessment. It puts the addressee not only at ease but in a mood to respond in kind, unless the address is for some reason regarded with suspicion or doubted in its quality or sincerity. As it comes from a warm heart, kindness often has power to dispel distrust and cynicism, unless it is misunderstood or out of place. An overture advanced in kindly terms may unfortunately be judged as evidence of weakness or dependence and may fail where otherwise it might be entertained graciously.

If an individual on extending his hand in proffered friendship and kindness of mien might as readily be slapped or kicked or spat upon as receiving a reciprocal response, social cohesion could not have been achieved. The refinement of social behavior would have been doomed as an impossible enterprise. The ego would have been without a potential basis of ameliorative behavior. Since the usages of polite society have in fact been established, hypocritical, and superficial as some of them may be, we can conclude that the basis of reciprocity existed in human character.

A difficult aspect of the function of kindness is encountered when kindness of response is suggested as an antidote to rude, hostile, or insulting address. The ego perhaps seldom comes under a more provocative temptation than it is when it is thus confronted. The ego may be trained to proffer kindness rather than rudeness or incivility to another person in ordinary relations, to the end of begetting a response in kind. There is at least a degree of self-interest to be served. If kindness of address may be expected either to beget a like response or at least a semblance of kindness in return, the atmosphere of relations may become more pleasant. Therefore something of value is gained by the person who initiates the first step of kindness, although such an ulterior motive does not comport completely with a sincere act of kindness. The latter demands no reward nor expects one. The ego, however, is not naturally so unselfish and self-denying. If kindness may be expected to beget kindness in return, the act takes on a pragmatic aspect, and we have previously remarked on the pragmatic inclination of the will-forces and the ego.

What has been said is to the purpose of demonstrating the greater difficulty of responding in kindly fashion to an unkind or even hostile address than to ordinary address. We have had occasion earlier to depict the difficulty of making a response on principle under the inciting pricks of provocation, not the least of which was pictured as the fear of being regarded as a coward.

One great difference between the act of dispensing kindness, on the one hand, on the initiative of the dispenser, and seeking to be kind under provocation, on the other, lies in the probable equanimity of the person on the occasion of the initiative and therefore relative freedom from inhibition. An act of kindness in fair weather offers no insuperable difficulty to the ego. It may indeed require training and dedication to exhibit kindness even under such circumstances; but to be called on to smile in response to an insult or a vile accusation is a demand that falls into a different spectrum.

The threshold of kindness on such an occasion is very different. In place of a tranquil inner sea on which a sail may be launched before a favonian breeze with happy augury of an easy and pleasant turn on the placid waters, in place of a fond expectancy on which to spread the sails of good will, we launch the craft in the face of dark wind clouds that have suddenly stirred an angry sea into wild commotion.

How launch a sail upon such fury-agitated waters, with leaping waves crashing upon each other, producing flying spume and acid spray?

The recommendation of kindness under the provocation or an outrage does indeed represent a counsel of perfection not easily obeyed. Yet amelioration of the raw-ego responses demands heroic effort in this direction. Behind the demand is recognition of the deadlock that would occur and persist beyond hope of resolution if no one ever had learned how to absorb an outburst or thrust of ill-will without response in kind. Amelioration of human relations could not have prospered.

It became obvious on reflection that any hope of preventing the right of might or of force or treachery from prevailing would have been lost if superior force or advantage had not learned how to bow to the considerations of human harmony and accord. This means something more than justice, for justice may be *imposed*. Kindness under provocation calls for a species of sacrifice. It means recognition and acceptance of a higher desideratum, a more encompassing objective, which is to say, deference to the interests of civilization, to the interests of the human species.

The acceptance of restraint on power, submitting to fetters on might and becoming amenable to a curb on available force— all the prefaces to amelioration of the ego—require withholding of available striking power under provocation.

Ability to absorb an insult, referring it to the office of under- standing and there playing on it a stream of good will as from a fire hose, thus quenching the fires of passion, is the highest achievement of man in the field of ego-taming and promotion of human concord and peaceful relations.

The pinnacle is not only not easily scaled; it is thought by some to lie beyond the reach of man precisely because of his nature. This supposed incapacity is really a reference to his ego and the mutual distrust fostered by it as a device to avoid sur- rendering the heady attractions of domination.

The difficulty is not the less real for its seeming irrationality. The whole struggle is one of the mind and moral considerations against the supremacy of the will-forces and the ego.

The equation seems virtually insoluble when it is considered in the light of man's vehemence derived from his primitive heri- tage. Yet, man has moved forward and upward from the savage base where the primary will-forces and the raw ego held sway with little restraint. This is not to say that a utopia is attainable on earth. It merely recognizes the advancement of man from the very rude base that marked his beginning. It is no more than a recognition of man's development of a variety of potentials seeded in him and pointing him toward the upward slope. That he was moved only part of the way should be evidence not of failure but of the fact that he had climbing ability and that there is no reason why he should not continue to possess it and to exercise it.

That man has climbed the slope a substantial distance is attested to by a number of historic comparisons. Today the sports arena is no longer the scene of lions and tigers loosed upon human beings, or even of gladiators attacking each other with brass knuckles or spiked fists to the delight of spectators. Sometimes the American game of football is cited as evidence of continuing brutality—or prizefighting or bullfighting. Nevertheless, it is a far cry from these sports to those of ancient Rome. Only bullfighting smacks of the residual savagery of the present-day civilization in sports. Cockfighting is also reprehensible in the depraved glee evident in spectators who watch as two birds, artificially armed with sharp spurs by man, fight to the death.

While treatment of animals leaves much to be desired today, a dawn of conscience is spreading over that field, and an amelioration of common cruelty is clearly visible.

The progress of the ameliorating quality of kindness, again, seems slow, indeed, and its acceleration could be welcomed; but when the nature and vigor of the obstacles are considered, we can applaud even as we shake our heads in regret over lapses, setbacks, and seeming retrogression.

The civilized ego that speaks for kindness and understanding in place of the angry or rude retort, sarcasm or disbelief, and other provocative forms of address and response has not lacked supporters; but in this very asset it has also borne great liabilities. Such is the nature of propagation, be it a philosophy, a doctrine, or religion, that it evokes suspicion, skepticism, and hostility in others. Even the virtues of kindness cannot easily be propagated without arousing contrary opinion. Good will can hardly be promoted without arousing suspicion of a self-serving motive, or fear in someone that something ulterior is afoot.

Even if kindness is acknowledged as a virtue and its praises are duly sung, differences will arise over the interpretation of particular behavior as representing or not representing an act of kindness. Yet greater differences may appear over methods of promoting kindness as a mode of conducting relations with others. Should exhortation be relied upon, or would the setting of example accomplish more? Should kindness replace the reprimand or soften an administered rebuke? Should scolding, berating, and reviling make way for a mode of address that recognizes the ego-sensitivity of the recipient of the censure? Or should the abrasions and contusions inflicted on an ego be disregarded if censure is unquestionably merited? To what degree does stern punishment act as a deterrent to future unsocial behavior? Does kindness lead a culprit to take his infraction of a rule or a law or a canon of good behavior less seriously? Would it invite further lawlessness? Is kindness in any event misused when it is extended to offenders against law and morality? Should kindness be reserved for the deserving, the innocent but unfortunate, who may suffer from various degrees of inadequacy before the complexities of the world?

A thousand differences may spring up over the answers to questions of this order and many more. Therefore the cause of the virtue of kindness, even if supported by the best of will, is not itself smooth and straight, and the reason is not far to seek. Because of particular temperament or character traits, some individuals seem to prefer animosity and antagonism to kindness as their posture toward the world. Others are distrustful. Lincoln Steffens warned against the quality of trustworthiness in those who incline to distrust others. Yet again there are those who discern ulterior motives behind almost every act to which some mystery clings. They seem to be unable to credit man with unalloyed good faith. On the recommendation of Steffens, they should probably look inward.

If these various diffractions of normal attitude are pursued to their origins, they will be traced to the ego or will-forces, but principally the ego and the experiences to which it was exposed in the past and to which upon repetition it reacted after a while with an acceptance of certain patterns of response. Thereafter it was no longer easy to re-examine and recast the patterns, and the same one was made to do duty on a wide scale or on nearly all occasions that bore any resemblance to the original situation when the response seemed to be adequate.

If the raw ego is to bow to kindness as a way of meeting the world, it will need extensive modification in most instances. Because all human beings are individual, they initially see the world only through their own eyes and interpret it in terms of themselves. If kindness is to take root, it must be inculcated unobtrusively before mental attitudes become set in the stone. Greater flexibility of future attitude may be anticipated if a high level of intelligence is present—which is to say that early attitudes are then more readily re-examined and recast if they are found wanting.

The influence of great teachers and moralists, as the influence of original thinkers, inventors, artists and others, has provided the beacon light in the cause of kindness. In them the mind had gained supremacy over the more pragmatic interests of the will-forces and the ego. Original teachings found followers and expounders who accepted the permanent values as superior to the passing interests of the appetites and desires.

They recognized a transcending value in principles. While the appetites and passions could not be dismissed as no more than lures to excesses and revelry, since man depended for his life on their moderate gratification, they regarded them as conducive to riotous living if they were not brought under the dominion of reason. Even Epicurus, whose philosophy has been widely misinterpreted, recognized the indispensable function of temperate usage if the senses themselves were to deliver their highest satisfaction.

If great seers recognized the ameliorative function of kindness and the balm that it might bring to the afflicted, the deprived, and oppressed, the problem was one of achieving an ever wider and wider appreciation of the worthiness of benevolence in human behavior.

Kindness does have the advantage of being positive rather than negative, and in this aspect its advocacy is less repellent to

the ego than the injunctions against the kind of behavior that is
most dear to the ego. Kindness is not an abstention or restraint
but an extension of the self into the very person to whom kindness is brought. Therefore the ego is merely to be offered a change
of direction—from strictly self-regard to inclusion of other-regard.
The change does not necessarily call for renunciation of the self.
It does mean admission of others into the inner circle and therefore entails some real effort at self-extension into the orbit of the
interests of others—not as a participant but as one who under-
stands and appreciates what others are concerned about. The scope
of such personal interest is, of course, circumscribed because of
energy, time, and place limitations. The more general attitude of
kindness may, however, be turned in all directions.

The interest of the ego may indeed be enlisted beyond that
of a species of passive kindness that merely speaks softly and avoids
giving offense. It may be brought to gain satisfaction from more
robust evidence of kindness, such as lending a helping hand in
need, going to some trouble to succor those in pain or under the
affliction of misfortune.

From indifference to the problems of others or even an inclination to avoid any likelihood of sharing a burden, the ego
may become ready to bring help and solace to others, to the
degree that it soon becomes a point of honor to it.

Once the ego makes the shift and is more than comfortable in
its new attitude, it will thereafter defend the new premises as it
previously defended the old. Conscience will inscribe the new
attitude into its own book, and when the person in whom it dwells
gives way to the prompting of the old ego, the raw and uncivilized
ego, and behaves harshly and boorishly, the new conscience will
be taken aback, offended, and feel regretful. It will feel shame
over the relapse into unworthiness by its host, and will prick him,
taunt him, and berate him for so base an example of behavior by
one who presumably had achieved a higher altitude in the level of
virtue. Time was when the same ego would not only have echoed
no remorse over a similar act of behavior but would perhaps have
clicked its tongue in rollicking satisfaction.

Surely this could not be the same ego! Yet, it dwells there

within the same person. The consciousness that lights the ego into reality also links its identity with the past. Yes, it is the same ego, even as it is the same person in which it dwells; but it has undergone change.

How could this come about? The person continues to live where he lived earlier. He eats the same food, his style of dress is unchanged. His posture is as it was; his manner of walking, standing, sitting, holding his head are as they were. To be sure, he is somewhat older, but he is recognizable readily from his external look as the same person of a few years ago.

What, then, has changed in him?

What is there of permanence in a person? The physical elements that are combined in him to give him his body are borrowed elements, so to speak. They are constantly changing.

Consider man as he is physically constituted. In a sense he is a veritable pillar of water held upright by his skeletal structure, ligaments, tendons, and muscles. Beyond that he is laced and suffused with a variety of minerals and chemical elements in a mixture that gives him special characteristics.

Contrary to how it seems to us who are human beings, we do not own the water that is in us. It merely acts as a medium of transport for minerals and chemicals to various parts of the body. It is no different from the water in the well or on the rooftops or in drops of rain. We do not in fact retain the same water very long. It goes on its way, unmodified or transformed in any way. At the same time, being inanimate, it is completely neutral about its whereabouts or destination. It is still as it was: H_2O.

The same may be said of the salt in us, the phosphorus, and all other minerals and chemical elements. They are inert and wordless. Man is, so to speak, a movable container temporarily filled with a specific combination of liquids, gases, and solids that have only transistory residence in any individual. After a period of time, we are no longer composed of the identical molecules and atoms as we were, even though we retain our personal identity and undergo but little change in appearance in a few years' time, with the exception of the years of growth. Physically we may be a completely different identity or very nearly so. We are like a gun that after years of use and repair has a different stock, a different barrel, and a different loading and firing mechanism, but is yet regarded as the same gun.

We put no personal stamp on the elements that serve temporarily as our bodily constituents. They are, to repeat, the same whether they are a grain of salt in the ocean water, in a strip of bacon, or in a human being, performing an organic function. The arrangements and combinations within certain defined limits are merely different from individual to individual.

The elements have each a physical continuity of its own. The question is how man achieves conscious continuity that survives complete replacements of the chemical elements. His sentiments go on independently of the exhaustion and replenishments; his convictions and beliefs may remain the same; his habits remain as execrable or tolerable through all the physical transformations. Of course, changes may be caused by illness or accident, but normally man's enjoyment of life, no less than his misery or melancholy, transcend the replacement of water by water, this salt by that salt, and this other mineral by a substitute. The ego may be insulted, but the waters, minerals, and chemicals are not affected and remain inert.

The physical comes and goes, but the nonphysical lingers, identified with itself today and tomorrow, this year and next, and on through the span of life—always excepting mental derangement or alienation.

Even as the aging process changes the individual and modifies his primary will-forces as the years pass and the person moves from stage to stage, the ego and the self-identity that it provides remain above the process.

The mystery is deep enough, but it should give pause to those who perceive no difference between the mental or spiritual and physical aspects of life.

So it is that the ego goes its way essentially without regard to the chemical changes of the body, so far as personal continuity and self-identity are concerned. To be sure, the ego may be affected in its stance toward the world by physical conditions, such as disability, deformity, or extremes of size and similar deviations from the normal; but even then the ego may undergo changes independently of the unfortunate physical abnormalities. The hunchback while remaining in his unfortunate physical state may undergo a complete change of outlook toward the world. From harboring an embittered ego he may be transformed into a veritable fountain of kindness, understanding, and good will.

This independence of the inner man from his physical trappings, far from absolute in all respects, indicates an independent source of power—a source that is not in the molecules of water, minerals, and other elements that constitute the body at any one time.

The continuity of self-identification, just now noted, may be attributable to the seed from which each individual grows. There, with the genes, must reside this nonphysical attribute, a companion to or a part of the life force.

The seed, if nourished, proliferates into the organism according to its kind. Growth, maturity, and all the changes supervening between infancy and adulthood do not break the ego's continuity. The octogenarian identifies with the boy of ten that he was seventy years before. Even in growth there must be some force or purpose that is independent of the molecules and atoms which it uses and arranges to its own end.

What happens when death overtakes the body? All the physical elements are the same as they were. They may be deranged or transposed to some degree, but they are no less water and salt, phosphorus and so on than they were. Whatever has departed, it is not the physical elements. This is a question for religion, and no answer will be attempted here.

It is enough for our purpose to say that the ego can and does change, without change in the physical constituency, in the part it plays in shaping human relations. It is true that a change in the physical constituency may change the ego in its relations with associates, companions, working mates. Drugs, such as tranquilizers, are credited with changing the tense and high-strung personality to one of serenity or placidity, and in so doing ameliorating problems of relations with others. However, such changes also occur without the influence of drugs. Therefore the ego may be transformed while the physical base remains the same or virtually the same.

Without a change of diet and without the use of drugs, an individual's mental attitude may undergo a radical transformation, for better or worse. Thus, while there is an acknowledged interplay between the ego and the physical base, the ego is also independent of changes in the base. To say this is not to overlook the influence of glandular activity and its abnormal excesses or deficiencies.

Long before the administration of drugs occurred, the modification of the ego was well established. Obviously the fortunes of civilization were not dependent on the administration of drugs or glandular therapy.

Much as the secondary will-forces have power to moderate and restrain the primary will-forces, so education or culture, belief and faith have the power to moderate and transform the raw ego. These moderating forces, while not always independent of the physical substructure, nevertheless have power to work changes of their own. That this power is not absolute may be concluded from the hopelessness of transforming the insane unless the substructure can first be modified by appropriate therapy.

How the influences of education, religion, or similar forces are able to modify the ego has already been touched upon. In the first place, of course, the thing to be modified must be amenable to change. The potential making the modification possible is closely linked with the capacity to learn; and man is a learning animal, as are some other orders of the animal kingdom.

The process of learning, as said elsewhere, moves forward basically through trial and error, supported by memory, reflection, foresight, and innate judgment. Seeking what is pleasant and pleasurable and avoiding what is painful and disagreeable represents the more primitive path of learning. It has the virtue of simplicity but also the liability of misleading him who follows it indiscriminately, for not all that is pleasant merits pursuit and not all that is painful is to be shunned. The qualifications and exceptions to pursuit of the pleasurable options may be supplied by the mind after much experience with the consequences of particular behavior.

The raw ego, like the primary will-forces, is not unlike some of the higher of the lower animals in amenability to training and instruction. A trainer of certain animals need not testify to his ability to teach such animals. He has but to demonstrate his success by putting his charges through exercises that no animal would perform on its own account.

The primary will-forces and the raw ego of man respond no less readily to teaching. Moreover, man's potentials are much greater; he is more apt and his capabilities more flexible or malleable, conforming more readily to a greater variety of teaching.

What is taught creates a response that is different from preceding responses. After a while, with sufficient repetition, the new response becomes habitual; subject, however, to yet further change if the mind is amenable to the new influences brought to bear.

It is the receptivity of the ego to modifying influence that accounts for the inculcation of a different style of response from the pre-existing one. The degree of possible modification no doubt varies from person to person. Children and adolescents are perhaps more malleable than older people. As the saying goes, the latter get "set in their ways."

We are not concerned here with the quality or character of the modifying influences, although it is of great importance. For the present, our concern is with the amenability of the ego to modification rather than with the character of the change. This might be good or evil.

The path by which the ego is reached, as has already been said, lies through the mind. If the mind becomes convinced that a particular attitude or mode of behavior is not desirable for a reason that the mind regards as sufficient, it will be in a position to influence the response of the ego to external events. To say that the mind is in a position to influence the ego is not the same as saying that it will do so or that it is immediately competent to do so through exercise of its potential mastery. It may be guessed that the greater number of people make little effort to change their typical and customary responses to verbal or other excitation once they have willy-nilly adopted a pattern. Mental laziness is a common ailment that represents the inertia of the mind at rest.

If a person fails to adjust, he will remain a captive of his home training or lack of it, his schooling or religious inculcation. If this background, as luck would have it, were beyond reproach,

the individual would be happily turned out in his mental or
habitual ego-response.

If man indeed has the power to interfere with physical probabilities, he has to that extent, as observed previously, an influence
on events, including inner ones. This fact might still not give him
the power of self-modification. Cold weather too has the power to
influence events, but that fact does not bestow autonomy on cold
weather. Weather is itself only the effect of a chain of causation.
Man, it may be argued, can himself bring about changes in the
weather—at least on a small scale—but the weather cannot change
itself. Therefore man can from an external position inject new
causes into physical processes or decide not to do so, as he wishes.

This is said in reference to the physical world. Inwardly man
has a certain but variable power to modify himself by consciously
interfering with the inner chain of cause and effect.

Of course, man has as much aptitude for wayward, mischievous, and evil contrivances in both the external and inner
world as for those that represented an improvement, a refinement
or perfection. The contest between the two has been the tension
of civilization. Which of the two potentials would achieve the
ascendancy?

It is readily imaginable that the wayward, mischievous, and
evil, not to mention the depraved, would have prevailed had not
a restraining force in the form of the possibility of a life after
death been introduced. The notion of refinement of the senses
and the impulses if sustained by experience as a superior mode of
living and if linked to the state of life after death, would produce
a strong incentive to frown on the wayward, to distrust the mischievous, and to despise and avoid evil. If the linkage were in the
form of reward for the good and punishment for evil, the effects
produced would perhaps be more fruitful if punishment were the
alternative to the reward rather than reward itself being the only
consequence without the counterpart of punishment for evil. Likewise, if punishment for evil without the accompanying reward
for good were held to be the order of reality in the afterlife, the
effect would be less fruitful because the positive inducement
would be absent. A sullen, fearful, or driven mood would fill the
air, not relieved by hope and sustaining anticipation.

Virtue for virtue's sake represents a noble sentiment, as does art for art's sake, but as we have previously had occasion to remark more than once, the primary will-forces and the raw ego are not candidates for the nobility. Elements somewhat more substantial than noble sentiment are needed to impress the primitive endowments.

These endowments do not modify themselves; they must be *modified from without themselves* if they are to be changed, even if from the inside of the person. We have attempted to indicate the agencies by which the modifications may be accomplished. The endeavors of the mind and the moral forces often need help both internally and externally since other minds may pull or push in opposite directions. Such opposition may be the result of difference of opinion or disagreement, the basis of which we have previously noted, and it may be sincere and may influence the minds of others.

However, as said just now, man has as much aptitude for learning and imitating wayward and noxious behavior as the exemplary variety. It goes without saying that the primitive appetites and desires have an open affinity for doing what "comes naturally," and civilization does not come naturally. It responds only to cultivation.

Therefore the fortunes of civilization are bound inseparably to conscious effort, to endeavor, greatly helped, however, by the secondary will-forces and the tutored ego, once these have been brought under the dominion of the mind; for these, too, and not only the primitive impulses, have moving and driving power. The secondary will-force seeking beauty, for example, will indeed be ranged against any primary will-force that in its excesses would despoil the fair, the comely, or the unsullied.

This reliance on the secondary impulses, of course, is neither without question nor absolute, since the secondary forces are themselves subject to corruption. We have but to consider justice, and the desire for knowledge and romantic love. These forces do not lead themselves to refinement; they must, if they are to be refined, be subjected to a course of refinement. Here the person and his mind are the master. Yet he, too, needs guidance.

Whence would this have come if not from parents or bystanders who themselves needed and still need guidance in some particulars? Once more we are driven to the exceptional individual in whom something new was born—an original who could teach others. His special capacity might, of course, be confined to a rather narrow segment of knowledge, behavior, or wisdom.

Turning and pointing the secondary will-forces in the direction that avoided the wayward and execrable usages of the primary ones or set them against the lapses of these, fell to those rare individuals whose special gifts attracted them to the various virtues.

We have previously noted the difficulty experienced by virtue in attracting adherents or practitioners. But for the appearance of individuals whose secondary will-forces were disposed in the right direction in one or more segments of behavior, as originals, who saw clearly the disarray and shambles attendant on certain courses of behavior, as previously related, and counseled, preached, or remonstrated against them, the secondary will-forces would have been left without a sense of direction, for these forces are not born perfected. They represent the behavior of man that is farthest from instinct and therefore needs the guidance of reason.

Clearly these originals, themselves being human, were confined in their originality to fragments of total behavior; nor was their wisdom necessarily the final word even in the narrow segments. New situations might arise, rendering obsolete the previously suitable standard of behavior. Also, their experience or possibility of experience was limited to the particular environment, and in early times this offered but little variety.

It was therefore not to be expected that a comprehensive set of tables governing behavior under all circumstances could be assembled by mere man, who was within time and influenced by his particular times. Because of the diverse environments and conditions of life of the different original trailblazers, the codes or fragments of codes of conduct could be expected to differ from each other in widely separated communities, where there was little or no intercommunication. What seemed or was actually fitting and acceptable behavior in one place might not be suitable elsewhere; or if it would have been acceptable, it would not be adopted on exposure to it because the line of learning and imitation had followed a different original and had become attached to that instead. Hostility might then be expected to greet something different if it came from elsewhere. Conquest, of course, would sometimes substitute one code or culture for another or lay the foundation for a mixture.

The ordinary man could only be perplexed until time healed the wounds or smoothed the junctures. What is called the relativity of moral codes became visible, and no doubt produced perplexity.

The contest between the virtues, the refined sentiments, and the decencies, on the one hand, and the rude, crude, wayward, and noxious, on the other, was an uneven one, the times and situations in some instances being more propitious to the one or the other side.

Aristotle found the virtues of justice, prudence, temperance, and fortitude as the basic substructures of optimum human behavior. It will be noted that none of these is an expression of the primary will-forces or the raw ego. So far as self-guidance is concerned and also relations with others, these virtues represented the ascendancy of wisdom over the primary inclinations. Had the latter inclinations, appetites, and needs not been given frequently to unseemly, damaging, or irritating behavior, there would have been no need for the virtues. The human race would have been like the bees. Human beings would individually have gone their ways always doing what they should without offending or hurting anyone else, except perhaps by getting in the way of others occasionally or stepping on their toes or jostling them unintentionally.

Since the virtues represented antidotes or preferable options to the kind of behavior that came naturally from the primitive impulses, it was not a welcome intruder to the young, even as today, nor to the adults among the primitives for these too were still young *as man.*

It goes without saying that man was reduced to groping for guides to behavior as more frequent and extensive mixtures among his kind occurred. What passed for suitable behavior in an isolated community could easily, as previously noted, fail under more complex conditions and greater diversity of human elements to be satisfactory elsewhere. The need for an *absolute* made itself felt, for man, as said earlier, seeks certainty, even if he can find it seemingly only in certain rather unpleasant inescapables, such as death and taxes.

One of the peculiarities of wayward behavior that has had the effect of promoting its own restraint in a roundabout circuit lies in the phenomenon that what delights, titillates, and produces wanton hilarity in those engaging in lusty gratification of the primary impulses often produces a contrary reaction in non-participants who observe the revelry or riotous gaiety and may be discommoded or disturbed by it. Their sensibilities may be strongly inclined to seek surcease from the source of the disturbance.

Therefore the inculcation of virtue in the nonvirtuous may be helped by outside reaction to their own behavior. We have previously noted the first steps of virtue-propagation as a reaction to the pain inflicted on the victims of rude behavior. When this occurred, someone who was among the objectors to the obnoxious behavior just noted, almost surely, once upon a time, called one or more of the objectors to account when they in turn misbehaved. He was probably the first man of all time to say or to indicate that it was not consistent to engage in the very same objectionable behavior against which they themselves had complained only a short time before. If the behavior was objectionable when others engaged in it, it could be expected to be objectionable to others now that the original objectors engaged in it. It is not difficult to imagine the response of this pioneer.

"We will give them some of their own medicine. What we are doing to them is no worse than what they did to us. Let this be a lesson to them!" This is the well-worn gambit of the *tu quoque,* which justifies self by citing a like evil committed by others. In group activity this device of self-justification usually prevailed, as it does even today, for the community or group ego is eager to find an excuse. To justify a wrong by pointing to an equal or worse wrong committed by others is a typical refuge of the ego.

We thus see that the difficulty of mounting a force of virtue is all the greater in view of this escape hatch because the opposing ego or will-force matched against the mind can always call on intelligence to provide exculpation and justification of itself by simply pointing to others who are equally guilty.

How the so-called golden rule, which is the reverse of the *tu quoque* defense could gain adherents, again poses a typically difficult question. It seems miraculous that such a rule of conduct could survive even if it made a beginning. It seems impossible to avoid once more the twin explanation already advanced, namely, that exceptional individuals had a natural inclination to good in the sense that they were both kindly disposed toward their fellow-beings and perceived the disarray and damage caused by certain disorders of behavior, which is to say misbehavior. In the latter perception, they depended largely on their own unhappy experience, over wrongs done to themselevs; for even though they had occasion to observe evidence of the ill effects of misbehavior inflicted on others, in the form of weeping and sad, oppressed, or angry faces among those with whom they lived, they could not have had a full appreciation of what they saw without similar experiences of their own.

Man being what he is, usually falling somewhat short of nobility and both led and driven by his robust instincts and impulses, is greatly assisted, as we have indicated just now, in his endeavors if he believes that in the absence of perfect mundane justice and judgment, he is assured of a reward for virtue in a postmundane existence, and retribution for his malfeasance and misdeeds committed in the course of his life on earth. Concern over his posthumous state will, by a reflexive effect from foresight backward, influence his current behavior.

If the golden rule is supported by a belief in an afterlife and is perceived as a means of gaining a reward and avoiding punishment, it will have a powerful ally. The mind, fixed on the final purpose, would find restraint on the wayward impulses more easily carried out. Hope of a reward represents a pragmatic consideration and is therefore at home with the will-forces. Fear of punishment may, of course, also exert a strong influence on behavior.

Man's effort to reconcile the two aspects of his dual character (animal and human) has brought him face to face with his limitation and finiteness, producing a restless uncertainty in his earthly existence. In some individuals, this state has produced a veritable torment. William James wrote of tough-minded and tender-minded persons, indicating a willingness of the former to take the world as they found it, while the latter sought refuge in the absolute. Since tender-minded persons could not find the absolute on earth, faith was their final haven; revealed religion was their guide.

Karl Marx was perhaps the epitome of the tough-minded, followed by Nietzsche, who, however, was a philosopher rather than a polemicist and agitator, as was the former.

Religion in Marx's view, as is well known, was no more than a convenient instrument used by the ruling dominancy, which in his time was the capitalistic structure, to assure the continuous docility of those who were mercilessly exploited. If these could be induced to keep their eyes on the next world while regarding present life as no more than a way station where the bearing of a cross was a badge of merit of itself, the dominant element could rest in full assurance that no one would revolt. They would be satisfied to accept present deprivation for the sake of future happiness.

That exploitation of fellow inhabitants is not an object of religion; therefore, that those who would use it for such a purpose would be in the position of violating what was presumably their own religion either did not occur to Marx or if it did occur to him, he ignored the contradiction or satisfied himself with the thought that capitalists were hypocritical and held to their own economic comfort on earth as the first consideration.

However, to say that a religion might be abused was not a condemnation of the religion itself since few if any human practices are free of possible abuse. Marx was, however, right in concluding that a belief that is essentially nonmaterialistic in its philosophy and that proffers a reward for a life lived in disdain of the material satisfactions beyond the necessities does produce a willingness to renounce riches and wealth.

That such a religion could be used for the purpose perceived by Marx can be conceded without establishing a necessary connection between capitalism and such cynicism. Perhaps there was such a connection in many instances.

As man was still in the preliminary stages of reasonable emancipation from the cruel yoke of material scarcity, the few who by superior acquisitive and organizational talents gathered unto themselves a great part of the wealth produced were prompted by their primitive will-forces and raw ego to defend their status with all the power and resources at their command. That they could do so without renouncing their religion only demonstrated the natural ego-blindness of man. The primitive impulses were not yet tamed—as they will not soon be wholly tamed in any event. Man therefore finds no great difficulty in accommodating himself to inconsistencies between his mind's professed loyalty to principle and the will-force and ego interests, particularly when he is defending his accustomed comforts. Indeed, much of the inner tension to which man is host is traceable to that very conflict. Hypocrisy, which acts as a release of the tension, is the bridge between the mind and its principles, on the one hand, and demands of the will-forces and raw ego, on the other. It might also be called the path to rationalization.

Marx, in his tough-mindedness, elected to use his indictment not as the base for amelioration of this conflict but as the foundation for irreconcilable condemnation and therefore revolution through class hatred. He devoted himself in consequence of his choice to forging an instrument for his own use not only to upset but to destroy the economic class that in his view used another type of instrument to maintain *its* power. His *bête noir* was the exploiters. His instrument was hate and the violence that could be generated through the incitation of hate. He would expropriate the expropriators, which is to say, substitute one economic class for another. That his plan would not dissolve the duality of inner man seemed to escape the penetrative power of his mind.

His justification, rather, we thus see, was the *tu quoque* defense. He was doing or suggested doing nothing more to others than they had perpetrated against the proletariat. Religion and the sinister use made of it, in his view, merely stood in the way. Therefore it should be dismantled and swept away. The better to accomplish this act of stripping and abolition, hatred, again, plus suppression would be the favored weapons. In other words, unleashing the primary will-forces and the raw ego would give the maximum assurance of success in this endeavor. Little did he know that he was set on a path that would soon bring him full circle to face the problem of inner man that he refused either to see or to recognize. Hypocrisy is not limited to a religion, class, race, or any other division of man. It is endemic to the species and will break out according to the mandate of attendant circumstance.

Primary will-forces and the raw ego are a common denominator of all mankind. Each child is born with an undisciplined new potential of these necessary troublemakers, and no form of government will produce a crop of angels free of the troublous heritage. The Marxian classless society would be no exception.

Unfortunately for Marx's philosophy and political approach, discipline would be as indispensable for his purpose as it is to any plan or program. The contradiction contained in these two conditions of success was never reconciled; for it would not be easy to discipline the unleashed primitive forces (hatred and violence) as a means to one end (overthrow of capitalism) while using the same violent forces, once unleashed, toward another end (building a new society). It is seldom if ever an easy or even a possible task to turn discipline on and off at the convenience of a dominant or ruling power. If the full benefit of the unleashed hatred was to be achieved, discipline must withhold its hand; and yet once let loose, the control of hatred could hardly be assured when its control became desirable.

Yet the latter course had to be Marx's practical choice. The result could hardly be other than extreme repression and a populace of robots with deadened senses, at one time hating on command in one direction and then not hating in another direction, also on command; and at the same time throwing discipline to the wind so that hatred could do its work, hatred being an undisciplined force; and then halting hatred once more for the sake of organization and discipline. Freedom could, of course, be given no footing under such circumstances.

The problem was necessarily one of how to exploit hatred

without risking the wild beast's turning on the master. If this was prevented by Draconian decrees, which is to say, by instilling fear through the harshest measures (Stalinism), the result could only be a cowed beast, which without a will or freedom of its own, would simply go through the motions spiritlessly after the manner of a West Indian zombie, described as a will-less and speechless being capable only of automatic, trancelike movement.

The incitation and use of hatred as an instrument is, of course, not confined to the Marxian program of achieving power. It is employed in wartime, from the tribal dances to modern nations which use propaganda to the same end. Nevertheless, the Marxian utilization of class hatred as an instrument of revolution must suffer from the same difficulty and self-defeating ordinance that attends the use of hatred at all times.

Hatred is a negative influence at best, but it is relatively innocent in its natural uncontrived state when it represents a response to frustration. It may then be brought under control. It is something different when it is incited as an all-engulfing and implacable medium, used as a means to an end, and made a way of life for generations, on a vast scale and as a cardinal point of philosophy.

Hatred, it should be understood, arises from the frustration of the will-forces and the ego. It is not a mental but an emotional reaction. It cannot be endorsed by the mind in good conscience but does readily gain the support of intelligence which may use it for its own ends.

It is anticivilization precisely because it takes its cue from the emotional responses to frustration. It is the instrument not of man as man, as distinguished from the lower animals that do not enjoy his high franchise, but of his animal heritage. This is not to say that animals hate. They bear no grudges, but man, having animal appetites and impulses that tie into his intelligence, can and does elaborate animal responses into veritable systems.

Civilization represents the degree of success of efforts made by man not to hate whatever may frustrate his desires but to understand the frustrations and to determine their merits. Moreover, mind, which is the hope and resource of civilization, seeks to ascertain whether frustration may or may not actually be a happy culmination of events. A sensible man may on occasion thank a mate, companion, or friend who restrained him from an unworthy act. After his passion of the moment has spent itself, his mind may assert itself and it may then reflect that he owes to the restraining agent a word of thanks for his act of frustration.

Hatred evicts the mind when the passion is at high heat, and misdirects human endeavor. Unfortunately, it has not only intelligence at its service, but it stimulates intelligence to subtleties that may ordinarily be dormant.

Hatred is the opposite of kindness and will have no truck with the golden rule. Indeed, it cannot traffic with kindness toward the object of odium because that would be self-defeating. If hatred is to be effective as an instrument, it cannot accept dilution of itself by thoughts of kindness, sympathy, or understanding. This would drain it of its force.

Of course, efforts can be made to channel hatred in one direction while retaining loyalty in another direction, which is, say, toward the managing source. In the Marxian world, this would be the State.

Such channeling may be undertaken by others than Marxians and often is succesful through propaganda efforts which picture the enemy as brutal, evil, greedy, and whatever other odious quality can be assigned to him. However, such hatred is not adopted as a way of life and may be relaxed sufficiently after scores have been settled to permit resumption of friendly relations after a few years. To say this is not to condone this style of hatred but to differentiate between it and the long-range instrumental variety.

Moreover, propaganda undergoes a decline in effectiveness after years of harping on the same subject. Renewed interest can only be aroused by offering new causes for hatred if hatred is to continue as a matter of policy. This may be accomplished by contriving incidents or encounters, the provocation of which may be attributed to the enemy.

Were freedom permitted, long-maintained hatred would disintegrate in time for lack of a flesh and blood enemy and because of internal disagreement. Hatred in perpetuity is unnatural. New generations are born without it, and efforts to inculcate it gradually lose much of it on the way.

Disagreement under a condition of freedom would be as certain as is difference of opinion, and the latter is a natural consequence of man's fragmentary knowledge, faulty judgment, and proneness to error—all deficiencies that are quickly noted by one person in others and often denied or hidden if found in himself.

Because of its knowledge of the certainty of disagreement under conditions of freedom and awareness that hatred will die if it is not renewed, a regime based on the employment of hatred as an instrument of policy suppresses freedom and fans hatred. It well knows that the management of hatred is a precarious undertaking at best, especially as a long-term enterprise, and that freedom would destroy the cohesiveness necessary to energetic prosecution of policy.

Such a regime finds itself in the need of an external enemy as justification for its repression of freedom. Therefore, should it find itself on the verge of reaching agreements that would establish friendship and therefore lessen the need for harsh measures against freedom, it would feel alarm lest its source of justification be destroyed.

Such a regime is essentially interested in preservation of itself; and this means preservation of the privileges and distinction of office of particular individuals. In the sense that it suppresses freedom, it denies to its dominees the privileges of the distinctive endowment of man that separates him from the lower animals, namely, a roving commission to develop his talents, not only in mechanical and scientific pursuits but in thought, art, religion, economics, and philosophy. Since new thought and philosophic or religious views under the leave of freedom might deviate from the official prescription, and lead to action in accordance with new views or at least to express them, such exercise of liberty could not be countenanced. Men might have thoughts but they would not only not be encouraged to express them but would do so at the peril of imprisonment, banishment, or worse. No right of individual self-expression could be recognized. Originality would be discouraged if not suppressed. Only if the state should sanction particular artistic or literary expression would it be safe to give vent to it.

The suppression of freedom would in time not only lead to

drabness and a colorless society; it would stifle all the more volatile endeavors that differentiate man from man. If man were naturally a spiritless creature, he would offer no objection to the suppression of freedom; but to the extent that he is spirited or Promethean, he severely resents and laments his loss, and is not satisfied to remain docile under a restraint to which his mind does not assent.

Thus the totalitarian regime that ascended to power on a platform of hatred and then found it necessary to suppress freedom lest disagreement and dissension bring it down deprives itself of the fruits of many talents of its people. Contrived fear, which expresses a primary will-force, deprives the regime of some of the highest fruits of the human mind.

Above all, the regime resting on hatred and seeking to build a new system would find in the end that preserving and using the primitive impulses and forces while seeking to repress them for its own ends would not in any case rid the human race of the inclinations that made hypocrites of capitalists, which is to say, professing loyalty to principles and faith while following the siren call for riches and status. It would only transform them and shift their base.

Any regime that engages in state economic planning, such as the socialistic state, and adheres strictly to its plans must also suppress freedom, but for a different end. Planning is a mental operation and as such represents one of the highest gifts of man. It need not rest on hatred. However, when a state plans economic activity, it soon recognizes that no plan is better than the quality of its execution. The best plan may be dissipated by indifferent or deficient execution, and it may be discredited through no fault of its own.

Assuming great confidence in the efficacy of central governmental economic planning, such as must be present if such a course is adopted, it becomes obvious that little or no interference in the execution of the planning can be tolerated. Little or no scope can be given to disagreement. We might as well expect a military commander to grant debating privileges to his subordinates. State planning cannot abide disagreement in the execution of a plan. It might tolerate disagreement before a plan is adopted; but once

a plan is placed in effect, it must be carried out if its value is not
to be dissipated. If subordinates had power to deviate from the
plan, it would soon lose all semblance of efficient execution. Friction and disagreement would sap any enterprise of its vigor.

Therefore all-encompassing state economic planning is inconsistent with the democratic processes.

What then is the alternative?

It seems clear enough that the development of the secondary
will-forces and the amelioration of the ego face many obstacles,
especially when the state intrudes and dominates the scene, since
the muscles of popular political self-control cannot be developed.
In the absence of such dominance, the obstacles are formidable
enough nevertheless. One of the most stubborn obstacles, beside
distrust, previously referred to, is found in the stumbling block
that may be called the peace-coward syndrome of human behavior,
or the kindness-is-a-sign-of-weakness fallacy of the same order.

We have devoted some space to this dilemma earlier under
conditions of individual freedom and found no egress save
through wit, practice, and an occasional show of force under circumstances that avoid emotional involvement. Each recourse represents a prescription that assumes control of impulses, aloofness
from hatred, and a font of good will, in a milieu of freedom.
Aloofness from the emotions that exude from an offended or
wounded ego assumes a degree of emotional control that is rare
indeed. Yet wit and good will are not easily maintained in an
emotional atmosphere. It is soon lost in mental confusion if the
hot blood of emotion or passion inundates the cerebral premises.
Good will is as quickly chilled and rendered self-conscious and
awkward at the onset of an emotional torrent. In the absence of
a totalitarian overlord, the individual has only his mind to
rely upon.

Therefore emotional self-control represents a first step in
pacification of human relationships. Whether the mind by itself,
even if aided by intelligence, is capable of rising to the necessary
dominance over the will-forces and the ego to be master in the
household is questionable. It penetrates, analyzes, classifies, brings
together, ponders, judges, concludes; but it shakes hands with no
one, is neither sympathetic nor antipathetic, and does not give

itself to kindness or hatred. It sees and resolves, or fails to see and fails to resolve; or yet again, it sees but fails to resolve.

It must go to the will-forces and the ego if any of its resolutions are to be executed. Therefore, we come back, as is usual, to the starting point, but hopefully with chastened and corrigible charges at the beck and call of the mind.

The mind is in the position of disciplining, often opposing and often being overridden by the forces it needs for its own purposes. The horseman must first break the stallion he hopes to ride; but once broken, the steed becomes a highly useful means of reaching destinations. Therefore the mind itself bears a high responsibility in shaping the person to whom it belongs toward the goals of civilization. It cannot be so cold that the forces it needs will refuse to follow it or support it, or even show reluctance in doing so. This was Woodrow Wilson's error.

In a sense the mind must hold conference with itself, to determine its own posture or deployment toward the world.

How will it go about such a course?

If it were under the domination of the state, it would have little need of such self-examination except in a narrow sector of private life. In a free society, it may take stock, so to speak, of its assets and liabilities. If it finds itself weak before the primary impulses, inclinations, and appetites, it will know that in order to gain control it must find a footing. This is in the form of purpose or motivation.

Why should the mind seek domination of the will-forces and the ego when so much exertion is entailed in the endeavor? What difference does it make to the mind what part dominates the person? The mind does not feel. It sees and beholds but it neither hopes nor despairs. It has no propulsive power of its own. This fact creates a problem of understanding how it begets action. It seems to have purpose and *acts* like a will. Yet, it only judges and chooses. It must and does use the will-forces and the ego to carry out its choices. Without their help it would be helpless, even as a paralytic is helpless to carry out a desire to arise and walk. Because knowledge is a mere state of consciousness, it too executes nothing of and by itself, but acts as a guide, a raw material for judgment.

The mind depends on the forces represented by the very elements it seeks to dominate in order to accomplish its mission. How can it make a beginning when neither the primary will-forces nor the raw ego enjoy frustration such as the mind's judgment may impose, but on the contrary object to it? The answer is the same as that offered with respect to the origin of kindness or the desire for knowledge. The *senses* bring messages to the will-forces or to the ego from internal or external sources. The inner forces react positively or negatively. Some action may then be automatic or reflex; but if a doubt occurs, the mind and its judgment come into play. Otherwise man would be mere animal. A decision is reached, but it does not carry itself out. The execution depends on the will-force or facet of the ego concerned. When the mind decides in the negative, the appropriate will-force stands checkmated; and the same with the ego. If the decision is positive, the will-force or the ego is free to carry out the decision, which is to say, to embark on the action which precipitated the need for judgment. Since the one or the other proposed the action in the first place, there is nothing further to halt the action unless an external obstacle intervenes.

The mind, in other words, must be the referee, but it needs executive power to carry out its decision. For this executive power, it looks to the disciplined will-forces and the ego.

The mind in its struggle would have been helpless had it not found the primary will-forces supersessible or supplementable by the secondary will-forces, and the raw ego not amenable to refinement and amelioration. Man would have remained pure animal. Having these potentials of modification on hand, it was able to assume (1) the office of judge through the power of decision between opposing forces and (2) the office of commandant by virtue of the power placed at its disposal by the trained soldiers representing the disciplined secondary will-forces and the tutored ego. The mind as the repository of reasoning power could modify the will-forces and the ego, and bring them, if it was successful, to do its bidding. Without the modified will-forces and ego, the mind would have been as helpless as a commander without troops.

The mind then holds potentially the highest office, and if it is itself of a high order, the individual possessing it is a man of wisdom. Such a one might indeed in the past have been chosen by his tribe or group as their leader or advisor. If he was chosen as leader, he became the judge and referee for the tribe or community much in the same manner, by and large, as the mind within the individual becomes the arbiter. The leader then had his trained and willing warriors and spear-carriers, or his hunters, as the case might be, to carry out his plans and decisions. Of course, if the leader were of evil bent, he would betray his trust.

We come around once more to obedience, for among the subordinates disagreements might arise. The leader might be challenged as in the individual the mind is frequently challenged. The leader exacted obedience as best he could. If he failed he was exposed—unless he was a local leader who was himself subject to a higher command, in which event the dispute might be laid before the next higher authority.

In the case of the mind, perplexity induced by complicated moral or other considerations would lead to indecision. In time perplexity over moral considerations led characteristically to a yearning for a final referee. If obedience was to be exacted, a final referee could settle the issue at least temporarily. The need of an absolute as distinguished from a relative point of reference was felt as a reflection of man's desire to live by certainty and to have done with changing opinions and new interpretations. He preferred to settle down to generally accepted routines with as little occasion for disturbed thinking and conjecture as possible, even if he seldom realized his preferences.

There was little hope of achieving such a happy state until a supreme law-giver might appear on the scene. Because of his proneness to error and therefore to disagreement which frequently led to serious and sometimes violent disputes because of the diverse will-force and ego interests, the need for a supreme law-giver, it bears repeating, became more pressing with man's multiplication in numbers and diversity of pursuits.

While the need was present, there was nevertheless no assurance that a supreme law-giver would be accepted as such by everyone. If there were no universal acceptance, disagreement might again divide the leading judges or referees and their retainers. Indeed, disagreement might be so vehement that a resort to violence might ensue.

With respect to the individual, his mind might, however, find a private haven in a different supreme law-giver if it found no flaws in the laws he expounded and had faith in his grasp of eternal verities. It could then refer its own questions for resolution to the supreme extra-mundane referee; and abide by the decision, regardless of the state of disagreement among the temporal ruling elements. Thus might the individual live in his private world and work out his own destination, even if the political order left him in a state of helplessness and veritable disgust. Meantime he might make such effort as might be open to him to bring about a better version of man's destiny by giving a good account of his own gift of life. Under a totalitarian regime, he might be completely helpless unless he were himself a highly unusual individual; and he might, moreover, be separated from all visible means of practicing the forms and ceremonies attendant on religious beliefs.

9.

Man's Quest

for Meaning and Purpose

IN THE PRESENT WORLD, the mind might occasionally achieve the post of supreme referee, assuming its domination over the will-forces and the ego—a condition it by no means achieves under all occasions. It enjoys the advantage of having the secondary will-forces and the refined ego at its command (with a variable degree of assurance) in *mundane* affairs, but it neither had nor has such forces at hand to give it power of command in the *extra*mundane field. In that sphere it was not, nor is it now, a matter of will-force and ego. These have to do with the biological needs and desires of the body and with relations among fellow beings on earth.

The mind, however, after the development of reflective powers, could foresee the debilitation and decay of the objects of concern of these forces. Death would still them all. Where, if anywhere, would it, the mind, then be left? If it went out like a light on death of the body, that would be the end of it; but consciousness does not so easily accept the lights-out view. Therefore the mind began to see itself deserted as the end of the mundane journey began to come into view as a dim but inexorable certainty. What if the light did not go out? Would there be a dark, cold void? Would the record compiled in this life make a difference in what might lie in store? No use to ask the will-forces or the ego! These would be dead!

It is a leading tenet of the Christian religion that the mind in and of itself cannot come to grips with the questions that thus

194

overwhelm it. Divine grace must intervene. This would be in the nature of a guiding light, and could be posited only if the supreme referee (also the creator of man and all else) were interested in man. Thus would the mind find a substitute for the will-forces and the ego in the extramundane sphere where these cannot enter.

The certainty that the mind seeks on earth must be elusive except in proximate degree in the physical sphere. In the sphere of the unknown, certainty is totally beyond reach, and therefore faith represents the only hope.

Faith in what? If the end of mundane existence is the final end to the individual, there is no occasion for faith. Only if it is thought that the spirit or mind remains after death would faith have any reason for being. Even the thought of independence of spirit is a matter of faith since there is no proof that such independence exists in fact. That man has long held to a belief that mundane life is not the end is supported by the practice among primitives of burying food and other usable items with the body. Such a practice is, of course, not proof of the actuality of spiritual survival. It is merely evidence that man has long held to the belief.

The mind must therefore be satisfied with *belief* in place of certainty. A variety of law-givers did appear on earth at different times and in widely different areas. Man had evidently been on earth many millennia before the prophets and law-givers of historical times appeared on the scene. It seems reasonable to believe that the historic prophets were preceded by others and that man lived in great degree by their guidance. Long before the Hebraic prophets set foot on earth and before Buddha or Confucius or Mohammed came on the scene, man had made his way through long stretches of time in far corners of the earth if the findings of paleontology are to be credited.

We have tried to sketch some of the early steps by which development may have proceeded. It was only after man had advanced to the era of thought, reflection, and philosophy that his concern with origins and destination could have a meaning for him. Until language was developed, thoughts on a subject of this order could not be communicated; and if they occurred, they died with the primitive philosopher. Man's mental development could not outpace his ability to communicate any appreciable distance because new thought had no place to go. Even after language made its appearance, its word-power, of course, remained very limited, awaiting the shaping and organization of verbal symbols. No doubt man often had more to say than the paucity of words permitted him to express. He then relied on facial expression, motions, postures, gestures, and a variety of ejaculations expressive of emotion. Ritualism might express what could not be spoken.

Surely the advent of seers and law-givers had to be paced by the ability of others, the possible imitators and followers, to grasp what could be communicated. Anyone who was too far in advance of the stage of language development was without an audience, except, of course, as the charades of rituals claimed attention. To be sure, even as language progressed, this or that prophet or law-giver who was appreciably ahead of those about him lost much of his value. After he was gone, his meanings were no doubt often garbled and distorted. What he said was subject to misinterpretation and lack of understanding.

Yet man, the Sapient, was not stopped in his progress. Therefore we must assume that he was possessed of a spirit of persistence in the face of all the most formidable obstacles that everywhere lay in his path, and that he made his way in spite of them. What an epic!

Discouragement? No doubt he encountered enough of it to halt a lesser breed. The device of renewal and replacement, substituting youth and vigor for the worn and the weary, saved the species.

To what purpose? To what purpose?

The question is inevitable to the reflective mind. To repeat, any effort of prophet, seer or law-giver to supply an answer would have been doomed to failure if it were out of pace with the stage of mental development and the mechanics of communication.

Can the hypothesis be avoided that purpose was walking with man on his way, a purpose invisible but of such persistence that it remained with him before he himself had a conception of it, and prodded him as he faced despair, lifted him when he fell, drew him on when he faltered? This was the mysterious life-force that moved him toward a destiny of which he had but little, if any, appreciation. To believe that man did this himself would be to think that he knew what he was about before he had the least notion of it; for he had moved forward a great distance, it seems reasonable to assume, before his mind was sufficiently developed to form such a concept. Just as a child takes all for granted before its mental development reaches a certain stage, man met the world as it was, before interpretative thought was awakened in him, and even then such thought no doubt first came to light in very few minds.

We come to the conclusion, then, that it was only after man had developed far beyond his primitive stages that he was ready to grapple with questions that required something far beyond his earlier capacity to comprehend.

The purpose that walked with him has always seemed impenetrable to his mind. Man was born. He grew, he learned, he worked in order to live, he reproduced with some exceptions, and died. His offspring followed the same pattern. The offspring's offspring did the same. Behold the teeming millions in the densely populated lands today! The process goes on and on, even as it did in primitive man.

What, indeed, is the purpose?

Man's will-forces and his ego kept him clinging to life; but the mere gratification of these came to fall short of expectations, the more so as he had more free time for reflection. He seemed to be pitched in his aspirations to insights that went beyond what these daily satisfactions could offer him. He was especially prone to ask about purpose when he reflected on the hardships, privations, and pain suffered by him under recurring circumstances, such as war, grief-laden bereavement, pestilence, and famine. Was it worth while? What was the purpose of these trials and tribulations? Did they indeed have a purpose or were they simply the result of the probabilities that ruled the physical world? If the weather produced no rain, man took the consequences in company with the lower animals. He had no special privilege. Some of the lower animals indeed fared better than he.

Was the world and therefore human life ruled by wholly impersonal forces as silent and unconcerned as the stars? When the cold winds blew and ice congealed the world, leaving every-

thing at the mercy of the elements which made no concessions
—what did it mean? Then, when the spring sunshine and rain
brought rebirth to all that had been denuded and so cruelly used,
what could be made of such a sequence? Was nature determined
alternately to scourge us and to delight us? If so, why? Or was
it all the result of a thoughtless, cold, unwinding sequence of
cause and effect, the chain links as cold as frigid steel?

Where could purpose fit into such a scheme? Evidently man's
mind could not answer the question. He found himself tangled
in contradictions when he tried. He was in need of a more penetrating light than came to him from within himself. Was there
such a light? He had relied on the special gifts that were bestowed
on rare individuals for his guidance and progress in many fields;
but the questions that beset him about the purpose of life, if any,
eluded even the most gifted among these. They could only say
that it was a mystery.

How much could he in any event be told in terms that he
could understand? He sought answers but he possibly would have
been unable in those early days to comprehend all that might
have been told him. If purpose was indeed his companion through
thick and thin; if it worked its design through man, as it seemed
to do, and spurred him on, it would not seem improbable that
the mystery that mind could not penetrate should one day have
been made explicit to him in his own words; but that could only
be after he was able to understand the spoken words sufficiently
to absorb their simplest meaning.

There would in any case be failure to understand all that was
said, and there would be misunderstanding and the ubiquitous
disagreement that is an abiding characteristic of man. There
would be those who would question the authenticity of what was
said and others who would deride the claims of authority that
might be asserted; for even if man seeks to know, even if he
thirsts for answers, he remains forever suspicious of those who offer
special insight—except the faithful few.

Man's ego and intellectual pride make him wary, but often
for good reason. He has been misled more than once; and he does
not enjoy being hoodwinked, or made to appear stupid—nor
should he. Truth is the most precious medium of harmonious

human relations, and its concealment, denial, or distortion deprives him of the value of his intelligence.

It seems to be man's fate to fail to recognize the certainty he so eagerly seeks if he does come upon it, for, aside from the physical field, proof is lacking. Therefore, uncertainty will continue to abide with him, and its presence will often make him uncomfortable and even bring him anguish.

Yet certainty would abolish faith, suspense, and much of the ferment of life that gives it zest and interest. Universal certainty would be the same as transparent determinism. It is the indeterminate, the continent, that furnishes the substratum of freedom.

Freedom, of course, for all its great attraction to the will-forces and the ego, may also be a torment when uncertainty is superabundant. Man wishes to be comfortable in the certainties but yet does not wish to be bored with too much certainty either. He seeks adventure, and uncertainty is the very soul of adventure; so he ventures and tastes the fruits of freedom.

Not only is man not easily satisfied; discontentment is the impulsion to progress, and were he willing to rest on his oars, progress would cease, not only in the material world, but in the search for final truth. Man is not made to rest like the oyster and have the world come to him. He is made for search, inquiry, and activity. Why? This is what he would like to know, but will never know during his mundane abode. The very process keeps him occupied on this earth. The questions whet his appetite and the inquiry proceeds.

Assuming a divine visitor, what would be expected of him? Presumably he should be a law-giver who would speak to man in his own language, saying how he should live with his fellow men to assure the greatest harmony without strife and bitterness; but he would also address himself to providing an answer to man's question of final purpose. Since man's life on earth is only temporary and man wonders about the sequel after relinquishing the familiar scenes among which he moved as a tenant in his abode of flesh, blood, and bones, the divine messenger would, it would seem, provide answers to the question that elude the human mind's capacity to answer.

This assumption would entail the further assumption (1) that a creator exists; (2) that this Creator has a purpose in mind for man; and (3) that the Creator maintains an interest in his creation and creatures, including man, and has not abandoned the earth, for all its diminutive dimensions and man's minuteness, to forage for itself without guidance.

Are these assumptions reasonable?

Ask man himself and you will receive a variety of answers. William James gave an illuminating account of the varieties of religious experience in a book of that very title.

Whether it is reasonable to assume that man came from a source other than himself as his own creator is a question that each individual must answer for himself. That he is a product of pure chance would represent a conclusion that would divest him of purpose. He who would elect to endorse such a conclusion is free to do so. Where such a disposition of the question would leave him would be his own concern. His life belongs to him alone.

If, on the other hand, one or more of the assumptions are supported in belief, other conclusions follow as a matter of course, and further questions also arise.

Acceptance of the belief that only a creator could account for the existence of the universe and its contents would not necessarily carry with it the further belief that the Creator maintains an interest in his creation. If inexorable laws control all the motion and activity of the universe, the Creator might be satisfied to allow matters to take their course without further intervention. If, on the other hand, man, one of his many creatures, is free and inclined to do no telling what, the idea of a degree of surveillance would not be alien to logic. Even the sending of an emissary would hardly be absurd. Man himself is given quite naturally to such a course when the need arises, and no one regards the action as unimaginable or ludicrous. On the contrary, it represents a quite sensible thing to do.

However, this is not a theological tract; our interest lies in seeking to understand man by his nature, his setting in outer nature, his inner constitution, his relations with his own kind, and what he seeks and what is his destination.

In what follows, we shall seek application of the principles governing the will-forces and the ego to some of the great problems that confront mankind. How man meets these problems will determine whether his release from total instinctual guidance and his accession to freedom and confrontation with multilateral options exceeded his powers of self-direction and self-government.

Whether his ability to live with himself and his own kind, guided by his mind and moral aspirations, his education and religion, will be able to prevail against his innate selfishness, impelled by his raw ego and primary will-forces, is a question that he must and will answer for himself.

10.

Travail of

Self-government–Part 1

MANY OF MAN'S GREAT PROBLEMS and his efforts to solve them or to come to terms with them may be assessed in terms of the dramatis personae of this treatise, namely, the primary and secondary will-forces, and the raw and refined ego, as guided by the mind and moral forces.

We have drawn on primitive man in certain imaginary situations in which these inner forces struggled for expression, but have not stopped there but traced the same forces in action in modern trappings.

The world today is a mixture of somewhat advanced civilization coexisting with intermediate and primitive forms. For reasons that may be somewhat difficult to justify, the less advanced countries seem to be bent on following in the footsteps of the more advanced ones. It might be hoped that they might exercise more originality and perhaps discover better forms of society and government than those that are in the forefront today; but the hope seems doomed to fade. Man seems to suffer from the starling defect, defined later.

Unfortunately, there is no prescription that might be given the lagging economies and cultures that would bring them to bypass or overstep the known and tried forms that have been found wanting. Perhaps, indeed, there is no other road, and an examination of the inner and outer forces encountered on the way indicates that the problems are much the same for all rising civilizations: man has to confront himself with his mind and subdue the animal heritage, or tame it, and then open the way to freedom, giving opportunity to his other endowments and gifts to unroll themselves. How else encompass progress as we have defined it? If shortcuts exist, they have not been discovered.

Self-government is one of the modern problems, and, of course, immediately upon its examination, we encounter the problem and complications of freedom; for self-government essentially represents an exercise in freedom.

We have previously concluded that what man believes greatly influences his behavior, his outlook of the world, including his relations with those who compose his human surroundings, and therefore his endeavors. Thus, his belief is an important factor in his development.

We have also given brief attention to the Marxist school, which is both nondemocratic and incompatible with freedom. It represents a totalitarian concept in which the state becomes the final arbiter in mundane affairs, and that is all there is. The materialistic pursuit is then the sole interest. Freedom, like religion, is an obstacle that is more than a mere hindrance; it is antipathetic to Marxian Communism's highest good.

If, however, as many believe, material abundance does not satisfy man's destiny, not all his eggs should be deposited in that one basket. Freedom of self-government would offer a higher and more attractive goal. Man's diversity would be a useless endowment if all individuals must in any case be pressed into the same mold.

Needless to say a regime that takes its inspiration from freedom faces a more difficult course than the totalitarian one. This follows from the greater scope given to disagreement and expression of a great variety of aspirations as reflected in the secondary will-forces and the refined ego. Both courses, the one of freedom and the totalitarian, face the common problem of taming the primary impulses. Beyond that, the course of freedom represents the Promethean spirit of maximum individual development. The most congenial medium for such development lies in self-government.

Comparison of the two courses of human development (which is to say, the totalitarian and the democratic) may provide a clue,

if not to man's purpose, to his most fruitful course of bringing out
the potentials within him. The difference is not merely one of
religion or belief in a supreme being, but of man's individual
dignity and the flowering of the potentials planted in him by
whatever put him on earth.

It would seem to be a misreading of man's ego to conclude
that it should be suppressed and wholly subordinated to the ruling
mundane power. The endowment of the human beings with an
ego would make a misfit of the individual (as indeed it seems to
do in many instances) if this unique force were not recognized
as the repository of man's potential for progress. The creative
source of man, responsible for his existence, must be thought to
be whimsical, sadistic, and irresponsible, perhaps gaining satisfaction and sport out of man's discomfiture and anguish, if the
ego's existence had no purpose and carried no compass.

Freedom (not license) of self-government offers the ego its
greatest opportunity either to stultify itself or to acquit itself with
credit. That the people given to self-government may produce
unseemly behavior, sometimes indeed bizarre, goes without saying.
Compared with totalitarian regimes, the democratic permissiveness
might be expected to produce freakish means of expressing odd
personalities, and much that produces at least an inner blush even
among the blasé occurs with indomitable frequency.

In the United States, one of the world's leading democracies,
a genius for bizarre buffoonery and ecstatic nonsense, noted principally for its loudness and shattering of all urbane sensibilities,
insists on manifesting itself at least once in four years, when the
political rituals that accompany the parturition of final candidacies
for the supreme office in the land are performed. While this ritual
lacks the war dances of the savages, it has the trappings of a wild-
West circus, together with the abandon of an uproarious back-
saloon hullabaloo. It sweeps along with the wanton abandon of a
stripteaser, shedding dignity and good taste as the act warms up.
It is a strange mixture of folklore, raucous irreverence, make-
believe, and bluff that is designed to gather an irresistible momen-
tum in behalf of this or that political aspirant.

A far cry it is from such exhibitions and the underlying

serious concerns and issues, and these can hardly be exhumed from
the cultural debris as it thickens on the floor.

There is much interplay, much controversy, in any self-
governing society. Many ingenious accusations and counter-accusa-
tions will be hurled in the course of the processes by which men
are selected for posts of government; much pretense, playing to
the galleries, as it were, or to the arbiters or referees who have the
power of election, meaning the people. An unconscionable amount
of exaggeration and reciprocal deprecation will be indulged; expressions of outrage, often sincere and serious enough, will be
heard; but so long as the rules are respected and fouls are not
de facto outrageous, decisions are reached and the results accepted,
usually, although not always, in good grace.

Not only are ground rules established as well as legal stric-
tures or practices but quite certainly as powerful if not more influential are certain unwritten rules and attitudes about fairness,
sportsmanship, and decency. Some of these are deeply set in the
folklore, and those who break them may find themselves condemned without quite understanding what went awry. Excessive
and obtrusive ambition may be such a source of silent condemnation. The person may simply not "get anywhere" and yet not be
overtly condemned. A species of silent consensus had taken shape.

Much folly, froth, and unseemly behavior may indeed be
encompassed in the process of freedom at work, mostly in the
political contests in search of popular favor. "Forgive them," the
more urbane onlookers may be moved to say, "they know not
what they do,"—while grinding their teeth in anguish and muttering at the price exacted by democracy. The wonder, they reflect,
is that anything decent and acceptable can come from such wholly
insufferable and insupportable antics, capers, and egregious pretensions. It is sickening, and yet they watch, half-fascinated and
half-groaning. If their side wins, all is forgiven. After all the *vox
populi* must be given an abundance of indulgence if it is to be
heard and given leave its wonders to perform! The losers on the
other hand will see the defects of the system and discern clearly
its horrors—until they themselves are returned to power.

From the foregoing, it may be deduced that a species of un-

suspected discipline does ride with all the commotion and confusion generated by the process of self-government. This esoteric
discipline does not have the appearance of discipline; rather it
impresses the onlooker and even many participants as indulgence.
It would be more accurate to say that the discipline has a wide
tolerance for buffoonery, execrable verbal usages, sometimes pur-
posely mangled grammar for effect, and perhaps too much of what
is called "character assassination." Yet none of this must be carried
too far lest the more sober public take offense. The atmosphere is
one in which liberal allowances are made for lapses that do not
offend common decency, and they may soon be forgotten.

In the sober body politic is indeed found a core of decency,
good sense, and even long-suffering tolerance, and this reserve
supplies the sanity and integrity that represent the saving grace.
In many encounters, contests, and controversies, it represents the
ballast that keeps the ship of state on a somewhat even keel and on
a reasonably straight course. In the absence of the totalitarian
command, an elaborately concealed discipline does come into play.

A democracy that lacks this disciplinary reserve will come into
trouble; and the discipline is not something that grows like berries
on shrubbery outside the door or like bananas in clusters on
stalks, to be had for the plucking. No! It is of slow growth, slow
refinement, developing hand in hand with the secondary will-
forces and the taming of the ego. It is a fruit that demands much
attention and prolonged and continuous effort for maturation.

In the United States, especially in New England, there was
an early Puritanism that was indeed a strong disciplinary force,
but a reaction against its external harshness forced it into hiding.
This phenomenon produced a species of inverse hypocrisy. Some
of those who continued to carry Puritanic principles in their
hearts were careful to disavow any intention to be good. Indulgence of the appetites and gayety was often simulated even when
it was despised. Outward piety was shunned, and much that
paraded as decay of morals was pretense.

The abandon and folly of the political conventions and campaigns might, by the same token, be misinterpreted.

The level of decency and propriety below which the public
recoils is, to be sure, not a thin, fine line. It is a rather broad

one, but a candidate or a figure in public controversy will trifle with it at his own peril. Despite the tolerance that goes with the artificial atmosphere that is often created, the line is not usually ignored. Cleverness at skating on the borders of thin ice may embolden some participants, but the risk is evident, or they would be less concerned about veering from the border when they have tempted fate. This is not to suggest the absence of corruption but to suggest that it is not a product of the folderol itself.

The existence of the line represents a species of modal behavior. Many are above the line, and it is they who suffer from the indecorum and coarseness that is characteristic of the contests. Those at the modal or dividing line, which may be a band of some width, such as the equator, tolerate the behavior without much laceration of their sensibilities. Those who are below this band may represent numbers large enough to offer strong temptation to the solicitous candidates. This is the gallery of catcalls, booing, and raucous yelling that deafens the ears of those who are at hand for better or worse.

The level at which the dividing band itself is located measures the general level of culture, or the degree to which the secondary will-forces and the ego have been cultivated and disciplined. This is, of course, a statistical concept, but may suffice to explain differences between diverse cultures.

We should not confuse form with substance. Horseplay and loudness under certain circumstances have been accepted as virtually routine and expected in a country in which frontier manners prevailed until recently. Even rowdiness must not of itself be associated with corruption. It may do no more than discomfit the genteel and urbane. Chicanery and corruption may indeed be concealed by the habiliments of gentility and breeding.

Among the principles that must be observed if disagreements in a self-governing regime are not to disrupt human relations beyond repair are sportsmanship and fidelity in cooperation. A public accustomed to expect fair play in sports contests and to accept penalties for infraction of rules is better conditioned to the fortunes of political contest than the one that has not been so exposed. There may be a wider gulf between the integrity of those who have learned to control their emotions out of considerations of fair-play and those who abide by rules because of harsh repression.

There are countries in the world—usually rather far away, of course—wherein ostensible self-government is but a form without substance. Political contests, while doing obeisance to lofty principles, nevertheless, are regarded in most cynical fashion. Often the philosophy of self-government is highly extolled in campaigns for office but promptly forgotten if success crowns the effort. At other times, the results of voting may be brushed aside without ceremony and strong-arm methods employed to seize power, sometimes with the excuse that the voting was fraudulent and sometimes without such an excuse.

In such instances, it is clear that the usages of justice as a secondary will-force and refinement of the ego will have been but poorly developed. Mere homage to a philosophy when ulterior motives of the ego, such as greed for power, run hot in the blood, is not only meaningless; it is deceptive and intended to be so.

Under such circumstances, it seems hopeless to bring the populace and its leaders to an appreciation of what is meant by the restraints of power, as expressed by Woodrow Wilson, when it has not hitherto been exposed to such a self-denying ordinance. Wilson was very aware of the temptations of power. Nevertheless, as President and as a student of civilization, he was a strong advocate of self-government, as witness his campaign for the self-determination of peoples. He saw clearly that acceptance of the restraints of power by those in power was a condition precedent to successful self-government.

Self-government by people does not go hand in hand with man's early organization. On the contrary, it is a latecomer on the scene. It presupposes a considerable degree of understanding and enlightenment, no less than much practice at self-discipline and self-reliance.

If the secondary will-forces have had but little development and exercise under freedom and the ego likewise has undergone little discipline under voluntarily accepted and imposed restraints, the hope of instituting such restraints when power is achieved by a people, often against great odds or after years of suppression, is not bright.

The mocking question of origins, so often lost in the darkness of prehistory, and therefore often assuming the problem of precedence as in the chicken-egg puzzle, stares us in the face once more. The desire for self-government is traceable to the ego, but how it gained sufficient force to assert itself successfully in the first instance can only be left to conjecture. We shall essay a few such conjectures as we proceed.

First, however, a distinction should be drawn between the circumstances under which self-government is sought by particular groups or constituencies of people falling under a common dominance or rulership. Wide differences may confront the aspirants under widely varying circumstances.

The approach, methods, and procedures and even the fortunes may vary according to the existing conditions of government. It may be one thing to depose a ruler or to force concessions from him from within the same society, as the Great Charter was wrung from King John in 1215. Thus might a chieftain, a prince, or a king be confronted by the people who are subject to him, but who are of his own blood, race, or tribe—relatively homogeneous and of the same culture. It may be quite different if a dominated people, perhaps previously subjugated by conquest or traded by treaty, who are of a different blood, culture, stage of civilization, or advancement from the ruling power, seek to throw off the yoke and then seek to institute self-government. It may be still different if a previously subjugated people are liberated to their own devices, or whose declaration of independence is not seriously contested, if at all.

Also variable are the vicissitudes of holding power against usurpation, the *coup d'etat* or other devices pursued by power-hungry individuals or factions who are not enchanted by the democratic processes where these are in being or have a foothold. Under this last condition may be mentioned independent people who have experienced different degrees of self-government and autocracy or dictatorship over different lengths of time: China, India, Egypt, Japan, Greece, Rome, European countries, Latin America, and the United States of America.

The principles of self-government will be the same under all circumstances, but the problems will be as diverse as the personalities engaged, the temperament of the people, the state of their advancement and dedication to the requirements of self-government.

Upon first taste, the "will-to-power" will almost surely over-rule suggestions of restraint, no matter what the conditions or circumstances. Power is so buoyant to a swelling ego that, once achieved, the very thought of restraint seems outrageous. The French Revolution erupted in wild excesses no less than the liberation of the Congo in 1960. The reaction is of the kind described earlier in our consideration of primitive men who were accustomed to domination of the weaker ones. Why seek power only to relinquish its fruits upon achievement of it? Let us first consider the condition in which a going government already exists in one fashion or another.

As we saw earlier in our consideration of kindness, if someone who has full power at his disposal did not on occasion refrain from its exercise even under the sway of temptation, no beginning toward the self-restraint of power could be made. Under most circumstances, such restraint would be regarded as a foolish luxury by those in power who are continually apprehensive of the loss of power to others who may indeed await an opportunity to wrest it from them. Unquestionably the problem is a real one where seizure of power by a *coup d'etat* is not uncommon and not regarded as the ultimate political sin. From experience, those who hold the reins of government at a particular time in such an atmosphere know or feel that they know that unless those who harbor an ambition to seize power are frustrated, by whatever means, they will indeed strike as soon as the time seems opportune. In some instances, seemingly harsh preclusive steps are therefore taken to avoid such an eventuality. Secret and often cruel methods may be employed to detect any conspiracy that might be forming.

In such a political milieu, the hope of self-government by the populace is remote, and any hope that the regime in power might honor the restraints that would make possible the practice of self-government by the people would be dim. Even the peaceful succession to power under such conditions is but poorly rooted, and resort to conspiracy and violence is not infrequent.

Under the circumstances, the dominance of the primary will-forces and the unrestrained ego over principles of good government is evident. A characteristic of such regimes is control or suppression of news media to stifle freedom of expression and criticism, and to forestall the flourishing of dissent. To press its imprint of power on the populace and to gain the appearance of popular support, likenesses of the oppressor are everywhere set much in evidence, often obtrusively and in execrable taste. The ubiquity of the image is made ostensibly to reflect the affection of the people. Streets may be renamed in honor of the henchmen who helped bring him to power. Statues are erected to the honor of the Great One even before his demise—sometimes only to be desecrated and torn down when the tyrant has fallen. The desecration itself gives further evidence of the political immaturity of the people, and it is this very immaturity that offers an opportunity to the demagogue or "strong man."

When the people themselves have not advanced far on the road to self-discipline, there will be inadequate social sanctions against the style of popular behavior that provides an opening to the dictatorial aspirant to power.

Public opinion has under these conditions not yet gained the force of expression and the unity that are necessary if it is to rise to the stature of social sanction. This necessary unity is not to be understood as opposed to diversity of political opinion or disagreement with respect to public issues but, rather, agreement on the rules of political conduct, including above all, fairness and honesty—rules that protect diversity of opinion and expression. If the people themselves are not wedded to the discipline that restrains wayward impulses and corrupt practices, they will be incapable of generating a force of public opinion of sufficient persuasive power to restrain objectionable political elements that are present in all societies, and their practices.

How much time is needed for development of social disciplines that will bridle at usurpation or, with more relevance, forestall it, cannot be foretold in any given instance. The attained level of culture, the degree of private discipline prevailing in the population, the attitude toward public service, and the philosophic orientation of the people would be decisive factors. Attitude toward public service would be one of the most potent influences. If tolerance for corruption is high, the outlook for self-government without the pitfalls of usurpations and dictatorial regimes would be crepuscular to say the least. If the public tolerates corruption, it will invite it in public office and will become the victim of venality, intrigue, and disruptive contests for power; for the rein on the will-forces and the ego will be slack. Public officials will be under little or no constraint to discipline their own impulses.

In view of the snail's pace of cultural changes and radical upward movement of the general level of education, it would be a sanguine soothsayer who would expect a transformation in less time than several generations from autocratic government to self-government. The older generation with their beliefs and outlook anchored in the past must give way to replacements that have accepted what for the elders would be new attitudes and standards of public service. A single generation would hardly make so radical a break with the past that a sharp differentiation would so soon mark the departure. Learning new approaches and accepting them is not a rapid process, as we have seen.

Disagreement would of itself retard progress, and hostility toward the new and unaccustomed would produce the same delaying effect. Whether national inspiration could be generated to produce the compelling enthusiasm that is needed to desert old ways and attitudes is a question that must remain without an answer in any given situation in the absence of happy examples. The transformation would almost certainly await the appearance of a resourceful, inspired, and determined leader. The populace does not lift itself by its own bootstraps. Without originality in leadership and the devotion of a crusader, a stolid people will have little inclination to change from the well-worn habits and attitudes that have the advantage of being familiar, even if they were oppressed. They know nothing better and are accustomed to a humdrum, lusterless life. It has the advantage of not exacting much thought and energetic readaptation. As we have had occasion to remark earlier, the populace is not imaginative nor ambitious for the extraordinary effort and exertion that radical changes in attitude and accustomed outlook would require.

A volatile and excitable people may indeed respond to intolerable oppression by highly eruptive reaction, but may soon tire of the prospect of settling down to responsibility and glitterless effort.

As charity begins at home, where it may become deeply set in the heart and in outlook and behavior toward the outer world, so self-discipline and fortitude or long-suffering effort of a people to achieve and refine self-government must arise within the people and be practiced by them before they can successfully *demand* and obtain integrity and devotion to duty of their public officials. The virtue-level of public service will not likely rise higher than that of the people from which the service is drawn. The problem here is analogous to that of the mind when it must enlist the help of the will-forces and the ego in the institution of self-discipline that is to be used against these very forces, as previously described. The people must generate the expectations that become sanctions against corruption, demagoguery, and the like, but *someone* must first lead the people and inspire them, increase their education and moral sensitivity, thus sharpening their expectations.

Here we also encounter the paradox of obedience. If the people are to obey their rulers, what will be the worth of their expectations of a higher morality in their governors? Who will provide the bootstraps and who will provide the upward pull?

The problem of obedience, to which we have also devoted some attention earlier, does indeed pose difficulties to the human mind in its contemplation of the processes of self-government as well as in other areas of human activities.

Obedience, we saw, is a necessity to human cooperation and even as a cement of society. The obedience of children is easily recognized as a necessity because of the immaturity of the child's mind.

We earlier saw, however, how the principle of obedience may be abused. Indeed, one of the most difficult of all human equations to solve in the consideration of the blessings of self-government and freedom is that of the peril-point of obedience. It goes without saying that in view of the frequent selfish nature of dominancies, obedience can be carried too far; that excessive

loyalty to it could truss the human spirit in rigidities that are
contrary to its genius. No far-reaching changes would be instituted. Society would become static. Yet, in asserting this truism,
no one had succeeded in fixing the fine line beyond which abuse
and excess set in and on the hither side of which obedience represents a virtue.

Permissiveness, tolerance, and indulgence are companion
questions walking hand-in-hand with that of obedience and assertion of authority. Few questions weigh more in the consideration
of the fortunes of self-government than these.

The less developed in the art of self-discipline a people may
be, even though of ancient lineage, still in a stage in which
obedience may be regarded as irksome because it was always in
response to *imposed* discipline, the greater their proneness to consider freedom as a release from the restraints that were imposed
to bring order into human relations. Nothing would, however, be
more certain than the disappointment that inevitably results from
an outbreak of libertinism on the advent of sudden freedom. Yet,
how say it? If a people is not permitted to learn from experience
what is excess and what is temperate, how will it learn the lesson
effectively? Yet, how can we be confident that the taste of license
will not linger among those, possibly the leaders and their
entourage, who did well under the new sudden permissiveness?
If an unhappy experience with a dubious venture of licentiousness following self-liberation to which the people gave itself was
not universally oppressive in its results but on the contrary en-
riched some elements because of their shrewdness or luck, the
whole body politic would not have been chastened by the experience. Those whom the libertinism brought riches or higher
status would thereafter chafe at the bit if stricter obedience of
laws and regulations were proposed. Since they had the necessary
acuity and shrewdness not only to escape the general unhappy
consequences of the debacle of freedom but to gain from it, they
would be expected to be sources of trouble in the future, and the
inspiration of instability.

Was it wise then, if indeed there was an alternative, to pay
out line too liberally in the first instance, thus providing the opportunity for the deplorable use made of freedom? Sometimes the

new rulers, not yet sufficiently entrenched, are powerless, and licentiousness and a blood-bath may be unavoidable.

This is the age-old question that separates liberalism and conservatism in their approach to government, even when the power of restraint is in hand. The liberal is more permissive, more tolerant and indulgent. The conservative thinks of the trouble that bad precedents will lay up for the future.

Fear of setting a bad precedent has no doubt laid a restraining hand more frequently on many ventures, enterprises, or relaxation of rules than pure negativism. The fear may be well founded that a bad precedent will soon blaze a trail to bad habit, and bad habits are difficult to eradicate. The idea that a stitch in time saves nine or that an ounce of prevention is worth a pound of cure stood the conservative in good stead.

Once indulgence of licentiousness, which means breaking the law or the moral code, becomes accepted by the populace from constant exposure to it, the primary will-forces and the raw ego which provide the impulse to license will become deeply entrenched. In the absence of an inspired leadership, it seems improbable that the tenacious grip of licentiousness could then be broken.

Who will indeed arise to provide such leadership will remain an unanswered question until he appears on the scene. *Meantime,* the private family, the schools, and the churches remain the principal sources of possible emancipation.

There is no prescription for the refinement of self-government by a people that does not begin with private morality and moral self-discipline. If the higher level is not otherwise attainable, a benevolent dictatorship may offer the best substitute. Such a dictatorship may frown on the corrupt practices of a dissolute regime or may confine them to a small circle, usually out of public view. The excuse offered by such a dictator will be the familiar one that this is the price he must pay in order to maintain his power. His benevolence may indeed bring the populace greater hope and some examples of good government that might profitably be made a guide to future regimes.

The cornerstone of democratic self-government is, of course, that of obedience to established law. If the law needs to be challenged or if efforts are made to modify or repeal it, the judgment of the community, as expressed in a referendum or other form of vote, must be honored. It is only in rare instances that a law may properly be tested by a violation. If the law is a new one and its constitutionality is doubted, a test case is sometimes contrived so that the constitutional question may be settled. If the judicial decision is final, as that of a court of last resort, the only proper recourse is a modification of the organic law or constitution. Means of achieving such a modification may be set forth in the basic document itself.

In a democratic society, unlike the totalitarian practice, appropriate flexibility is provided for. The very purpose is the accommodation of a variety of legitimate interests that express the diversity of temperaments, aspirations, and developments of the people. A rigid form of law might produce inequities or might not be suitable to changing conditions, and thus might close the door to freedom.

In a pluralistic society such as is found in the United States of America, special flexibility may be needed to accommodate different social backgrounds and cultures—at least for a period long enough to permit amalgamation.

Permissiveness and obedience were everywhere related to each other in the past as master and servant, king and subject, or commander and soldier. There was little civic freedom. Obedience had little flexibility. Such flexibility as existed was the result principally of permissiveness. In a democratic society, the actuality in individual cases may indeed not be as far removed from the king-subject relationship as theory would have it. The right to challenge a law is more theoretical than practical; for very few individuals are in a position to initiate or support a challenge. Their only recourse, then, is to obey and while obeying seeking change.

In view of the need for stability in law, this is as it should be. If everyone could enjoin enforcement of the law if a given law did not meet his approval, the people would spend all their time in court. Also, the ordinary business of day-to-day living could hardly be carried on because of a chaotic legal climate.

Nevertheless, if really important issues arise over the law, criminal, civil, or municipal, the possibility of effecting a change is much greater in a democratic society than in a kingdom or dictatorship. If discontent becomes general in a regime based on popular sovereignty, the people, reacting to general frustration of their will-forces or their ego-interests, will soon find a common scapegoat and some style of leader. The danger is a tempestuous outburst of emotion that may be exploited by a demagogic aspirant to power. Only if the people are well-established in self-government and have had much experience in distinguishing between demagogues and responsible governors or aspirants to the supreme office, will they escape the consequences of their emotional demands. Factionalism is almost sure to be fatal. It traces itself to the ego-ambition that seeks self-advancement rather than the general purpose. It destroys cooperation and fosters distrust.

Should, of course, the populace have no voice in its own government, the probability of eruptive sequences as a means of forcing a readjustment would be more probable unless the dictatorship were well entrenched. If a people can and do feel that they are participants in the processes of readjustment, they will have an extra measure of patience. Their will-forces will be more amenable to restraint. Even under these circumstances a demagogue may succeed in coming to power by promises of delivering the people from their oppressive economic frustration. The only hope of preventing such a course of events lies in the alertness and vigilance of the electorate and in their fortitude and self-discipline.

Loyalty to principle, rather than following blindly the feverish prompting of the will-forces and the ego, will offer the best but the least popular course.

In a democratic society, permissiveness comes from the lawgiver, and this is the people themselves. Permissiveness under these circumstances should indicate a trust in the integrity of the constituents of society or the citizens. The more responsible these are, the less is the need of surveillance and the less the law will be in evidence. Under conditions of a high level of lawabiding behavior, the law as a force withdraws into the background and needs infrequent invocation. Thus the fruit of self-discipline inculcated by a self-governing people will be found in less oppressiveness of the law and the least intervention of its forces in everyday affairs.

We reach the conclusion that individual self-restraint and understanding of the law reduce the need for law. Of course, popular self-restraint is hardly destined soon to reach the state in which the burden of law is cheerfully borne by the primary will-forces and the ego; for it is the restraint of these that is the very purpose of law. It is the heart of the contest. A degree of individual self-restraint so closely in harmony with the law that law would enforce itself could be dismissed as a utopian dream, particularly because not all elements of the population are equally enlightened or devoted to the principles of self-restraint and self-government.

Origen said, "Discord follows in the step of sin." Who is without sin?

In view of the growing permissiveness and consequent indulgence that appears to mark present-day democratic societies, there is no immediate prospect of achieving the degree of self-discipline that would make of the police force an obsolete order.

Progress in self-government may therefore be regarded as a product of the level of self-discipline of the citizens, however this might be achieved.

When the will-forces are not restrained, the behavior of one person will by its excesses arouse the animosity of those who are upset, injured, deprived, or disadvantaged by such behavior.

If they in turn are not disciplined to exercise restraint, their responses will be of the same order. An unrestrained provocation will beget an unrestrained response. To maintain order excessive police surveillance will then be necessary. This force will in turn be either too repressive or corrupt. Justice will be lost in the chaos.

The state can govern only by suppression of freedom under these circumstances. Thus, indulgence in too much individual freedom and license will result in conditions that can only be brought under control by excessive use of external restraints. The society as a whole suffers. The state will need an army, even if the country is poor and backward, and the men will be taken out of production. The army pay must come out of the treasury, and the treasury must be replenished from the productive resources of the economy. The country will be all the poorer—not better off economically. The people will have fewer goods, poorer farms, neglected schools, underpaid teachers, more politicians sustained by the taxpayers, worse and fewer roads and highways, teeming slums, littered streets, defective sewer systems or none, abominable telephone service, and combination hospitals and morgues.

Many of the so-called self-governing countries of the world suffer from the wasteful and weakening effects that flow naturally from undisciplined behavior of their people. No lasting remedy can be found unless the cause is removed. Economic assistance from abroad will not overcome the basic weaknesses until the necessary self-disciplinary steps are taken. Whether the incentive exists to undertake a task so arduous is questionable unless, to repeat, a leader is found who is able to awaken a lively desire to sacrifice self-indulgence in the interest of the general good. Some of the populace is already so sunk in poverty that no further sacrifice from them is possible. Where then would the discipline and restraint be of avail? The people, however, will more surely respond if they trust their leaders for their proved honesty and integrity. Cynicism born of betrayal offers the poorest springboard for progress.

The necessary discipline must come from the individuals who are foremost in their communities, those who may inspire by example and impress by instruction and teaching. It is they who must promote schools, support education, and inculcate honesty and other moral virtues.

Simply instilling a desire for a better life into a people, however, encounters the risk of their readiness to accept the benefits without the accompanying resolution to shoulder the burden. Yet no benefits will be permanent if they are not the result of individual exertion. There will be no appreciation of the price of advancement if the price is not individually paid.

The problem is not unlike that of self-betterment in other departments. Without motivation and understanding, little will be accomplished. The question is where the motivation will come from. It must in the end come from an internal source, even if the *initiative came from the outside.* Unless external inducement or persuasion modifies an inner disposition and turns it into a positive force, the individual will not be engaged and will not respond in a meaningful fashion. This is the test of leadership.

In a community, people are not all on the same level of energy, ambition, intelligence, and initiative. In order to move a community so that it will be receptive to new ideas, to take an interest in producing changes, the community's moving spirits, as said just now, must be engaged. They in turn may be able to arouse a response in the more indifferent, indolent, and even the torpid if they themselves see a hope of solid progress, as inspired by the leaders on the various levels that taper to the apex.

What is the source of progressive leaders? Almost any society produces a few men of sufficient ability and mental and moral endowment to become good leaders. An inspiring leader who can arouse the whole populace to a high endeavor is unfortunately a rarer specimen. He cannot be exhumed from the past, as one whose qualities are already known. He has to be tried before his qualities can be established. A prospective leader may on trial fall far short of needs and expectations. It is for this reason that self-government provides for the dismissal of particular leaders by the people, to make way for someone who may do better, but who may also do worse.

There is no guarantee in these premises. A people must have hope and live with fortitude. The road is rugged. How to imbue a people with upward-sloping aspirations is an art, as leadership itself is an art, that does not lend itself to ready transfer to others.

Yet, peoples have in fact developed and moved to higher levels in terms of behavior. Their primitive will-forces have been put under restraints and secondary will-forces have appeared and led the way to culture and elaboration. The raw ego, too, has yielded to amelioration and bowed to finer sensibilities.

Therefore, as the task has been accomplished to some visible degree in different parts of the world, it seems fair to conclude that it can be accomplished elsewhere and can be carried to a yet higher degree where the greatest progress has been made. There remains abundant scope!

We may turn now briefly to those people who have been

under foreign domination as was common under the colonial system.

When self-government confronts a people who have not hitherto governed themselves, many changes in attitude and outlook are necessary before the people can hope to exert much influence upon the course of government. Colonial people newly liberated will find it difficult to change their attitude toward those who exercise power. The people cannot think of themselves all at once as the source of government power. After all, government is invisible. It is not something to be grasped and manipulated. It is of the stuff air is made of. Even power, other than that of the police or the army, is not readily comprehended.

To learn to think of oneself as exercising power seems like a fairy tale. Freedom will readily be confused with license; and when freedom's nature is brought home to the people, in the sense that it is not license but that much responsibility goes with it, it may soon lose its luster and become burdensome. To exchange a life regulated by routines determined by someone else—just as one may be accustomed to sit down to meals prepared and set out by others without so much as a thought from oneself finds himself at a loss and incompetent—to exchange a system of government under which all was done by others for a system in which one is expected to concern himself about the affairs of the community, its schools and roads, keeping order, helping devise and paying taxes, looking after sanitation, and defending the country—this is something that had not been envisioned or very intimately imagined. The word "freedom" had had an uplifting ring about it. It stirred the ego and evoked vague notions of something great and glorious; but this, this—is so different! Nothing romantic, only difficult and mostly incomprehensible! There is something synthetic, artificial, and unreal about it! It does not fit! Perhaps the old life was better after all!

Obviously time will be needed to make the change in attitude that will bring responsibility into focus. A new generation, as previously suggested, must be awaited before self-government will seem natural. For the populace to learn to respect those who had so long been governed by the rulers of empire but who now sit in position of statesmen themselves requires a psychological readjustment. When for all known or remembered past time someone else, someone from the center of imperial power, was always the overlord, it is seemingly a make-believe world now.

The radical change is outwardly really almost invisible. The sun comes up and sets as before. The patter of raindrops has not changed. The trees and vines, shrubs and flowers are the same. The landscape is as it was. The animals, the birds of the fields, the insects and bugs take no note of anything different.

Yet there is a difference. People talk about it. Some say it will not change anything. Others feel a vague hope of better things to come, but cannot define what it will be. There is something in the air. It is difficult to define, but it is expectation, not unmixed with some anxiety. Can it really be true? Do we now really belong to ourselves?

From such a psychological state to the time when the expectation of the people, once secure in their freedom, and accustomed to its feeling, rises to the level of political sanction, may still be a far distance. When the people have so advanced in their culture, refined their moral standards, and achieved so high a degree of self-discipline that they expect high standards of conduct from their public servants and are sufficiently mature politically to enforce their expectation through the ballot, they will have passed the test of self-government. They will then have reached that state of advancement in self-government that will enable them to suffer patiently under an elected regime that may be disappointing, waiting for the years to pass until the happy day when they, the people, once more have the opportunity of throwing the rascals out!

This great terminal point will not seem so glorious and glittering either! There is much need to bother about how things are going while the hope of influencing events seem pitifully shrunk to almost nothing. "What can I do?" comes to be a refrain frequently heard as an exculpatory exclamation from the ego. If all that I can do is to vote once a year or even less frequently, and if my vote is only one in tens of millions, as in countrywide elections (in the larger countries), or one in several million or hundreds of thousands in provincial or state or metropolitan elections, or at best, one in thousands in more local polls—what is the incentive? My vote is buried as one grain in a heap of sand.

Such reasoning or rationalizing, of course, evades the issue. Just as the body of animals and plants and of man too, are composed of cells, each cell, though only a most diminutive entity in the vast ensemble, has a very important function to perform. If each cell sought to excuse itself from doing its work on the ground that the part it plays among the billions with which it is associated is so infinitesimal that it would make no difference to the organism as a whole; and if the notion took hold and ended in the idleness of an appreciable number of the cells, such as a quarter or a third of them, the organism would die. The body would be unable to function as a whole.

While the analogy is not wholly apposite, it nevertheless demonstrates the dependence of healthy self-government on active interest and participation by the citizenry. If this is lacking, systemic deficiencies will develop. Corruption, misfeasance, and nonfeasance will plague the body politic. No one will wish to shoulder the blame while many will complain.

Self-government will no more yield its best fruits than will a poorly attended orchard. As the orchardist prunes his trees, exterminates the weeds that would soon choke them and take much of their nourishment from them; as he sprays the blossoms and the new fruit periodically to prevent disease, borers, and worms from ruining the fruit; as he replenishes the soil with plant food and loosens the soil for aeration and retention of moisture, he exerts himself. He overcomes his inertia, his aversion for unpleasant work, and the soothing whispers of indolence. He well knows that his yield will be poor, the quality of fruit inferior from insufficient nourishment, the ravages of insects and worms greater if he does not spray or dust, and that his cash returns will be sadly reduced if he does not rouse himself and apply his energies to the best effect.

Why should it be thought that self-government is something apart, something that will thrive and yield its best fruit when it is neglected, given third or fourth or even lower priorities in its claim on the time and attention of those upon whom it depends?

One of the difficulties encountered by self-government lies

in the absence of an immediate and visible reward. The orchardist or horticulturist or farmer soon sees the results of his energetic devotion to his agronomic pursuits. If he operates in a free enterprise system, he will be able to market his output and enjoy the proceeds in cash. This prospective reward enlivens his will-forces no less than his ego. Cash receipts will enable him to buy what he needs in order to live, to house himself and his family and to clothe them. If he applies himself with yet greater vigor and intelligence, he can increase his yield per acre, if it is not already at the maximum. Success will enhance his outcome.

He may then be able to set a better table, enjoy a more comfortable home, and he and his family may wear better clothing. He will have emerged from the world of the strictly primary forces to that of the secondary will-forces. He and his family will not eat merely to live. They will become patrons of the culinary art. They will not live in a shelter that is a shelter and nothing more; they will have comfortable furniture, with pieces that are agreeable to the eye, reflecting artistry in the making of them. They will not wear homespuns, calicos, and ginghams only, but will have more changes of apparel, clothing made of finer cloth and more elegantly cut or tailored.

His ego, meantime, will also be deeply engaged. As a successful farmer or horticulturist, he will be esteemed in his community for his accomplishments. His neighbors will treat him with a degree of deference, will not pass him by without a nod or a greeting. He will be engaged in conversation and asked to take part in community affairs. He will become, if he likes, a real participant in the process of self-government.

He will begin to perceive the effect that government may have on his own activities, through taxes, expenditure of public funds and the building and repair of roads, and other activities or lack of them. His interest in the operation of government and in the officials and other persons who perform public functions will grow. For the first time he may have some ideas about alternative methods of public administration or plans of doing the things that affect him. Also he begins to wonder if someone other than this or that public official might not do better if given an opportunity, and before he is aware of it, he will have stuck his bare big toe into politics.

As he learns more about how government operates, he begins to form judgments of his own. Perhaps better methods or new undertakings would help in his own occupation or remove obstacles in the way. It would soon become obvious to him that while visible quick rewards do not flow freely from the process of self-government, the possibilities of helping to shape public affairs are more numerous than he could undertake. Instead of his own life and welfare being a mere end-product of a government far away and untouchable, he would find that there are all about him many means by which to take a hand in self-government. Not all of these possibilities would be confined to influencing formal governmental activities.

He would become interested in the education of his children. Why should he not then take part in the community's educational activities? Looking about, he would learn that he might belong to citizens' associations that devote themselves to the needs and problems of the schools. Soon he would learn that education does not spontaneously develop and administer itself any more than crops plant, cultivate, and harvest themselves. Someone must devote time, thought, and effort to both fields if the best results are to be achieved.

He would find that the same is true of other aspects of local affairs. Water, roads, sanitation, maintaining peace, and similar activities may also be subjects of concern to citizen groups; and these groups would be open to him. If he is able to contribute ideas and to inspire energetic activity, he would soon find himself asked to serve on this or that commitee. Later he would be asked to direct this or that function of committee activity. He would soon be asking others to serve on committees.

It would become clear to him that voting from time to time is but a small part of the activity open to him in the process of self-government. During the weeks and months intervening between election dates, the great stream of self-government flows on.

On reflection he would recognize one of the most widely ignored principles of self-government: self-government is open to all who wish to participate; participation is voluntary and there are no entrance fees. The citizen has the widest scope. His limits are his own, both with respect to the extent of his participation and his competence. Strictly speaking, his competence, capability, and willingness to devote himself to the activities of self-government are his only limitations—unless, of course, his ideas are radical to the point of being subversive of the existing government and he is not content to leave the question to the electorate but rather seeks the overthrow of the very institutions of government.

If he is in a minority group, he need not forever be helpless; but the obstacles in his way might be formidable indeed. However, progress has in the past been achieved despite seemingly insuperable obstacles. Stubborn obstacles did not await arrival of a minority status. Many were perhaps more forbidding than those that face minority groups today. The latter today often finds allies among those who are a part of the majority and obtain much help in their struggle.

Aside from the opportunities of the citizen to help shape the community in which he lives, he also has open to him numerous other activities—more in fact than he can possibly find himself able to accept. These have to do with his occupational, professional, or business interests. If he is an apple grower, he may become a member of a growers' association. A physician may join an association of the medical profession, local, state, or national. Physicists, chemists, teachers, members of the bar—it matters little what the professional or economic activity may be; membership is open to qualified individuals. If no association exists, one may be organized, and if properly led may increase cooperation, promote common attack on mutual problems, and lift the individual's horizon.

The citizen is therefore far from helpless even though he has only one vote in the selection of public officials.

The citizens' groups and professional, economic, commercial, and civic associations are themselves instrumentalities by and through which much of the effort or self-government is channeled. Associations devote much time to the affairs of government and often participate in the fomentation and promotion or defeat of legislation at various governmental levels. If all groups are equally active, one tends to offset the other, but between them the subject under contest may be well aired before the public. This is an advantage in turn to the public that is no part of either interest. Legislators, indeed, often find safety in the array of opposing forces that set forth conflicting claims.

Similar interests in the economic and business world may form alliances for the achievement of particular aims. This phenomenon is not unlike the alliances formed by will-forces for the promotion of mutually acceptable ends or the alliance of one or more will-forces and the ego. Each will help the other so long as the interest is mutual, but cooperation in other fields does not follow as a matter of course.

Sometimes a public defender comes on the scene lest private "interests" gain advantages at the public expense. Elected officials, through conviction or political acumen, may take the part of defender of the public interest. Veritable political careers may be forged by pursuit of this course. As a result, it is sometimes difficult to judge the sincerity of the protagonists of the public interest. Other political aspirants ally themselves covertly or openly with particular interests, especially if these are heavily concentrated in the constituency of the vote-seeker. He is then happy to be openly associated with the particular interest. A constituency containing a large industry, such as lumbering, fishing, mining, or manufacturing, would be inclined to seek election of candidates who express themselves as favorably disposed toward the welfare of such industry. If there is division in the constituency so that one half might favor one interest and the other half an opposing interest, a neutral candidate might have higher hope of victory at the polls.

In self-governing countries, the contest of the so-called interests is a common phenomenon. Since there is a great diversity of interest, much mutual frustration results; and if there is a separate public interest, it may find its greatest hope of prevailing precisely because of the conflict in equally active private interests.

The citizen in a self-governing society need not suffer from boredom. If he is in fact bored, an accusing finger may properly be pointed at him: he is not fulfilling his role as a citizen. Perhaps he has no taste for public service. Perhaps he is disgusted with "politics." This would of itself indicate that he should exert himself all the more to the end of lifting politics to a higher plane.

Some citizens will indeed participate in civic affairs, both locally and on a broader scale, not so much because they are imbued with the spirit of self-government but as a means of furthering their own careers or personal fortunes. The effect on the quality of government will soon be reflected in favoritism, corruption, and inferior service.

Self-government is not a static process. Constant vying of interests for attention and accommodation proceeds daily and continuously.

It is to be expected that much conflict and controversy will attend the business of the world, including its efforts to draw from raw nature the goods we need (production, trade, transportation, and similar activities).

However, controversies can be resolved if understanding of differences is substituted for the chafing of the primary will-forces and the raw ego. Sometimes it becomes necessary to live with differences and unsolved problems.

One of the byproducts of self-regulation is a species of cross-surveillance. If members of a group practice self-restraint, which may be irksome to the will-forces of each person, they are not pleasantly disposed toward other members of the group who do not practice the same restraint but "cut corners" or "feather their own nests."

A veritable growling disposition is exhibited toward those who "cheat," and the latter will adopt as cunning means of concealment as their skill and artfulness will be able to devise. If they are found out, they will make efforts to prevent a general exposure, and depending on the level of their moral index or quotient, they may employ persuasion by entreaty or by threat, blackmail or bravado. If one or another overture fails, they may attempt bribery. If the discoverer or discoverers of the fraud or other reprehensible act which the perpetrators sought to conceal are themselves not above corruptive collusion, bribery may be accepted, and the coterie will become confederates in concealment.

If, however, a higher level of conduct has been achieved by the discoverers, the culprit will be denounced. The course in any given case will therefore depend on the degree to which moral self-discipline has been practiced by the individual members. If most of the group have not adopted a code of conduct or adhered to one inculcated at home or accepted from some other source, such as associates, school or church attendance, their view may be overruled or dismissed by the others, usually by some form of raillery or display of good fellowship—unless one or several of them should exhibit a stern determination not to be mollified or diverted. Should the morally disciplined members be in the majority, the minority might display a different attitude, not wishing to be associated with the culprit. This would be an act of intelligence since intelligence would be at the service of the primary will-forces and the raw ego. The minority would fear the consequences of their association with corruption. Their egos would be concerned with their standing in the community, and their primary will-forces, counseled by intelligence, would fear the effect on their economic standing or their future income. Their compliance would, of course, not represent honesty, but merely expediency.

The mediation of the intelligence is necessary because hunger, cold, home discomfort, and similar results of vanishing incomes are conditions that are *felt* and, of course, are unpleasant; but conditions do not think. Intelligence, as previously observed, under these circumstances, taking its cue from experience, and exercising foresight, would arouse the primary will-forces attending the conditions. The will-forces would then provide the person with feelings of apprehension. This feeling would in turn influence behavior.

The irksomeness of restraint and self-discipline is such that even those who are well disciplined do not look with favor on someone else who, despising self-restraint and being seemingly congenitally opposed to it, seeks to harvest the fruits or reward of self-discipline when the opportunity arises, without paying the price.

It requires but little of perception to observe the force of disfavor that is quickly visited on someone who seeks to go to the head of a line while others are patiently taking their turn. The resentment is really out of proportion to the small additional waiting time that such an act of intrusion will cause; nevertheless it radiates its heat. The irked will-forces, because they would rather have the person in whom they dwell going about his business, whatever it may be, or getting under way to his destination, can barely abide the act of someone else of equal or lower state stealing a march by short-circuiting the same course of irksome waiting as the others endure.

So it is with moral restraints. Were these not irksome and difficult to maintain, there would be less, if any, resentment over the breaking of the law by someone else. There might, to be sure, be concern over any immediate personal deprivation that an act such as theft or fraud might cause, or resentment over discomfiture caused by some act of law-breaking, but the deep objection to someone's "getting away" with violation of the law that is so commonly felt comes from the will-forces and ego interests that are restrained. They too could enjoy a few hundred or, better yet, a few thousand units of coin or paper of the realm, without having to work for it. Holding themselves aloof has been at the cost of self-discipline, and this cost is remembered. Therefore, if someone else filches the contents of the exchequer, the restrained impulses say, "Go get him," and they are not disposed to be very charitable to the culprit.

The will-forces and the ego, in other words, submit to restraints under protest, so to speak, and if others are released from the restraints, a feeling of outrage answers from the inner depths. This feeling at the same time echoes the community interest. The restraints, after all, are instituted in behalf of the community, and the irksomeness may then appropriately be charged to the community.

It may be observed that the proclivity to alliances that is characteristic of like-tending will-forces and ego interests is also present among those who obey restraints and moral precepts. A community of interest springs up through a species of mutual understanding, and it is this that forms a demand for obedience of the rules of conduct by others, and calls for punishment of violators. The alliance, however, is not one of pleasure. Rather, it is one of equity, which, in this case, means distributing the burden of civilization equally or as nearly so as circumstances permit.

It is a subject for the secondary will-forces and the tutored ego.

Man's community of interest and the fact that individuals do not live for themselves alone but share their interests, their plaudits, their aversions, and reactions is thus exemplified. It is useless to say to a man that it is just that he pays his taxes for the upkeep of the community and maintenance of law and order and that therefore he should have no complaint, when he is aware that some people capable of doing so pay no taxes or very low rates. It is not the act of tax-paying but its irksomeness, which is to say, the deprivation it causes, that pains the will-forces. Reflection on the injustice, however, comes to rest on the basic fact that man is deeply implicated with his kind and is a unit among many, and this affects his ego. As an individual, he wants no one to steal an advantage over him. If someone is to have an advantage, it must be justified. If it is honestly justified, it will be accepted, even if it causes some pain to the ego; but if it is not justified, both the ego and the primary will-forces will rebel.

Whether the public will protest strongly and in really menacing tones or evince only slight interest or outright apathy will depend on the degree of self-discipline that has in fact been achieved. If an insufficient number of people have practiced self-restraint, there will not be present a great composite force of disgruntled will-forces expressing resentment over the injustice and inequity perpetrated on them. No self-governing people, no matter how well established their forms and procedures, is free of the self-centered indifference, nonconcern, and evasiveness of civic duty that will erode and subvert the principles of both freedom and democracy. Self-government will not soon outgrow the call for alert concern and vigilance.

11.

Travail of
Self-government–Part 2

WE HAVE TREATED THE INDIVIDUAL as the ultimate constituent of society, and so he is; but he is subject to so many influences that these must be given some further attention. As the influences modify the individual, they affect the fortunes of self-government.

We have already had occasion to consider the influence of the family. A few more words may, however, be in order within the present context. Next, the community will demand some attention, as the unit next higher than the family. This was formerly the tribal village perhaps.

It is in the family, as we have previously observed, that consciousness first emerges and the earliest and sometimes the most lasting attitudes are formed. For this reason, it hardly needs repeating, the outlook, behavior, tone, and moral attitude of the home, in which nearly all human beings are introduced to the world and receive its appearances and impacts, goes farther in the shaping of citizens than perhaps any one other influence. This is especially true of the average human beings—and this means most of them. Some who have a degree of originality may the sooner reflect on their own rearing and may overhaul some of their attitudes and forms of behavior. Even a juvenile rebel or adolescent or adult may be more beholden than he suspects to his early environment and training for his present outlook and behavior. Some further repetition may therefore be justified.

Since parents are the principal source of the atmosphere that permeates the hearth, their responsibility is of the highest degree.

After some years, as the children are exposed to the world in school, in church, on the playgrounds, they begin to help shape the home atmosphere by bringing in outside impressions. The outer world begins to penetrate and influence the home. Yet, the attitude of the parents toward school itself, toward teachers, toward the taxes that maintain the schools; their attitude toward religion, toward society; politics; their outlook toward the world, such as business, occupation, employers, fellow workers; what they think of local officials and other public officials and national leaders; and what they say about them at home; how they regard truth-telling, honesty—whether their outlook is one of cynicism or rather one of understanding, of suspicion or of trust; their attitude toward success of others who have surpassed them in career or earnings—and a hundred other subjects that claim the attention of the family and form the burden of conversation, reading, or discussion—all exert a molding influence on the children, and therefore on the fortunes of self-government; for it is not too much to say that self-government has its cradle in the home.

Whatever the general cultural level of the home may be, it may leave lasting marks on those who came up there. Is there indeed discussion of public affairs, of school events, of neighbors, of news, of books or magazines, of music, of local or national problems—and if so, in what atmosphere?

What is the attitude toward manners, toward dress, hygiene, habits, posture, bearing—toward learning, toward relations with neighbors, good ones and those who may not be exemplary? The whole spectrum of life will pass through the environment of the hearth. Members of the family become ill. How are they treated? Neighbors may suffer misfortunes. What does the father or mother say? Are they concerned or are they indifferent? Are they secretly glad as reflected by side remarks? Do they call on them and help them?

What is practiced at home, attitudes that may or may not be consciously inculcated at home but nevertheless imitated and adopted, will contribute to the *community* attitude because the family is part of the community. The attitudes and views of the parents in turn are influenced by those of relatives, friends, and neighbors; or by the economic or social class to which they belong, or the racial strain from which they sprang. Again a hundred different influences may pour their contents into the family and help shape attitudes. What these attitudes are in general, what the consensus of outlook may be from family to community, and from community to community will go far toward determining the fortunes of self-government.

When a whole community is affected by some condition so that all the members must adopt an attitude toward it by the mere fact that they live there, it is not uncommon to find a community attitude, and this will likely be expressed by the individual members when they go elsewhere and have occasion to express themselves. This uniformity is to be expected especially if the community interest is involved and if this differs from that of other communities. There is then a common cause among those from a particular community. Just as a common enemy unifies people who otherwise differ quite readily and even vehemently on other subjects, a common community interest will often beget a common attitude by members when they are outside of it or encounter someone from the outside. Of course a community of interest may be of a wider scope than a locality. It may reach far beyond the local community, and it may or may not be geographical.

In saying this, we merely recognize that common interests may be provincial, regional, national, racial, or of some other form of mutuality or extension.

In the United States of America, the southern states for several generations turned toward the outside world a remarkably uniform attitude toward the rights of colored people. There was not much to discuss. The discussion, if any, or rather the sentiments, had all been given voice at home, and the attitude induced by the impressions was absorbed by the members of the family. From the family, the attitude suffused the community and the region. If there were dissenting opinions here or there within the family, such opinions quickly disappeared or went into hiding when the members of the family encountered people from other parts of the country. Exceptions began to appear, no doubt, but openly only after many years placed the Civil War into a receding perspective.

Beside regional communities of interest are those that do not necessarily depend on a common territorial base, although proximity may be a supporting factor.

The attitudes, the propensity toward alliances among similar interests and the reactions to injustices and similar offenses against the public seem indeed to be quite automatic. For example, the disciplined ones in a society are automatically offended or taken aback by the unrestrained and licentious conduct of others. No one needs to incite the resentment. The like-thinking ones will be drawn together by their like interests, even if they are not neighbors. These are the natural responses of the will-forces and the ego. Those who think alike are quite alert to any affinity of interest that may lurk in any situation. On the other hand, the licentious ones will also be drawn together. They seek aid and comfort from each other against the common enemy. However, they suffer from the disadvantage that they cannot be sure of the trustworthiness of those with whom they would seek an alliance.

In the "climate" of the moral attitude of a community, the phenomenon of automatic response above referred to may be detected. If the community has by one process or another or one influence or another adopted, accepted, or absorbed an attitude of strong condemnation of lax conduct in sex relations, for example, there is little doubt about the reaction toward anyone who transgresses against the mores. Hawthorne's *Scarlet Letter* provides a good example.

Some of these attitudes may in other times come to be regarded as too severe. There may be a relaxation because of the inculcation of a more kindly feeling toward those who sin if the sin may be regarded as not so heinous after all. The charitable view may soften the severity of condemnation—perhaps after much reflection on the prayer in which one asks forgiveness in the degree that he can find it in himself to forgive those who sin against him or offend or injure him.

Thus, it seems clear that although the community reaction may be virtually automatic, its tone or quality may not always remain the same. Any change would be attributable to one that has already occurred, or that had been worked, in the secondary will-forces or in the instruction of the ego.

If we wish to know how the community reaction can be so automatic, at least under condition of well-settled attitudes, we must still inquire into the individual; for the community's unit consists of individuals. There is no community attitude or opinion as such. We use this terminology because on many occasions there is so much similarity in reaction among the members of a community that the individual attitudes, since they are the same or nearly the same, are lost in the composite. Most members are followers, some of them passively so, taking their cue from the leader.

Nevertheless, each individual does react, even if only to nod approval. Were this not true there could be nothing that we could call a community reaction. There would be no consensus, no community opinion or community response.

The individual's attitude, his opinion, and his response are, as we have seen, a reflection of his will-forces, his ego, intelligence, mind, and general belief, as exemplified by his religion or lack of it.

In many fields, these attitudes and opinions may vary widely because with respect to them each individual may be left to himself. The community has no interest in the individual's attitude toward poetry, for example, unless it be a community of poets, or toward art and similar subjects, because these predilections do not affect the community in any manner that would be regarded as vital.

In other fields, the influence of the community, meaning the other individuals composing it, on the individual may be more than minimal. If a home-owner burns his leaves in the autumn, no one will be concerned if there is an abundance of surrounding space, if smog is not a consideration, and if there is no danger of a conflagration. If the opposite conditions exist, or only one of them, there will exist grounds for a community attitude toward leaf-burners. There are then grounds of common concern, and if the individual is properly sensitive to the comfort and welfare of his neighbors, he will arrest his inclination to do as he pleases.

This is a simple example, but it may have a thousand variations. Other inclinations to do this or that might have more proximate and irritating or perilous consequences. The rights of his neighbors would then clearly outweigh the individual's freedom to do as he might like.

Community sentiment, representing the interests of the other members of the community, would become a consideration that in turn would come into the individual's consciousness when he contemplates some action the consequences of which would be expected to reach beyond the borders of his own habitat. How much weight would he give to such considerations? It would depend on the degree of self-discipline and the scope of his reflection on how his behavior might impinge on others. If he had sensitized himself so that he would be aware of the range and character of the effects, he might or might not refrain from action that would discommode, annoy, or injure his neighbors and the community.

He might, of course, even delight in being obnoxious and vexing his fellow-beings, but might or might not wish to stop short of doing them damage. Depending on his disposition, however, he might deliberately inflict injury on them if he thought that by covert maneuvers he might escape discovery. The ill-will that would lead him to such behavior, aside from a deranged mind, might represent a reaction of his raw ego to some slight insult, real or imaginary, or evidence of disfavor in which he was held by the community. His ego might then become a smarting center demanding revenge, and only a strong inhibitory voice within him would be able to halt him.

If the moral sense of a community or a people is highly developed because the individuals that compose it have been taught moral precepts and have accepted them, with less than major exceptions, a moral atmosphere will prevail. Individuals of the community will be aware of what is expected of them. When they are confronted with a temptation to behave in a fashion or to participate in a covert transaction that would violate the moral principles to which they have been sensitized, the temptation which elicits the response of the primary will-force interested in what the temptation offers or suggests simultaneously arouses moral reflection. If the individuals who are tempted have a sensitive conscience, they will "trump" the temptation without much ado. They had "made up their minds" far ahead of time.

They fear more the consequences of wrongdoing than they crave what is offered. This fear may not rest entirely on the probability of being discovered. Even if no doubt existed about the complete secrecy of the act, the moral sense might condemn the solicitation and bar the temptation outright, not allowing it to reach the interested will-force or ego-facet that might be tempted. Again, they had already made up their minds. Religious considerations would produce the same effect.

Secrecy that would be proof against exposure or being found out would be no defense against total reality or omniscience and would therefore offer no cover to a person convinced of the omniscience of God. Further, the idea that the individual's status in a post-mortem existence might be jeopardized would act as an inhibition against the action. Which inhibitory influence would be greater: the fear of losing standing in the community, with friends and associates, or the fear of eternal condemnation, would depend on the individual's moral orientation. Morality is not necessarily indissolubly attached to religion. Where there is no such attachment, the conscientious individual would be deterred by the mundane social considerations, such as the state of his esteem among his neighbors, rather than by religious reflections.

Of course, if neither concern is present, we have before us the potential criminal, which is to say a person who is devoid of the inhibitory reflexes that are evoked simultaneously with a temptation. His only concern is discovery and the punishment that might be expected to follow. He devotes thought to means of avoiding discovery and runs his ingenuity over crafty imaginary dodges and artful evasions of pursuit, but is not concerned about community opinion, the discomfiture, hurt, or injury that his acts might cause the victims of his misdeeds. As a result of his mental attitude, he is not halted by reflections such as restrain the religionist or the one in whom a feeling for fellow beings is ever present and alert. It is for this reason that society is justified in removing him temporarily or permanently from social intercourse, if he succumbs to his evil impulses.

We have said enough to demonstrate how the fortunes of self-government are linked to the character of the people who seek to govern themselves. This is not to say that problems of production or economic development are not important. They are indeed crucial; but unhappy results may be foretold if a low level of self-discipline and a flaccid moral atmosphere prevail. Much of the energy expended will be dissipated in economically ill-conceived enterprise and in the disarray caused by disorderly ambitions and passions.

A people who have placed only the loosest curbs on their primary will-forces and tolerated only the most flexible leashes on the indulgences and pretensions of the ego will be disproportionately eager to expend the fruits of their effort on consumption and will therefore encounter great difficulty in building the capital substructures needed for economic growth and development.

The attack on scarcity of the means of satisfying human needs and desires will not be crowned with gratifying success if the people are too eager to consume and not at all enchanted by saving. By using their time in producing for consumption, there is little left for improving the *means* of production. Output per man will remain at a low level unless time and energy are devoted to the improvement of tools and mechanical contrivances employed at production. When methods are improved because time has been diverted to that purpose, more abundant goods can be produced in the same amount of time as before; but even then the means of production, which consist of tools, machinery, equipment, energy needed to operate them, and similar instrumentalities, cannot be neglected without courting stagnation.

The problem of "capital formation" is one that plagues many of the countries that have not developed as rapidly as some others and have been left behind in the march of industrial progress. The reason is not so abstruse that it cannot be made comprehensible.

The possibility of growth and economic progress is provided by nature, as already remarked.

Consider something as simple as a seed of corn. If this seed is planted, it will, if properly cared for, reproduce itself several hundredfold. If the planter should consume all the surplus corn but the one seed which he would keep for planting, he would not move far afield. If, on the other hand, he should consume only three-quarters of his crop and should retain the remainder for planting the next season, he would soon have much more corn than his needs would call for. He could then give the remainder away or purchase other goods with it, or perhaps use it as feed for cows or pigs if he had them. If he should continue to consume less than he produces, his productive expansion would soon be phenomenal. The cows and pigs also reproduce, although not as freely as corn. Should he refrain from slaughtering them, he could have the use of the cows' milk in addition to the increase. Milk has excellent food value, and would reduce the amount of food the producer must buy elsewhere. Corn is also prized as food for chickens. With his savings he could obtain a few of them. These in turn lay eggs and breed rapidly. A flock may be produced from one pair in a few years, assuming that the grower did not eat all the eggs as a consumer; or if he should keep some eggs for hatching, and did not eat all the new chicks as they become broilers or roasting stock.

The equation is simple, but it becomes more complex as more is produced and as greater variety is sought by the consumer.

Let it be said that production is not an end in itself. Its purpose is to produce goods for human consumption. Therefore, consumption is an important factor in any economy. Our present concern is the means by which man may so increase his product that he may have more to consume without retarding or setting back his productive processes.

As our man reserves some of his corn each year for planting by restraining his desire to consume, and does the same with his cows, pigs, and chickens, which is to say, instead of consuming all but one pair each year, he refrains from so short-sighted a practice, he will soon be on the road to affluence. Meantime, he and his family have developed a desire for a greater variety of goods than those needed simply to subsist.

However, he finds his output limited by the tools and implements he uses. He can plant only so much corn because time runs out on him. Also, he can only harvest so much because it takes time to break off the ears from the stalk, to husk the corn and put it in bins.

Our beleaguered agronomist needs tools—labor-saving tools and machinery. If he is able to make some himself, it will help him to plant more corn and perhaps to harvest it in less time. If he is not a tool inventor or mechanic, he may exchange some of his produce for the services of a toolmaker or machine-producer. Since he has not regularly consumed all that he has produced, he will have a surplus that can be used for this very purpose. This will represent his "cash crop."

By refraining from too eager consumption, our grower had made possible the "capital formation" that was destined to catapult him still farther ahead. He had restrained his will-forces in behalf of futurity. The future as it was foreseen reached back to discipline the present.

If others in the community should follow the example of our entrepreneur, a thriving people would soon greet any wayfarer who might pass that way. A busy people, moreover, would have less time and inclination for the wayward behavior that disrupts human relationships, calls for guardians of peace, causes anger, arouses passions, and generally makes of man a poor husbandman and provider because his time is diverted to other pursuits and wasted effort.

If the future has little power to discipline the present, much of the effort that is dedicated to futurity will not be put forth. Why should the youngster undergo the discipline of school and study? Is it because he is dedicated to the future? He is told that he must prepare himself for his estate of adulthood. If futurity stirs little response in him, he will probably languish at the foot of his class. However, he might be spurred on by the attitude of his fellow-students toward laggards. This would depend on the sensitivity of his ego; but the question of the origin of the fellow-students' attitude itself would arise.

Evidently they would be reflecting a tradition or a community attitude, and this in turn would require further tracing to its origin.

We have already had occasion to mention the discipline imposed by climate, and especially the rigors of winter in the so-called temperate zone. It is easy to trace what seems to be a likely explanation of the corn-planter's cerebration if he lived in a latitude far enough north or south to experience the change of seasons. If he did not produce enough corn and did not store a quantity of it sufficient to last until the following spring or summer when other foods might become available, he would experience a corn famine. If his dependence on corn was radical, he would fare very badly and verge on starvation. If others were more provident than he, they might out of charity or by putting him under a burdensome obligation help him with a sufficient daily or weekly ration to keep him alive.

We may be sure, nevertheless, that he would not be selected as the most popular man in his neighborhood or named as the most likely to succeed. On the contrary, because of his dire need and his utter dependence on others, he would find himself in a very unenviable position. What might be exacted of him as a borrower might border on slavery or a lowly status in his society. This would represent the social discipline imposed indirectly by his fellow-men in reflection of winter's harsh discipline of them. It would be a small matter to them to share their goods with him if it had not cost them much work, worry, self-denial, and other burdens to produce what they needed. His improvidence would not be condemned if there were an abundance for everyone, to be had without effort. No stigma would attach to him. In fact, his unconcern would not really represent improvidence because nature would not withhold her abundance from him; but such a state of nature's generosity would not be encountered in the latitude we have assumed as the scene of our observation.

As remarked a little earlier, it is only because their own will-forces and ego-inclinations had to be curbed, and because this is an irksome or painful exercise, that those who are called on to share from their own store of goods with those who did not practice like restraint on their desires, and did not exert themselves as did the others, will find sharing a burden and an unwilling undertaking. This reluctance would be modified or might disappear if the shortage afflicting those in need were not the result of their indolence or negligence but rather resulted from ill-fortune over which they had no control.

We may believe, as we have had occasion to observe earlier, that a people that has lived since time immemorial in a winterless latitude where the need to make preparation for a long season of nature's withdrawal from seed, berry, or fruit production was not present had no reason to develop the foresight and the worry that prodded husbandmen in the northern latitudes to make special effort to lay by supplies for the period of relative destitution. If such winterless people were asked or were expected to learn to worry, they would need special instruction, devoid of an inner feeling that would of itself demand foresight of this order. It would be necessary to recast their attitude toward the need of producing more than enough to meet the barest human needs.

The rudiments of capital formation through saving are easily understood but are perhaps not so easily accepted as a guide to everyday activity. In the winterless areas, education of children would offer the greatest hope of overcoming the natural unconcern. Inculcation of foresight and ambition to make nature yield more of her bounty so that more needs and desires might be met would be more readily accomplished in those areas among the young than among those who by custom had already become habituated to the status quo. The usages of incentives designed to enlist the interest of the secondary will-forces might be available from external sources.

The problem facing such an endeavor would be encountered in finding means of avoiding the ascendancy of the primary over the secondary will-forces and the primitive ego over the tutored ego. Incentive of a monetary character alone would, if left to itself, merely stimulate the more primitive and undisciplined will-forces and the unrestrained ego toward more desire for goods, and might lose its potential civilizing and progressive influence. Unless the more refined will-forces were stimulated and promoted, and the ego properly modified, the dangers and unhappy fruits of corruption, of which we have drawn a sketch, would be an eager menace.

What has been said demonstrates that there is no necessary

connection between self-government and economic development. Self-government may stagnate or fall under the domination of corrupt regimes that have no interest other than self-perpetuation in office. The plunderers may be satisfied to leave the people in a low state of economic development—in fact, may seek to keep them in such a state by the very withholding of education and vocational training.

If self-government is to be linked to economic emancipation and development, special attention to the means of forging the link becomes imperative if the effort is not to end in a cynical rejection by the people themselves. Unless they are offered the opportunity and the mental orientation necessary to improve their economic lot through self-discipline, they will find themselves in a trap, so to speak, from which they cannot extricate themselves; they will not know whom or what to blame, and apathy may overtake them.

Corruption may indeed render economic progress if not impossible, at least very difficult; for corruption in public officials may reflect a corrupt populace, or one that does not demand with sufficient determination that official corruption be halted; or the example of official corruption may in turn corrupt the people.

Therefore, if a people are to help themselves, it behooves them to seek the eradication of corruption. This objective deserves the very highest priority; otherwise economic development will have a dubious base. If a people is to be helped from external sources, the same prescription is germane, and failure to have it fulfilled will jeopardize the undertaking.

If monetary assistance is supplied from outer sources, the danger is all the greater that it may be dissipated by converting it excessively into consumer goods and away from producer goods. Great sums may thus be dissipated without achieving substantial economic development.

The principle may be illustrated by reference to the loan of $3.75 billion made to Britain by the United States of America after World War II. Had the British used these funds to import French wines and perfumes, German beer, Italian silks and shoes, American beefsteaks and costly automobiles and other luxuries, the proceeds of the loan would soon have been spent without adding strength to the British economy. If, on the other hand, the funds had been used to re-equip obsolete factories, building fertilizer plants, improving the railroads, and otherwise overhauling the production facilities of the country, as in great part the funds were used, the loan would have been highly beneficial. Had the British people clamored for diversion of the funds to consumption purposes, as they would have been inclined to do had they not had a high level of self-discipline, the results would have been dismal. The value of the pound would have fallen, prices would have risen, and inflation invited.

We therefore come to the need for self-discipline, whether the subject is one of self-government or economic development or both. Therefore, self-discipline is a basic need of both a worthy self-government and economic development.

In view of the basic value of self-discipline to the human aspirations just described, it may be asked how self-discipline might be initiated and promoted. Unquestionably self-discipline will need inspiration of a high order if it is to flourish. While it is necessarily an exercise that devolves upon the individual, the latter may be motivated by external sources and seek inspiration from elsewhere as a means of making a beginning. Possibly the merit of self-discipline may be brought to the attention of a people through their educational institutions and religious establishments. It would be far better, of course, if the notion and inspiration came from within; but unfortunately those who are most in need of it sometimes are often the least interested in disciplining themselves. It is indeed difficult to perceive how the undisciplined can become interested in what their will-forces and ego find repugnant. If a people has no aspirations in this direction, it is something in the nature of a mystery how it can be brought to dedicate itself to such an alien course. We are driven once more to the conclusion that the initiative must rest on the shoulders of an interested individual or group of likeminded individuals who must assume the leadership. The most fruitful possibility would again lie in a great leader of state who could arouse the people with an inspirational zeal. This conclusion brings us full circle to the same critical question as in the field of self-government. The two are so intertwined that a separation is not much more than an artificial division made for the sake of demonstrating the heavy burden that rests on self-discipline.

This is, of course, not the only style of discipline, since the variety that comes from outside of the individual is the most common of all. The value of self-discipline lies in the greater understanding of the function of discipline that it bestows and the greater freedom that its practice brings the individual. Also, self-discipline may be expected to become more firmly established in the person and thus exhibit more fortitude under challenge than the imposed variety.

He may, however, be at a loss over initiation of the endeavor, and may undertake to rely on his "willpower" to carry the burden, and so may find the task too arduous for his stamina. It is no easy undertaking to change well-entrenched habits that he would do well to eradicate; or to change mental attitudes and to overcome indolence. These attitudes and habits may be very dear to the person, and he will be loath to change them. Perhaps the most needed of all supports is what, for want of a shorter and better word, is called motivation. It is a source of incitement, prompting, or stimulus that acts as a spur to the individual to engage in some form of activity or to refrain from it.

The individual under ordinary conditions needs no motivation to eat, sleep, or breathe. Hunger acts as the spur in the first case. This style of behavior owes its incitation to the primary will-forces. The raw ego supplies its own quota of activities or styles of behavior. No special motivation is necessary. No one needs an intent to breathe.

In fact it may be some of these very styles of behavior that need modification if man is to rise to a higher level. We face again the question of how man can interfere with his accustomed manner of behavior and turn it into new directions. Once more, too, we come to rest on the secondary will-forces, the refined ego and the sources that moved them in turn to higher levels; for, as we have said, while the cause of justice, for example, is expressed by a secondary will-force or the ego, justice or its administration, unlike hunger, is not an automatic phenomenon of behavior. It must be guided by the mind and the moral sense. It needs refinement.

What we are asking the person here who is concerned with instituting self-discipline is to find a motive, or his endeavor will soon founder on the treacherous rocks of the primary will-forces and the raw ego. This question was faced earlier, and we may now assume that the motivation has either been achieved or not, as the case may be. If a desire for self-discipline is present, no matter how it was generated or what its source, the person would be ill-advised to trust to his so-called "willpower" since it does not exist.

He has one or two courses open to him or a combination of the two. One is a process of inward self-instruction. The other is the setting of a contrary will-force or ego interest in opposition to the habit, attitude, or manner of behavior that the individual wishes to eradicate or change so that it will not stand in his way.

The first alternative is treated at some length in the author's book entitled *The Philosophy of Self-Management.*

The principle invoked is that of speaking to and instructing the inner self on the assumption that the desires, habits, and impulses may be addressed directly and that they will not only "listen" but after an appropriate course of concentration and repetition will obey the suggestions or instructions.

The inner inclinations and impulses are likened to the higher levels of the lower animals. These respond to training administered by competent masters. Our primary impulses and appetites are of animal origin and will obey the master if he is consistent, logical, and persistent. If he is inconsistent, inconstant, confused, and self-contradictory, an indifferent or disappointing response may be anticipated.

With persistent effort, the individual might become master in his own household. He might then as a citizen offer a good example in his community and be able to overcome the temptations that might accost him, such as the eagerness to overconsume or to participate in corrupt practices. Moreover, his influence might inspire others in the community to follow his example. If many others should indeed follow his course, the outlook for self-government would be greatly improved, as well as the prospects for economic development. A public leader would then find his hope of achieving measurable progress perceptibly brightened should he dedicate himself to improvement of the moral tone of government and the welfare of the people.

The interrelation between the inspired or crusading leader who seeks to bring his people forward to a recognition of the principles of self-government and to a greater loyalty to the necessary principles, on the one hand, and a people that on its own motion is performing this very function, without governmental prodding, on the other, is one of cross-stimulation. Each helps the other. Alertness of the people increases the hope of a higher level of official functionaries, while an inspired leader will promote the desire of the people to overcome the traits of indolence and apathy that underwrite corruption, incompetence, and inefficiency in government.

Corrupt leaders would be called to account more quickly by the public and given a choice of mending their ways or being turned out. The power of popular sentiment would not only be taken up with achievement of the legitimate desires of the primary will-forces and the raw ego but might also be aroused against abuses of good government and wayward and wasteful economic practices. Once the secondary will-forces and the disciplined ego were provoked by the corruption of public officials and by lax and debauched economic practices, the community's moral indignation might rise to great heights. Common interests would be linked. The foundation of reforms might thus be built on the reaction of the irked will-forces and the offended egos.

Needless to say, such an advanced form of democratic competence is not soon attained, but its model as a goal may be helpful to those whose function it is to awaken the people to their birthright and opportunity.

It should be noted here that one of the rarest accomplishments of those who seek to instill a sense of public service within a community or broader area is found in substituting loyalty to duty and competence for loyalty to friends and political patronage. The hope of overcoming corruption rests in a high degree on success in making this substitution. Public attitude is a crucial factor in the equation.

The content of self-discipline, if it is undertaken, is therefore not a matter of indifference. It might indeed be misdirected or ill-conceived, or fail of its mission if it is too narrowly based. The Brown Shirts of the Nazi regime were undoubtedly highly disciplined, and much of the discipline was perhaps self-imposed. It is therefore of more than passing concern to avoid fanaticism in either self-discipline or discipline administered by others. The mind must be the arbiter, and it must obey the wisdom that comes not only from trial and error but from innate good sense and moral inclination.

The family that is agreeable to virtue and to self-discipline would do well to reflect that obtrusiveness will quickly rob such virtue as may be practiced of its value as an example. Also, it would wish to draw a distinction between virtue inculcated by authoritarian methods and virtue that is accepted and practiced because it is understood and makes sense as understood. Virtue that owes its practice to authoritarian inculcation may have only the shallowest roots and may provoke rebellion rather than acceptance. Damage is then done to the attractiveness of virtue, and the rebellious reaction may more readily attract imitators than the practice of virtue itself.

Virtue in any case is seldom if ever attractive to the primitive impulses, with one exception: namely, when its possession is praised in a particular person. It is then attractive to that person's ego, but, unless the praise is judicious, it may arouse envy in others. Self-discipline, like virtue, may be peculiarly unattractive to witnesses when it is practiced with too great fervor, and the more so if it is flaunted as a mark of superiority.

Newspapers bear a heavy responsibility in the field of attitude toward moral conduct and some are aware of it. The schools and the trustees are further sources of the climate of community opinion. The magazines that circulate, the books to which citizens are exposed, the radio and television fare, the films offered by the moving pictures, and the churches, if they are attended—all these and other media have access to parents and exert influence over them.

It is not a mark of Puritanism, which may be regarded as an extreme form of condemnation of appetites and impulses that man needs, to recognize the great influence that is wielded by the various media of culture or nonculture. The media that play to the primary will-forces, lusts, and pruriencies need no stimulation. They are self-starters and would soon conquer the field as weeds soon overtake a garden if they were not restrained by the virtues that man has developed for this very purpose: namely, to help him accept his status as man and to moderate and play down his animal heritage.

It is therefore a matter of good sense to be concerned about the tone of newspapers, their catering to the primitive impulses for the building and holding of circulation. The same observation applies to radio, television, and literature. Those who are deeply concerned about censorship, as everyone should be, nevertheless have a towering responsibility to discourage the stimulation of the animal heritage in man if they are interested in developing his higher and finer potentials. It is not enough to deplore censorship as representing an interference with art and expression. It is better to help create a community climate that frowns on excessive stimulation of the lower inclinations of man, so that pornography will not pay. The animal appetites are ever ready for titillation and indulgence. It is man's hope to restrain, to moderate, and hold the raw impulses within limits, so that their usefulness may be enjoyed while their excesses are avoided.

The pecuniary interest is plain enough. Pornography, obscenity, and lascivious display would offer lucrative returns if left unbridled; and indeed they do in a variety of communities throughout the world. They are hardly to be encouraged. A family of which the parents are devotees of the lowest in culture will seldom generate an atmosphere that is conducive to self-discipline or any other variety of discipline that reflects abhorrence of the base fare that is offered in such a family. It is families that either patronize the vulgar and sensuous, or wink at it in permissiveness, for want of or rejection of a better culture, that permits the newspapers and the Al Capones to justify themselves by saying, "We only give them what they want." A further escape from moral responsibility is seized in the form of the blanket justification that says, "If I did not do it, someone else would." The attitudes thus reflected are essentially cheap certificates of irresponsibility.

Should the patronage of the lust-dominated media cease or fall to an unprofitable level, as it would if the family atmosphere were alien to the vulgar fare, there would be no need for censorship and infinitely less concern about the right to corrupt the morals of a people, which in turn is little else than a license for the subversion of the foundation of self-government.

If man is to move forward into the potentials that are planted in him, he must perforce resist the dissipation of his capabilities by doing too much homage to his primitive inheritances. This is a matter of degree, but it is important to man himself that he learn what is the optimum degree. The question of degree of indulgence is of a kind with the balance between the means of production and consumption. The dissolute ones indulge too freely; they would also consume too freely and forget the means by which goods are made available for consumption. Good government, good economics, and good family and community relations are the fruits of self-restraint and refinement of the ego.

12.

Man's Predatory Instinct
—Aggressiveness
and Belligerency

REGARDLESS OF THE CLOSE LINK between individual self-discipline, social discipline, and amelioration of the ego, on the one hand, and a high level of self-government, free of the saturated corruption that afflicts a dissolute people, and a highly productive economy, on the other, these disciplines do not of themselves overcome the belligerency of man as represented by the nation-state.

Strange though it seems, man undergoes a radical change when he is under the stress of military necessity, but the change is not beyond the reach of explanation. A man who would not think of shooting his neighbor or anyone else will kill in war with a clear conscience. If he is not himself killed and returns home, he is soon reintegrated into his community and is the same peaceful man he was before he went to war. A few exceptions, of course, may be the exceptions to the rule.

What causes the transformation?

One immediate answer is suggested by the man's surrender of his freedom of action and the substitution of a higher command for his freedom. He receives instruction in the use of weapons, both for offensive and defensive purposes, and if he is a good soldier, he will learn how to use his weapons effectively.

His responsibility is narrowed to a small radius and that lies within rigid limits.

He fights for his country. He is afraid to be a coward, and in any event, cowardice might have fatal consequences.

If we wish to know why the arms-bearer fights, we must first inquire why nations go to war. Once his country is at war, the citizen is caught in a force that carries him along either with or against his mind or reason.

Several considerations bring a nation to go to war; several others create a force that sweeps the individual down the stream.

Wars in recent times have had strong economic motivations. A spot in the sun or *lebensraum* may underlie a rationale that seeks war, not for war's sake, but for the purpose of making certain readjustments of resource-control or means of access to important resources.

The innocent citizen protests that he does not wish to burglarize another country or to take by force of arms what belongs to other people, and he is probably saying what is in his heart. However, he is not responsible for the management or direction of the nation's affairs. If he were, he would be confronted with considerations that would hardly occur to him if he did not have the responsibility—if for no other reason than the simple fact that he would perhaps not be aware of the considerations that would confront him were he in the position of manager, prime minister, or president.

As the responsible director of national affairs, including policy-decisions, he would soon learn that international affairs follow certain patterns, and that certain expectations rule many actions; and further that distrust is fostered by the fact that nations are not responsible to a third force, previously referred to as a referee.

Distrust arises from self-observation and from observation of the historic behavior of other nations as described by historians who are often nationals of the country in which they write their history. The motives of other countries are generally suspect in time of conflict, and naive trust in the honor of another country's statesman borders on treason in time of war.

Nations have needs and appetites no less than individuals,

and they also have what corresponds to the individual's ego. Usually it is called patriotism, and it may be sensitive to slights, insults, and other provocations. It is, of course, registered in individuals.

In the days of dukedoms, principalities, and kingdoms, the national ego might be centered in the person of the duke, prince, or king. An insult or humiliation aimed at his highness was an insult to his people. Likewise, an insult to a citizen was an insult to his highness. A proud prince would not allow an insult to a subject to go unchallenged. To do so would assuredly be taken as evidence of weakness and would invite future insults or worse. The princely ego therefore could not with equanimity let an insult pass. It would be regarded as high policy to repay an insult quickly even if it were not meant as one, for it might represent a test or probe.

As individuals have will-forces that express covetousness or envy, so may a nation. If a rich fishery lies offshore in the waters of one political area while an adjoining area enjoys no such resource, we may be sure that the fishery represents a strong temptation to those of the poorer fishery resources whose glances stray across the waters. The prince will merely express the desire of his fishermen if he has designs on the fishery of his neighbor. The fisherman is not then so innocent if his highness seeks to seize the fishery. After all, it is not the prince who expects to go out and spread his net, but rather his subjects. As for the women and children at home: surely they are innocent! Yet, it is their stomachs that have to be fed, and it is the business of the husband, son, or father to bring home the fillings. So, again, innocence may be innocently implicated. Do the wives, mothers, sisters, and children renounce eating so that no one needs to bring home fish from the sea? Are they willing to go hungry if the fishermen honor the territorial boundaries and remain content to bring home only half as many fish as they might net if they encroached on the neighbor's waters?

Such cruel questions are not asked, but the prince is condemned for his aggressive action, and the fishermen have been guilty of trespass.

It is only necessary to substitute other riches for fish to discover the same motives. In modern times, the resource might be coal or oil or other minerals; or it might be a strategic point or a pass that could determine the outcome of a contest in the future. It is the responsibility of the prince to exercise his foresight in behalf of his people. If the pass or the point has great strategic defense value, he would be remiss if he did not seek to secure it. Again, he will not himself seize the area; he will send his soldiers or mariners; but he does it not only for himself but for the defense of the women and children as well.

The soldiers will now kill or will try to kill or to capture or to drive away those who will contest the control or who will seek to wrest it from the prince if he took prior possession.

The interest is conceived as a common interest, and the will-forces supply the motivation. It is not the purpose to kill; the purpose is to secure and hold the pass. If the pass could be possessed and held without killing, it would be occupied peacefully. If it could not be possessed without killing or maiming, the killing and maiming would be undertaken.

The objective is not aggression. It is security of the home people. If the security cannot be achieved without aggression, then aggression it will be. Obviously aggression is often a substitute for wit.

Seen in this light, aggression is not an unreasonable form of behavior. It is sparked by needs of the body or by the desires expressed by the secondary will-forces or the ego. Perhaps the desires are not reasonable, but given the strong impulse, the act of aggression is understandable as a reasonable one. At the same time, the response to aggression in the form of defensive combat is also reasonable.

The trouble lies in the fact previously observed, namely, that despite difference in tastes too many people too vehemently desire the same thing; and if the object is scarce, a rivalry is inevitable in view of the character of the will-forces and the ego. Man typically is caught between his animal heritage and his estate as man. Since the latter has not risen to a position of domination within him, he is in the uncomfortable position of being half animal and half man—with variations of the proportions. Christ Jesus was all man in the sense of what man aspires to be at his

highest reach, and He suffered the consequences of being confronted by man's divided loyalty, arising from his station part-
way between animal and man. Jesus was able to say in his agony,
"Forgive them. They know not what they do."

Meantime man continues to be anchored to his animal heritage in a manner that makes him realize that he is not what he
should be under the stress of overwhelming circumstances. What
mortal has not at times realized to himself that he is not able to
meet what he himself expects of himself or would like to expect
of himself? It is all very difficult. The words were well spoken:
"Let him who is without sin cast the first stone!"

These words quite surely were not meant to excuse oneself
but to suggest understanding of the lapses and shortcomings of
the one whom one is about to condemn. This was followed by
the further suggestion that one should not condemn another for
doing what oneself might under the same circumstances, considering all human limitations, also do.

How inadequate, indeed, one can be when suddenly confronted with untoward and mixed circumstances, one has to act,
with so little time to do more than make a quick consultation of
conflicting feelings! Unmerciful! And what an ignominious thing
one may do thus pressed, giving pause later to think about the
egregious failure of one's preparedness. No matter how good the
general intent, inadequacies before specific events may descend in
a flock, and the grossness of the human heritage is revealed in its
nakedness. Even good Peter in his affliction was inadequate and
made three denials!

So it goes with aggression and defense against aggression. To
be sure, the occasions are not always on so swift a wing; but the
more time there is, the greater the multitude of considerations to
be entertained! And the considerations: how can one weigh them
in delicate scales when it takes time to read the scales, and,
further, when one cannot be sure of the scales themselves, while
yet so many considerations are to be weighed, with the first one
half forgotten before the last one presents itself? And yet further,
though nudged by doubts because of the well-known fallibility of
human judgment, one has nonetheless to grope through the
crowding considerations, some earmarked, some obscure, others

strange, while dubious motives crowd in from the sides urging one's own interests. Where does truth reside?

It must be obvious that when considerations of community, of the kingdom, or of national interests are at stake, the individual enlisted or drafted as a pawn must take his cue from command. The final questions and decision then devolve on the supreme commander, civil or military as the case may be. The perplexities, bewilderments, and confusions must be surmounted by the commander despite the inadequacies that beset his mind on all sides.

Aggressions and defenses against aggressions soon become intermixed, each side in its profusion of errors giving the other side adequate grounds for holding the other to be the aggressor!

Oh, Man, how poorly thou hast acquitted thyself and yet how hast thou done so well?

The victors in great battles of old no doubt asked themselves this question a thousand times while the disorganized groupings and broken lines swayed and gave way, flanking movements worked or failed to work their purpose, and thus mixed confusion with confusion.

In *War and Peace,* Tolstoy depicts the quandary, perplexity, and helplessness of the commander while a great, far-flung battle is raging. Only when the smoke and dust have settled and perhaps not even then, but only later, can it be known who prevailed.

No doubt man has given himself at times to naked aggression: Alexander, Caesar, Napoleon, Hitler, for example. To feed their consuming ego or megalomania, they drove to remote points, far beyond any practical need to feed or clothe or defend their people. Ambition for glory, an insatiable reach for dominion so that their names might be wondered at and spoken in awe and recorded in history: that was what fired their ego!

As for the men who filled the ranks, what was their mission? They were under command. Their freedom was surrendered to or appropriated by the commander. They had in any case little voice even as private citizens before filling the ranks. If their commander won victories, they shared in the glory. Their ego absorbed the glory reflected by the great one. This reflection buoyed their spirit, made them proud, and they fought the harder and willingly endured the forced marches, the fatigue, and the wounds—willingly, as opposed to the alternative. The why of it was a luxury they had little occasion and less account to waste their reason upon.

It was not territorial protection that drove either them or their commanders, nor extension of resources as such. It was the play of the great leaders for the stakes that gave them the highest satisfaction—the irrationality of a magnified ego, supported by uncommon skill and far-ranging military vision.

Other wars were of a different species. In them the rational considerations are visible in the rivalry for resources and strategic points, and the men who manned the guns, swords, and other weapons, while also performing the function of pawns, nevertheless participated in the purposes, such as those mentioned in the preceding pages. While they were pawns, those whom they left behind were at least possibly or presumably beneficiaries of their sacrifices.

Aggression, as defined by Konrad Lorenz and others and as exhibited in the animal world below man, is relatively simple. In man it may also be simple, but the intrusion of the ego vastly complicates the equation.

The simpler forms of human aggression consist of those that have been displayed through the ages by many mobile species of animals. "Territorial defense" simply means guarding the home, the breeding and hunting grounds, and is entirely rational in view of the scarcity of need-satisfying means and of comfortable shelters and resting places. If no one or no animal had need of shelter against the elements or need of rest, and if food were everywhere as readily available as anywhere else, there would have been little need of aggression, and this form of behavior would perhaps not have appeared—except in man, because of his ego. In the lower animals, selective mating would perhaps have offered some justification for aggression.

It does not seem appropriate to classify the killing of edible animals by the carnivorous species as aggression. They must eat in order to live. The killing process to them is no different from that of breathing. It is not a matter of ambition, cruelty, or hatred; nor is it so understood by Lorenz and others.

The so-called ranking or pecking order in some animal species may give the appearance of a rudimentary ego, and so it may be; but it has a practical usage in the survival sense, namely, in the sense that the stronger is assured of food in a situation of scarcity at the expense of the weaker. This idea, however, has some weaknesses. It assumes the presence of the stronger one at the right place at the right time and also that the deprived ones are not deprived merely because they are not yet fully grown even though potentially strong. If they are pushed aside merely because they are physically unequal to the strong one that is fully grown, some potentially strong specimens would be sacrificed in their childhood or adolescence, and the survival of the fittest would be thwarted to that extent.

Aggression, as a term, needs a little more refinement. Man has classified certain animals as predatory. Indeed, he has set about the systematic extinction of some predatory species in some areas of the world. This fact, of course, makes of man himself a predator, but the indictment weighs but little on him. His interest in exterminating the predators is very practical and almost wholly selfish. He seeks to prevent the wolf from eating the lamb because he wishes either to eat the lamb himself or to have it grow wool for him or to produce other lambs or sheep that he may either eat or shear. The wolf then is a predator, and man "hates" him—not because he "loves" the lamb more, but himself. After all, the wolf is as beautiful as the lamb and in many respects more admirable. Even birds are placed on the predatory list by man when they eat his peaches and apples on the trees or seeds of grain in the fields. In Australia and elsewhere, rabbits are looked upon as predators even though they are wholly herbivorous and kill no other animal. In the United States, the golden eagle is hunted and killed because it kills and feeds on lambs.

It is clear enough that aggression is not necessarily coextensive with predation as man defines the term. The rabbit is not an aggressive animal although severe fighting does occur among individuals, but it is a predator, not as a wolf, but as a herbage eater. The wolf or fox, ordinarily regarded as aggressive, is also a predator, but he kills in order to live. His predation on other living things is no different from the eating of plants by herbiv-

orous animals. Man "hates" the wolf or the fox for its depredations—the killing of lambs or robbing of the hen house. He
"loves" the lambs and chickens. Translated, this means he "loves"
what is useful to him and sees in it a remarkable variety of virtues. He "hates" whatever deprives him or would, if it could, deprive him of what is of value to him. He then manufactures
words to express his interests and aversions.

That this is true can easily be demonstrated by observing
the person who has tamed a fox or a wolf, and keeps it as a pet.
He "loves" the animal for its many fetching virtues, and would
not trade it for a "stupid" lamb. As for the fox, what could be
more lovable and adorable than a quarter or half-grown fox cub
—to one who has tamed and owns one? Any enemy of such a fox
would be an enemy of the owner, or would at the minimum gain
his disfavor. Should a rooster going about his duties as master of
a roost peck a young fox to death, which would be the aggressor
or predator in the eyes of the owner of the fox?

The common denominator, in the true sense of the word,
which has to do with naming things, is man's interest or assumed
interest. Bird-lovers "hate" cats if they, the cats, go about being
cats and killing birds; but they may "love" the cats for killing
mice.

Perhaps the best hope of staying in man's good graces would
go to the saprophyte, which does not kill but feeds on decaying
matter in the form of an excrescence on the outer side of such
things as fallen tree trunks or superannuated stumps. Parasites,
on the other hand, may, like the foxes, rabbits, and wolves, be
either good or bad. The mistletoe, which is reputed to be a parasite, may be a veritable symbol of love at Christmas, but when it
debilitates the maple or black locust it quickly loses favor. The
orchid, also reputed to be parasitic, is forgiven its sin by man
for its beauty. It is especially prized by the human femme covert
as irrefutable evidence on the wedding anniversary that romance
has not withered. It therefore is a highly prized ornament despite
its reputed parasitism, which is a state of livelihood universally
despised among thrifty people.

The happiest form of life, one would be led to believe, is that
of symbiosis, of the variety that is advantageous rather than

antagonistic as is the parasite. Symbiosis of the advantageous variety is well illustrated, without reference to taxonomy or other source of ornithological name-making, by the hippopotamus bird. Its feet are especially adapted with egregiously long toes, webbed as in wading birds, for walking on the backs, heads, and faces of the hippopotami. It makes its living by pecking, catching, and eating certain forms of diminutive animal life that uses the big animal, in turn, as a source of livelihood, often if not always no doubt to the annoyance and discomfiture of the broad-nosed behemoth. The bird takes its time covering the landscape under foot as it walks over the great animal, which in turn is highly contented. It even opens its mouth, as if to say "Ah" on command, while the helpful bird inserts its head into the yawning cavity and gathers the tidbits to be found there. The bird has absolute confidence that the open jaws are not a trap such as great clams may set for their own food or Venus's flytraps use to catch flies. The bird "knows" that the behemoth is a friend— herbivorous and not interested in fish or fowl as food.

The man-dog relationship could perhaps qualify as a form of symbiosis; and the same might be said of cats, chickens, horses, cows, sheep, and other domesticated animals in their relation to man.

Man feeds his dogs and they in turn are loyal to him and may be useful in protecting him in a variety of ways. Sometimes they may do little more than to sound an alarm, but under some circumstances this is a useful service. The relationship is generally one of mutual benefit.

If man's heritage in so many of its less inspiring features is traceable to the lower animals, there would seem to be no necessary obstacle to his inheritance of some of the more admirable forms of behavior from that source. Therefore, there should be some natural good in him even as there is many animals, and no doubt there is, as we have remarked earlier.

His fighting propensities have made a destructive species of him to the degree that he has been able to devise destructive weapons. He is now near the ultimate weapon if he does not already have it.

If man were weaponless, he would still no doubt fight both

individually and collectively, but his destructive capacity would not be great. Physically he is indeed virtually disarmed, having neither fangs, claws, nor stingers. The deficiency, however, has been more than compensated by his intelligence at shaping and using tools. This compensatory feature is not unlike his growth of intelligence to compensate for the disappearance or virtual disappearance of instinct in many of his activities.

If we examine the function of fighting or aggression, defined as an *unprovoked* attack, it will be seen as representing activity generated by one of the will-forces or the ego.

An unprovoked attack, however, does not dispose of all forms of attack. In a battle, defensive forces return attack with attack. Also, even provoked attacks are not themselves all in response to an attack. An irritating agent that itself is without militancy may nevertheless provoke an attack. Some provoked attacks, for example, are in the form of abating a nuisance or an irritation. While such provoked attacks are not in response to an attack or a defense against aggression they are nevertheless not in the class of unprovoked attacks. The provocation may, to repeat, be non-belligerent but may nevertheless provoke action designed to drive it away or eliminate it. Such would be attacks made to abate unpleasant presences of whatever form.

Probably one of the most common forms of aggression arises from encroachment on an existing preserve; another takes the form of widening a preserve already held or finding a new one to take the place of one that had to be abandoned for some reason, possibly because of being driven out.

It is easily imaginable that no small amount of fighting occurs when birds and other animals are driven from their natural habitat by man. If man opens a field for cultivation or extends urban developments into hitherto wooded or grassland areas, he disturbs the balance of nature by forcibly evicting many animal residents. If the adjoining areas are already saturated with animal life or nearly so, an invasion of existing or "owned" habitats will occur in the bordering areas. Then begin attacks designed to find new habitats and as many defensive fights to ward off the expropriation. Tribal migrations of man countless times created the same conflict, as rainless seasons or pests rendered existing territorial habitats inhospitable.

This style of battle, which is to say aggression in response to a vital purpose, such as finding a place to live, breathe, and forage, naturally provokes efforts at defense. Encroachment is resisted.

There are other styles of aggression, not limited to man, but nonetheless a favorite form with man. One is the act of plundering for booty, marauding, and banditry. Individual acts of the same order are in the form of robbery, burglary, and the like. So far as animals are concerned, such acts are as innocent as the act of a cow eating grass. If a wolverine plunders a cache made by a trapper, it is not in the schema of a robbery; the animal is merely in search of food. To man, of course, it seems like foul robbery. The same is true when a bear "robs" a bees' nest. He has found honey. He likes honey and having found it he undertakes to eat it. The bees fight back and stick their stingers into him but their spears do little more than annoy the bear. He has no idea that the bees worked incessantly through the season to store the honey. He perceives no relation between the bees and the honey. He is hungry and eats the booty he has taken. No compunction, no conscience!

In raw nature there is much plundering, pillaging, banditry, and robbery, but it is all innocent.

The animals merely obey their instincts. Nevertheless, the damage to a bees' nest is none the less real and devastating for having been done innocently. Even so, as far as responsibility goes, the damage might as well have been the ravage of a storm. There was no creative responsibility.

Man, however, is in a different estate. His motive for marauding, plundering, and robbing is perhaps no different from that of the bear or the wolverine; which is to say that he, too, must eat, have a habitat and shelter. What then is wrong with his taking what he can by stealth, main force or by stratagem appropriate or grasp?

Evidently man could not have survived if all members of the species were bandits and robbers. Someone must do the work necessary to wrest from nature sufficient provisions to maintain life. If half the men at work hunting, fishing, digging, climbing, or gathering, could, by applying themselves continuously, provide just enough for everyone, the other half need not work but might be drones or even bandits so long as they took no more than their share. There would be enough for everyone's subsistence.

If the task of feeding, sheltering, and protecting everyone required the efforts of all, there would be no room for drones or bandits. If the work of only *nearly* everyone were needed, a few could live without working and might be fed by the others. We may be quite sure that such feeding would not have taken place except in special circumstances, such as governmental status.

If one who was not in the special status undertook to help himself when he did not contribute to the store, his popularity rating would quickly drop. It might do more; it might sink below the zero level, and he might do well to make his getaway.

The will-forces of those who do the work would react in a definite form—not because the men do not wish to work, but because many aspects of work are disagreeable, sometimes involving actual hardships. So interrelated are human beings that but for an adequate excuse they expect everyone to do his share—and the excuse must be acceptable. Even then much grumbling may attend the exemption.

Even the ego becomes involved: "Who is he?" is the inevitable question—"Who is he, that he should be spared?" they ask. "Why not I or you?" This question is designed to produce consciousness of favoritism, and it is a well-appreciated fact that favoritism is anathema to the ego unless its own host or owner is the beneficiary. Then it is regarded as a mark of distinction and as such is greatly treasured; and the pleasure is accented by a slight feeling of guilt and a feeling of superiority.

Therefore, if the person who contributed nothing in the form of significant effort had no credentials of exemption, it would go hard with him. If he were no favorite of someone of higher rank, he would indeed be driven out or would be so beleaguered that he would be glad to make his getaway with a whole skin. He would probably in any case gather contusions and abrasions as evidence of his radical unpopularity.

Once out of reach of his fellow groupsters he would soon feel the pangs of hunger, but there would be no food within reach. What to do? At first he would feel little concern, but as the stomach's command became more imperious, his intelligence would begin a course of feverish cogitation. What, indeed, could he do? One idea and then another brought up for consideration by his mental effort would likely be discarded.

Finally, beside himself from the inner gnawing, he would decide to go back. The approach would offer some delicate problems of tactics and face. How would he present himself to avoid being set upon again? He would wait until only women and children or old men were in the precincts, scattered as they might be. He might prevail on one or more of the women who, seeing his state of hunger, might take pity on him and give him some food. Failing that approach, he might walk in and overpower the female defenders, but such rude action might make his lot still more difficult. He might instead try to insinuate himself into the sympathies of the women by showing them a deference to which they were not accustomed. He might thus gain a few mouthsful of food and then must be on his way before the stalwarts returned.

By this process of hyenalike approach and disappearance and keeping his distance he might survive, but on one or another occasion his presence might be detected by those who had sealed his exile and so it happened, let us say. The women were severely used by their consorts for their softness, and the next time he appeared he readily sensed the changed atmosphere. The women avoided looking at him and applied themselves in concentration to their tasks. He would not dare to raise a noise or create a commotion and would perhaps beg with eye and gesture once more to unlock the bank of mercy, but, sensing the ways of human cunning, the women suspected the hidden presence of a sentinel who would be on the lookout for the beggar, and, of course, were right. There was a sentinel and he was alert.

The outcast, not without a sense of cunning of his own, seized a joint of meat from a hidden spot, made a threatening sign of silence to cover his unwilling companions, and stole away. He knew, however, that this was his last trip, and that he must devise a better method or either starve to death or deliver himself to the untender mercies of those who had cast him out. The latter idea made him shiver. He had seen some examples of displeasure vented on others, and he was not a candidate for such an exhibition, with himself as the star attraction.

His wit worked overtime as he skulked in the dusk, hoping to find some means of sustenance. All avenues now seemed closed. His hunger grew worse, and he seemed destined for the vultures when he saw in the distance a lone hunter who was returning to his domicile. He was carrying a half-grown roebuck, a spear, and some accoutrements of his clan or tribe.

Here was a last desperate chance: the possibility of acquiring not only some food but also a spear. How to execute a plan so difficult held him in his tracks until his instinct as a hunter began to move his feet as his body assumed a crouch. He moved at an arc beyond some cover, accelerating his pace with the idea of intercepting the lone hunter before he reached his destination and before he neared it or came within earshot of those who had already returned.

He soon reached a slight eminence alongside the path the hunter was following at a rather slow pace. The hunter limped slightly and was among the oldest ones who still went afield.

Should he accost the hunter as if he himself had come along at a late hour, and then seize his spear and snatch his kill away from him and run, hoping to outdistance the limping victim of his assault? Would the latter recognize him in the dusk and spread word of the assault and robbery?

The pursuer no longer had time to think but sprang from behind on the back of the older man and bore him to the ground. Despite his own debilitated condition from lack of food he gathered sudden strength in his desperation. In the ambush the older man grasped and gripped and twisted, but his assailant was too fast in his movements. In a trice his assailant grasped the spear and jumped to his feet. Not an instant did he hesitate but threw the spear into the older man's chest, jumped upon him, pulled out the spear and thrust it once more deep into the gasping victim. Pulling away he seized the roebuck and threw it over his shoulders and stole away.

Thereafter he lived by spear as well as he could but prowled the dusk with the hope of repeating his feat of robbery. He became the object of search but evaded his pursuers. It is not recorded how long he lived. His life was difficult, lonely, and without balm or the possibility of ever again feeling the warmth of human kindness.

At other times and other places similar incidents occurred. As the number of people increased, the number who were averse to working as their companions did also increase. Lone outcasts and roamers might meet in their wanderings and after overcoming mutual suspicion and distrust, might form a band held together by common interests. In place of one robber there would now be two or more. In this doubling or manifold increase of manpower, there was advantage. One could keep watch while the others forayed. A band would multiply the advantages, but it would not all be gain. The larger the number, the greater the risk of betrayal, and the more pelf to be divided.

Such a band could sweep down upon small and remote settlements and plunder almost at will. The career was exciting and it was not necessary to work from sunup to sundown, as before, with seldom anything to call your own, always under command and having to account for one's behavior or lack of success.

The greatest drawback in such banditry lay in the mortality tables, in the rigors of life, the frequent hunger and the lack of a future. There was a great disadvantage also in the smallness of number, and yet it could not be otherwise. Those who remained behind in the settlements or habitations did not produce a sufficient surplus to support more than a small plundering band, and it was not practical to kill many of the inhabitants because such a course would only reduce the surplus.

The hostility of the loyal ones who stayed at home and carried on the toil and activity that was necessary for survival toward the bandits needs no elaboration. Human beings, except under special circumstances, do not like to share necessities. It goes against the primary will-forces, and unless there are overriding considerations, such as concern for mate, offspring, or companion, it is not a welcome disposition of the fruits of labor. Much less do they wish to be robbed or beaten and perhaps maimed and also stripped of their food.

Little doubt then that the elimination of bands or robbers stood high in the general dedication of society to desirable ends.

We have asked the question of what distinguishes the act of the bear or the wolverine in robbing bees or a trapper's cache, on the one hand, and similar acts of human beings, on the other. What sets bandits, maruaders, and plunderers of the human species apart from the lower animals that engage in similar depredations?

The animal is innocent; man is not. Why is man's act in catering to his needs not innocent if he does it in one way while it is without blame if he meets his needs in some other fashion?

The answer is no doubt to be found in man's sense of justice and in his capacity to love his own kind. To say this is, of course, not an adequate answer. Why has man a sense of justice and a capacity for love, and of what do they consist?

We have given attention previously to the function of justice in human society, but why man has the sense is as unanswerable as the question of why he has a capacity for love and friendship, in other words, why he is man rather than a lower animal. We can only say he was made that way.

In outer nature, justice is nonexistent, but the function it performs or seeks to perform in human society is performed by the law of probabilities in outer nature. The law of probabilities or the occurrence or sequence of events in the physical world is a deterministic phenomenon. It suits the animal world and explains the innocence of the bear and the wolverine, but man's mind was given power to interfere with the probabilities by inserting his hand into them and rearranging the pawns.

Where in this milieu, does the question of justice arise? Was it antiselective in the Darwinian sense?

We noted the capacity of the stronger ones among early man to elbow others out of the way and thus to take more than their own share of the scarce goods that were made available by constant effort—assuming men lived in a place other than paradise where he had all he needed without effort.

As previously said, "Justice or the notion of justice interfered or was designed to interfere with the ordinary course of the primary will-forces and the crude ego. An external consideration was injected into what were thoroughly natural relations."

Had this not occurred man would simply have been no more than a short-armed, nearly hairless type of gorilla.

A believer in the role of natural selection might have been alarmed at the interference of justice in the battle for survival, because in many cases it might award the contested prize to the weaker of two contestants. Would such soft-headed or heart-born folderol not soon undo the work of natural selection? If the weak were recognized as entitled to as much as the strong, the weak would survive as readily as the strong. Mankind would be the loser.

On the other hand, without denying the function of natural selection, a defender of justice might say that it was desirable to change the direction of evolution. When man reached the stage at which physical strength and agility were no longer his greatest assets in the struggle for existence, the time had also arrived when it was desirable to redetermine the correlation between physical strength and intelligence. If physical strength was not a correlative of wit or intellect, a process of natural selection would have militated against the survival of the fittest in the human sense if it had continued to favor the physically strong.

As the most intelligent individual was not necessarily the best physical specimen, the progress of the human race toward civilization would have been retarded if the bases of survival had not been changed.

Man outdistanced his natural enemies in the form of ferocious beasts not by evolving a race of bigger, stronger, and more agile creatures but through his greater intelligence and adaptability. His tool-making capacity and his ingenuity at using them were the assets that would enable him to overcome the beasts that in other physical respects overmatched him completely. Instead of providing him with horns, thick skin, and hoofs, it gave him intelligence and the equipment that his intelligence could use.

Except in primitive warfare among his own kind, physical prowess was then no longer so important. Even in his internecine warfare, the invention and fashioning of tools was not reserved for the strong and robust. These were reserved for the fighting and were therefore the most likely to be eliminated.

The selective process thus really was weighted in favor of the stay-at-homes who did the thinking and inventing. If these had been killed off regularly, progress in toolmaking and other arts would have been retarded and man would not have advanced as rapidly in his efforts to make nature yield her products to him as he did; for those who were spared for making tools that were useful in warfare also made tools for peaceful pursuits.

The institution of justice may therefore be regarded as a veritable instrument of evolution since it produced the effects that operated in behalf of the preservation of human specimens that might be intelligent or even highly intelligent while they were not necessarily superb physical specimens. First, it deterred (in time) the stronger physical ones from lording it over the smaller and weaker ones in the communities in which they lived. They could not snatch or grasp the food away from the weaker ones with impunity. That they eventually lost this power seems of itself to provide evidence that they were outwitted by the weaker ones. How else could a reign of justice have been established? The evidence would indicate that the biggest ones in the community were not necessarily the brightest, or their type would have prevailed. Second, as observed above, those who did not don war paint and did not do the combat service because they did not meet the physical specifications suffered fewer casualties. More and more as the toolmakers and other constructive members were spared, victory would more likely go to the tribe or community that was the most inventive and ingenious in its weaponry.

By remaining behind, the commanders and higher ranks also contributed to the survival of the higher intelligence. Yet it was the warrior who received the garlands. He was the visible element of victory and of protection and was therefore the obvious earner of gratitude, even though the arrowsmith or inventer who gave the warrior a new tool may have contributed more to the cause of victory than was recognized. The warrior had, of course, risked his life, and was therefore entitled to special gratitude.

The institution of justice, which was a very difficult and long-drawn-out feat that has not yet been completed, represented an example of man's interference with the deterministic forces of nature. It changed the basic conditions of natural selection by changing the definition of "the fittest." In a sense, this change was an act of free will, much as that of a card dealer who interferes with the natural grouping of the cards in successive "deals" by withdrawing cards from the deck. He interferes with the probabilities by an act of free will.

When administration of justice, which is man-made, interferes with the will-forces of the strong and active, and prevents their domination and deprivation of the physically weaker members of society, the natural probabilities are upset, as we had occasion to observe earlier. Thus both the Marxian economic and the Freudian biological determinism are to that extent undermined.

Justice may thus also be seen as an agent or force that may interfere with aggression by acting as a restrainer. It acts as an ameliorative force insofar as it holds back the vehemence of the primary will-forces and the raw ego. It accomplishes its objective by two means. Sometimes it calls for restitution of what has been unjustly taken. At other times it punishes, and in so doing acts as a deterrent to future acts of injustice through the function of memory. Altogether it serves as a pacifier of passion or emotion and therefore acts as a civilizing influence on behavior.

If we look upon aggression and examine it carefully, we will find it closely linked to frustration of the will-forces or the ego. One of the simplest forms of frustration is familiar to everyone. It occurs sometimes in the form of simple obstruction, as when someone interposes himself across the line of vision and prevents a spectator from seeing what he has been watching intently. The obstructive act will annoy the spectator, and he will move his head or body to one side to regain his line of vision. The frustration of his vision will annoy him in the degree of his interest and the situation in the activity he is viewing. If the moment is one of suspense, his irritation will be the greater.

Of the same order is the outbreak of noise when a listener is intent on hearing a conversation, a speech, or a musical performance. If his hearing is obstructed or "scrambled," he, too, will feel annoyed. Many other examples could be produced, but the reaction is the same.

The annoyance is a feeling of distinct displeasure, and this feeling stirs in the organism a strong desire to remove the cause or, if it is an animate entity, to strike it or push it out of the way. If noise traceable to someone close by is the offender, motions, sometimes threatening and aggressive, are made with intent to silence the source of the noise.

The action in either case would be of an aggressive nature, the intent being to restore the unobstructed line of vision or to quell the noise so that clear hearing might be restored; but the provoked feeling itself usually calls for a little more such as a loud reprimand or an actual push, again depending on the depth of interest and on the degree of self-restraint. If the interest were lukewarm or of low intensity, the provoked feeling would also be of low intensity.

When spectators are deeply engrossed in watching an athletic spectacle and if one of the teams or one of the contestants is about to score in a very "tight" contest, the spectators may be moved to shout "down in front" when other viewers rise in their excitement, wave their hands in the air, jump up and down, and otherwise succeed in blocking the view of those to the rear of them.

In yet other instances, of a wholly different nature, as might occur on entering a conveyance or a room or other place of assembly where vacant seats are available, one may hope to sit next to another person, perhaps a friend or something more, only to be displaced by a stranger. Immediately the innocent but intruding person is seen in an unfavorable light. Even though he is obviously innocent, he seems rude, inconsiderate, ill-bred, a person of low cultural attainments who for the good of all should really be thrown out. If the will-forces and the ego had their way, an act of aggression would certainly be committed unless the offender's physiognomy offered sufficient discouragement to quell any aggressive impulse.

We may conclude that in even such simple instances of frustration as these, aggressive actions would occur but for external or internal restraint. The external restraint might be in one of a number of forms. One has just now been mentioned. The object of aggression might act as the most effective discouraging agent by nothing more than being what it is in terms of space displacement, musculature, countenance, or other evidences of prowess as an adversary; or a different form of outer restraint might be present in the form of a guard, or of a yet different variety, such as the presence of genteel people who are given to a kindly and refined manner, among whom a rude response to a rude provocation would not be regarded as a mark of good breeding.

Internal restraint, as described earlier, would come into play principally as a reflection of reciprocal regard, by which we mean the internalization of external restraint, through memory of unpleasant responses to aggression in a variety of forms, or as an echo of words heard at home or elsewhere about unseemly behavior such as rowdiness or the like.

In any event, it seems clear enough that the natural aggressive response to simple frustration may be halted or modified before a movement is made. The restraining influence acts on the provoked will-force or ego interest. Only a partial movement of aggression might occur, or none at all. The impulse might be stifled inwardly as we may stifle a yawn or a sneeze. A certain amount of inner turmoil might be registered, but under the influence of self-discipline, it would soon subside. Even the ego might be enlisted in the process of abatement by the reflection that a low threshold of annoyance is evidence of the absence of noblesse or of the presence of vulgarity; or that if a low threshold is present, it should be compensated by a determination, all the higher, not to succumb.

From these simple examples, we may pass to more complicated vital and enduring frustrations of the primitive appetites and ego interests, such as result in hunger, suffering from inadequate shelter or body-covering, or longing and anguish from frustration of the mating instinct and the like, or resentment of harsh insults to the ego or dignity inflicted in the presence of fellow beings in the sight of all who might be present. Such frustrations and inflictions would be expected to produce much more intense impulses to aggression, and these would be more difficult to restrain or to bring under calming influences than the simple ones. Efforts at stifling the impulses might not drain them but might produce festering ill-feeling that in turn might be driven underground.

From the less serious frustration or partial frustration of the kind described, we pass next to the frustration of the primary needs. Here we encounter many impersonal forces, such as may be contained in economic and political practices and conditions: social attitudes, institutional forms, political dominancies, oppressive regimes, corrupt alliances, and the like. Yet the principles will be the same, but the effects may be much broader and farther-reaching.

It is one thing to find one's vision blocked at an inopportune moment while watching an entertaining spectacle. The experience is annoying and provokes an inclination to a local act of aggression dedicated to removal of the obstacle. It is something quite different to be confronted with a frustration that threatens to prevent satisfaction of the need for food or shelter. This form reaches to the very foundation of life itself. The response will be something more menacing to the obstructor than a mere shout to unblock the view. In extreme cases, of course, the effort to overcome the frustration would become an act to assure self-preservation, as in a case of famished hunger. Once more, in the absence of inculcated self-restraint or overpowering external restraint, the aggressive action would be of a kind best designed, within the limits of intelligence, to procure sustenance. This might be robbery, grasping, snatching, physical engagement with use of weapons or whatever else might be found opportune as a means of accomplishing the end.

The task of restraint would obviously be more difficult than in a minor frustration even if only one person were afflicted. If the number were considerable, police power might be needed to pacify or contain the straining will-force.

Oddly enough, if the famine condition were not regarded as the fault of anyone, but the result of weather conditions, and if there were no question of maldistribution of food, the attitude of the famished would be more passive. They might simply suffer in silence. It is thus a question of locating a cause on which to vent the displeasure and pain, if they are to be vented. Sometimes an object is found or even contrived if no true one exists. This is what we call finding a scapegoat.

The secondary will-forces and the secondary ego would come into play if injustice in the distribution of food should actually exist or *were thought to exist*. A feeling of outrage would be added to the hunger pangs, and a more menacing atmosphere would be produced. The impulse to aggression would be magnified. Hatred of the actual cause or of the scapegoat would rise higher, and only a spark might be needed to set off a riot.

Frustration of the secondary will-forces or the ego need not, however, rest on a frustrated primary will-force. A sense of injustice may be aroused when no hunger, mating instinct, or need of shelter is involved. This sense may become so refined that a variety of considerations of the ego may evoke it. Injustice may be perceived as a reflection of simple inequality. The ego may then enter the lists, so to speak. If someone other than oneself is overpaid, the sense of injustice is not invoked because of the overpayment but because of discrimination.

I have not been paid as much as another person, and even though I was paid within reason, I wish to know, perhaps unjustifiably, what accounts for the difference. This is my ego speaking. It may hurt my ego more to know that someone else is favored over me than any underpayment of myself would arouse in me. Moreover, I begin to ask what accounts for the favoritism. My imagination will run the gamut from some imagined concealed relation to conspiracy and what-not.

However, aggression is not so likely to break out under these circumstances. It may take the form of gossip, down-rating of the one dispensing the favor, or other efforts designed to hurt his standing.

In the situations in which the government or the group exercising power and dispensing "justice" is thought to be responsible for privation, hopelessness, drab and uninspiring or actually ugly, grim and rundown environment, the general frustration may identify the object or cause with the government or group at the helm. Inclination to aggression will then center on the removal of the cause, in the belief that things would be better if someone else were substituted; but such a belief may not even be necessary. The resentment against the ruling dominancy may be so great that the ego and will-forces will thirst for the scalp of the scapegoat quite regardless of the sequel—as in the French Revolution and on other occasions. It is not necessary to believe that a change would be for the better. The frustrated will-forces simply want to be avenged on what is believed to be the cause of the general destitution.

The principle here adduced is that frustration of the will-forces and/or the ego makes man ill-disposed. He wishes to remove and, for good measure, to punish the cause of the frustration if it was personal. If he is ill-disposed over a period of time, his whole humor will be infected, and he may even "take out" his "ill-will" on innocent associates, subordinates, or whoever may have whatever to do with him.

His aggressive instinct is aroused, and if he finds the cause or thinks he has found it, he will vent his spleen according to the intensity of the will-force or ego-interest and the degree of frustration.

It would seem from this equation or formula that mankind would be in a perpetual state of ill-humor. Frustrations are encountered on all sides. They are a part of the daily fare of life, so to speak. Why is not everyone "out of joint" on nearly any hour of the day?

In the answer to this question lies the principal hope of the amelioration of human behavior—even to the extent of raising the threshold of national aggression or war.

It needs no scientific proof to tell us that the responses of the will-forces and the ego to frustration may be reduced, abated, or even dissolved.

We of the human race would indeed be in a state of constant irritation or turmoil if we did not learn how to cope with most frustrations. We begin very early in life to learn that we must adapt to some situations, or, as the saying goes, learn to "live with them." We learn, for example, that some obstacles are too big or too heavy to move out of the way if they are between us and something that excites our will-forces to seek possession of it. We learn to go around these obstacles if we can find a way.

If there is no way, we learn to forget about our desire or we resign ourselves to reality.

These two tactics, namely going around, over, or under an obstacle or if this is not possible resigning ourselves to the facts of life, help to overcome the pain of frustration and may drain us of our inclination to aggression. Children would do better not by being constantly helped but by being allowed to learn for themselves how to overcome obstacles.

Again, we may reflect that things change and that on another occasion the obstacle may have moved itself or have been moved by some other agent. Finally, as a fourth alternative and last resort, we may call for help; but we may or may not obtain a response. If we do not, we may once more feel frustrated, this time not by the object but by whomsoever failed to respond. The ego will now come into play because a personal factor has been introduced.

Of course, the help may come, and our ego will be assuaged if the help is useful and the attitude is one of good will. Even if the assistance also fails to move the obstacle, our ego will not cavil if good intentions are in evidence. We may be disappointed, but recognize the stubborn nature of the obstacle. If the attitude, on the other hand, is negative or is one of fault-finding or leads to accusation of stupidity or the like, neither the ego nor the will-forces will be inclined to pacification. Aggressiveness of word if not of deed may result; although allowance may be made for the fact that the person did answer the call.

What is indicated here is that the response to frustration need not be a helpless surrender to the will-forces or the ego, as the case may be. After all, sources of impulses and desires belong to each individual. Unless he is an abject weakling, he does not belong to them. They belong to him, and he is not their slave unless he elects to be.

For this reason, mental attitude toward appetites, desires, ambitions, and aspirations becomes a decisive factor in behavior. As we learn to demobilize our desire to reach a goal that is beyond our reach because of an immovable obstacle, or learn to bypass a physical obstacle or to seek help in removing it rather than kicking it or pounding it with our hands in frustration, and thus expending our aplomb and dignity, so can we adopt a reasoning attitude with respect to other types of frustration or disappointments.

One of the elements that may determine the threshold of frustration is the level of our own expectations. As remarked earlier, it is not wise to let them run too far ahead of our capabilities nor yet behind them. There are, of course, as also remarked earlier, an assortment of expectations of us harbored by other people and these, too, may exert a great influence on the kind of response we might make. There is, further, something that might be called community or social expectation, again as previously mentioned, or other more generalized forms of the phenomenon. These may help to shape our responses, although in some instances that may become a source of exasperation.

Therefore, the fact that we are constantly beset by frustrations need not be regarded as abnormal or as a continuous source of aggression. It is always possible to confront frustrations with a solvent attitude or philosophy. Also, we will recognize the happy function of wit and humor, of song and music, reminiscences and tales, poetry and drama (for those who respond to them with receptive sensibilities), games and other forms of recreation, and convivial fellowship as activities that buoy the spirit and help us past adversities and oppressive anxieties.

The expectations of the community or of friends or members of one's family will produce their effect, whatever it might be, on the ego. As is easily observed, to repeat yet once more, not everyone is as sensitive toward the expectation of others as are some individuals. In some instances, indeed, there may exist a veritable delight in causing discomfiture or shock to others.

In the absence of such a distorted attitude, the opinion or reaction of others to an individual's behavior will be of some concern and may act as a restraint on the will-forces but especially on the ego, if the intelligence notes or senses disapproval. This influence will extend to the inclination to indulge in aggression. One who contemplates committing an act of aggression may resist the inclination out of unwillingness to face the opinion of others. The power of reason, in other words, intrudes itself upon the scene, so to speak, and lays its hand on the shoulder of the inclination and bids it desist. It may not obey at all times, but if reason persists, the will-force or ego may be brought under control.

When the light of freedom shines brightly within, we have less difficulty resisting the animal or native inclination that would have us turn to aggression or other action that would be unworthy in our own eyes. How brightly the light of freedom shines in us is a question about which, in turn, we need not be helpless.

Freedom, which is to say the exercise of choice without compulsion, requires exercise for its perfection, and it is in the exercise for its perfection that the hope of subduing the inclination to aggression, as well as the conquest of other wayward conduct, lies.

Yet we must not fall into the error of believing that private self-control will lift us out of the sway that public excitement may exert on us. Private self-control will assist in the effort to remain calm and to rise above the storm, but forces of extreme magnitude may nevertheless overwhelm us, driving reason to cover. This fact, of course, is recognized universally, but its recognition does little to overcome the virtual helplessness of the individual.

Yet, from the nature of the phenomenon of public "hysteria," it would not be beyond control if the community were sufficiently enlightened. If individuals are able by self-discipline and endeavor to enhance the voice of reason as an inner arbiter, the community is not without hope of capacity to thwart "hysteria"—if its probable onset is recognized *before* it asserts itself. If its incipient elements can be apprehended in time, an enlightened community would be able to disperse the telltale forces before they congregate to form an irresistible power. There can be no question about the power once it is constituted, nor about the helplessness of the individual once he comes under the full force of its sway.

Prevention offers the only hope of escape. The quandary is not unlike that of the individual who fears his downfall before certain varieties of temptation. He does poorly to leave his preparation to the moment of the temptation. Instead he should prepare himself long and far in advance by the many means at hand or available to him. He should look to his ego, to make it invulnerable to assault by deliberate adoption of a code. One can easily wonder how those who daily are exposed to the temptation of taking money, as a teller in a bank, become impervious to the temptation. They train themselves not to entertain the least inclination to consider what possession of the money might mean to them. They place themselves by a mental decision above the reach of temptation. They may, of course, be greatly helped by their training at home and by the family attitude toward honesty and honor. In some instances, of course, temptation may still prevail.

The concept of justice has been implemented in what is called municipal law. This is the law that pertains to the internal affairs of a state or nation, as distinguished from international law. The establishment of courts of justice represented the practical application of a concept that in turn was generated by contemplation of a need of human society, just as an automobile represents the practical elaboration of mechanical principles.

Imperfect as the administration of justice is in municipal law, it does no doubt produce an ameliorative effect on human behavior, including the inclination to aggression. It acts also to protect those who go about their affairs in peaceful routine against the rapacity of those whose primary will-forces and raw ego are without proper restraint. Under the principle of natural selection, it has thrown its weight on the side of the least aggressive and the meek against the most predacious and combative.

While municipal law has been elaborated and refined into endless minutiae that fill vast arrays of thick tomes, international law remains still much in the seed, as a concept that man has not been able to employ as an instrument of justice. This inability is perhaps one of his most telling defects. His intelligence at contriving tools, as has been universally recognized, has outpaced his capacity to rule himself as a species.

It is most difficult to find a reason for this discrepancy. That man should be so slow in his adaptation to international government, held back by animosities, suspicions, and aggressive attitudes, compared to his scientific advancement may be regarded as an evolutionary error that may be his undoing. What is needed is obviously a complete reorientation of the human heart, and this means a redirection of the ego.

It is not the will-forces that are at fault in the sense that their reorientation is not possible. They will respond to economic rearrangements. This is to say that if the means of earning a living is dissociated from national fixation or anchorage, the will-forces would become amenable to denationalization. A person who finds his fortune in an alien land and even in an alien culture, will also find that his will-forces will not revolt against his enjoyment of the fortune. The saying that where a man's treasure is there his heart is also, arose from a clear insight into the tranmutational power possessed by that which in turn has the power to gratify human desires. As a man seeks the means of satisfying his needs and gratifying his desires, he soon becomes attached to the place and the surroundings that are generous to his quest. This is a matter of association and infection by affinity. Changes of citizenship sometimes reflect the sentiment.

One of the most convincing examples of inner transformation and attitude may be encountered in the milieu of romantic love. This is a soul-filling attachment to which we have already paid our respects. It is not an unusual experience to see a veritable transmutation in the regard or attitude of one who comes under the sway of this influence, toward a place, locality, community, or country. From what might be considered an initial intense aversion for such a place in, let us say, a young man away from home, there may soon emerge for seemingly no reason at all a tolerance that may be detected in a period of silence which replaces the wonted frequent deprecatory references to the less inspiring aspects of the place. After a while, but not so much later that the words do not create a somewhat startling effect, the youthful fellow may surprisingly be heard to say, "It's not such a bad place." After the wand of romance has remade the soul, the words will come out in a yet more astounding form. Says the smitten one, not at all embarrassed, but secretly relishing his confession, "I like it here."

Yet the place had not changed. It was as drab as always, as devoid of interesting diversions, no less lacking in those cultural delights that some other places have in abundance. The change was in the person. What was depressing in the environment is now quaint; what was insufferable is now gladly borne. The opposite may, of course, also happen. If the human associations are displeasing, even paradise would lose its attraction.

To repeat, such transmutations are not unusual. More than one student has become fond of mathematics for no better reason, or lost his interest because of antipathy to the teacher.

What is the heart's attachment? What has prestige for it? What lifts it from the floor and gives it a remote and loyal attachment? What builds its morale? What gives it a mystique? Where is its beacon or has it none? If it lacks one is it possible to give it one?

Precisely because mankind did develop in compartmentalized fashion over the millennia, first perhaps in family or tribal form, then in somewhat larger aggregations and finally in nations, reflecting in varying degrees racial groupings, his heart became centered in the grouping to which he belonged. That is where his satisfactions, his romance, his sorrows, his joys were. That is where he was at home. There his language was understood. There he knew how to play, and to shout, to laugh, to quarrel and cry. There is where he understood others than himself, where attitudes of everyone toward alien things were much the same. This is where one could know tranquility, or if one did not have it, one could hope to have it. The dress of people was natural and customary—no "outlandish" costumes, no strange headdress, oddly cut coats or other body drapery, no overdone differences in colors and costumes. His ambitions were centered there. His schooling, study of history, his religion were all a part of his native soil. The history he studied was kind to his country, and because it pictured his homeland as so noble, he came to have a special regard for it. In its wars, as he read about them, his heart was with those who fought its battles to drive off brutal invaders or to punish the horrible enemies on this side or that. The display of his country's flag on days of memorable events gave him a deep feeling of attachment, fidelity, and even a willingness to acquit himself bravely and honorably, perhaps even with a distinction, should the occasion arise. Yes, it was his land, his country, his home, and these were his people. They were his kind, and whatever was alien and hostile to them aroused his own hostility. His heart had its attachment to the way of living under which he grew to maturity. He was taught songs of praise that pictured his land as the most select of all. He was so conditioned in his heart's attachments that it was beyond his capacity to question the goodness of his homeland, and in times of stress he had only one love and that was his country. Of course, there would be a few questioners and even rebels.

Obviously it would be a superhuman undertaking to change the anchorage of his heart—with a few exceptions, as noted.

How give his heart an attachment to international substitutes for his existing fixations? Either it would be necessary to dissolve existing loyalties and attachments and then to replant those of an international matrix in the heart or, finding this process an improbable undertaking, to begin with the earliest years of life and making the substitution then, thus awaiting a new generation's development.

Immediately the difficulty of such a departure from the customary looms as virtually insuperable. Who would consent to his children's weaning from patriotic sentiment? The sense of treason, of outrage and betrayal would oust any suggestion of such a reorientation. The first question would come with a crashing force against the proponent. "What would happen if we should eliminate patriotism while our potential enemies did not follow suit?" The result would make our defeat an easy task for the enemy. The dilemma is of a kind with the one that confronts disarmament proposals. Who can trust the other? Who will be the referee? Half-way trust is insufficient.

To foreswear patriotism without a substituting attachment for the heart would leave man without the object of dedication that has most readily produced the selflessness that represents one of his highest aspirations.

Can man find a devotion to life sufficient to sustain his will-forces and ego at the proper tension unless he has an object of dedication? As previously observed, merely living does not fulfill life's aspiration. It may answer the primary will-forces, but man, as we have seen, if he is of any consequence, aspires to more than a sated stomach, a warm body, and reproduction. His secondary will-forces may indeed be satisfied by the endeavors and exercises to which they lead. A scientist, an artist, a musician or mathematician may have an all-consuming dedication in his work. To these *humanity* is more easily acceptable as a substitute for patriotism than it is to the more competitive undertakings and enterprises where national rivalry plays a part.

The ego, with its ramifications which identify the individual with the group, offers the principal obstacle. After all, my country *is mine.* Nothing is more closely associated with the ego than what is "mine."

Is it possible to substitute humanity, or the human species, for a narrower grouping? It is readily conceivable that if the earth were invaded from the outside, so that humanity would have a common fear or a common enemy, supreme loyalty to our species would not only become possible but would soon be precipitated. Such an event, however, whether probable or improbable, is not predictable with any such degree of certainty as would be necessary to produce a unifying influence on humanity.

This lack of imminence brings us back to where we are and have been since the advent of man. The question then is whether the hostility induced by rivalry over economic assets and territorial position and occupation can be abated or perhaps sublimated without the confrontation of a common enemy.

Man has engaged in what from the point of view of his species would be called internecine warfare. Nevertheless, he has reached settlements. He is uniquely a creature of tit for tat. He proceeds by elaborate formulas of *quid pro quo.* He congenitally seeks something for something, or even something for nothing. He is a trader. Even the system of reward and punishment which is a universal phenomenon, is based on this for that, or something in exchange for something else. This is perhaps why in his religion the idea of a reward or punishment holds so high a position.

The settlements that hostile or rival groups, tribes or nations have made, this side of complete subjugation, have been expressed in agreements or understandings, in latter years known as treaties. Something was traded for something else. Usually it became possible to live side by side, at least for temporary pe-

riods of varying lengths. If the war was a deadlock, an uneasy
peace might be the result. Each side would be biding its time to
gain an advantage over the other. Then hostility might be
renewed.

In many instances, one side would gain sufficient military
advantage to retain possession of conquered territory or a part of
it. Settlements awarding territory had their limitations because
pacification and governing of conquered people brought peculiar difficulties of their own. It might be costly as an economic
and military overture. Again, even though the conquest may have
been the result of a decisive military victory, victories were never
permanent. Perhaps the victory was the fruit of brilliant general-
ship, and generals are mortal or fade away. The vanquished
group, having lost only a part of its territory, might later produce
a great general of its own, while the erstwhile conqueror might
come to be weak in that department. Then the tables might be
turned, and a new settlement might be reached. The conquered
territory might be returned, and on occasion some additional
acreage might be signed over. The bargains depended on the
relative strength.

Why the settlements? If distrust was so great that no group
or country could rely on the word of another, why go through
the farce of a settlement, since settlements were nothing more
than words? Evidently there was a margin of trustworthiness, and
in time, as people began to have a voice in the state's affairs, a
species of public opinion grew up—an opinion strong enough
(in terms of expectation) to compel national leaders to take it
into account. That is why it became so important to see that
blame always be placed on the other side. Probably without exception in modern times no country was ever guilty of the original aggression in a war in its own account to its citizens and to
the world.

This very fact provides some measure of the strength of
public opinion. It could no longer be ignored, or at least that
was the judgment of the rulers. Even if they were the aggressors,
they felt compelled to make their own countrymen feel that the
war was defensive or at worst represented an effort to right
grievous wrongs previously committed by the enemy. It was

sometimes necessary to strike first because the enemy was really poised to strike at any moment; therefore what appeared to be unprovoked aggression was really a defensive act. Thus could treaties or settlements reached earlier on occasion even be called scraps of paper if it was inconvenient to honor them; or it could be said that necessity knows no law (Bethmann-Hollweg)—thus equating a national ambition or need with necessity in its universal sense.

Always, once the die was cast, the citizenry rose to heights of patriotism, fired by oratory, newspaper accounts and opinion, martial music, marches, parades, and flag displays.

The resort to these devices was explained or justified to conscience by the fact that the great mass of citizens are so immersed in their daily routines and interests that the national needs, concerns, and worries are lost in the fogs of indifference. Thus, even if the head of state and his advisers were de facto confronted with a menace to the nation from without, they would find it necessary to resort to the usual devices of arousing the public. It is understood, of course, that if the enemy followed the same course of arousing the masses, it was propaganda, rousing the rabble and generally fracturing all that civilized people hold to be decent and honorable!

Such characterizations of the enemy are a clear confession of the activity of the will-forces and the ego. The blackening of the character of opponents is the favorite instrument of the frustrated will-forces and especially of the ego. After all, aggression is not mounted on indifferent or unprovoked will-forces! If heavy exactions are to be made on the populace, their will-forces and ego interests must be not only awakened but brought to a high degree of intensity against the image of the enemy.

As the exactions of war become in time more onerous and painful, including their impact on the people at home, a bigger reservoir of reluctance and skepticism builds up. More penetrating questions will be asked of the national leaders, and these will be confronted with unaccustomed difficulty in explaining the need for looming armed action. In a sense they are then placed in a position of explaining to the people its own self-interest as interpreted by those responsible for the national security.

This is another way of saying that the people are naturally for peace, but possibly because they are blissfully ignorant and therefore indifferent, perhaps culpably indifferent, to the dangers confronting the nation.

The attitude of the public has shifted toward a point of skepticism that is nevertheless still on the side of patriotism. Should a fully powered international referee exist, those who question the judgment of national leaders in the vortex of conflicting national ambitions, fears, and distrust would be justified in making a demand for settlement by arbitration or adjudication by an international court. However, in the absence of such a referee, force remains the final arbiter. In a dispute, especially between two powerful nations, there is today no alternative other than diplomacy to force or the show of it, because no referee has the power of enforcement.

Under such circumstances, there can be no guarantee of peaceful settlement. Each country has its position to maintain, and if it has certain claims to put forward or denies the claim of the other, it is compelled to stand its ground on pain of being considered weak, vacillating, or irresolute if it retreats. If the citizens of each country are in support of their leader, even if only after being aroused, they can hardly suggest a retreat or diminution of their country's demands. Thus a deadlock becomes inevitable, and unless that stalemate can be held in status quo, hostilities can hardly be avoided. However, so long as an exchange of advantages and disadvantages that might be attractive to each side, for reasons of its own, were kept open, the possibility of a settlement would remain.

Sometimes the outbreak of violence is but a substitute for lack of wit. Each country, supported by the national ego, will still seek to achieve its ends. The will-forces of the people having been aroused either by stimulation or by force of appetite, the diplomats will find amelioration of their own demands on the other nation most difficult. They may find themselves victimized by the home opinion that was so laboriously contrived. Every move is debated in the press and by self-appointed commentators who have the ears and the minds of the people at their disposal. The demand for open covenants openly arrived at will deprive negotiators of some of their most effective instruments. The notion that negotiations should be conducted in a "goldfish bowl" represents a naive oversimplification of what is undoubtedly the most difficult mediation ever imposed on the resources of human intelligence.

Two factors put in their appearance to the further complication of the equation. One is the force of the *quid pro quo* consideration, and the other, the struggle for dominance, which is the province of the ego.

The *quid pro quo* equation represents some approximation to justice or equity, but it is not in pure form. The one side will seek advantages to buoy the ego, and, of course, the other side is under the same pressure. Commentators will write and speak in oracular tones, and will seek to impress the public with the acuity of their insights and prescience. One day, in the midst of the negotiations, one leading diplomat or national representative, such as a foreign minister, will be lauded for his shrewdness in gaining this or that concession, thus by inversion awarding a scroll of stupidity to his opposite number at the negotiating table. This interpretation will produce the effect of making him more adamant in adhering to his position in the future, and he will be supported the more stubbornly by the national ego of those for whom he speaks.

A recent example, although mild in its context and tone, will serve as an illustration. In a daily London newspaper, a three-column headline proclaimed "How Wilson Plans to Outsmart de Gaulle," Wilson being the British prime minister, on the eve of a state visit to the French president.

Those who raise their voices in a regime of self-government, as is their privilege under constitutional guarantees of freedom of the press, have a heavy responsibility of their own. The constituents of self-government, who may in the end become the victims of irresponsible journalism, will have a stake in the establishment of journalistic codes of conduct and responsibility. The spectacle of freebooting commentators applying the customs of sportswriting to international affairs is a luxury that a self-governing people may not wish to enjoy.

As for the possibility of bringing the *quid pro quo* objective under control, it is obvious that the national ego offers the most stubborn stumbling block. Woodrow Wilson's notion of peace without victory represented an effort to do without this time-honored principle. It was naturally not a popular proposal. Franklin Roosevelt's demand for unconditional surrender was of the opposite extreme at the end of World War II. The Wilsonian idea, of course, collided with the national ego. To withdraw from a field of battle without victory is to ask the ego to forego its raw satisfaction, and reason has little power to prevail against the aroused ego. This assertion assumes that victory is regarded as the undoubted outcome when the proposal is made. To suggest peace under those conditions assumes that the proponent has the upper hand.

Inasmuch as a good *quid pro quo* will possibly satisfy the will-forces, both primary and secondary, since it wears at least the semblance of the robes of justice, the notion of peace without victory becomes essentially a question of how to propitiate the ego—of satisfying the heart, so to speak.

If we keep in mind the predilection of the ego for dominancy, we immediately grasp the difficulty confronting the proponent of peace without victory. To any one of the old school such a proposal would immediately be regarded as emanating from someone who has no stomach for war. Why, it would be asked, would he make such an offer if he had victory within his grasp? It would be unbelievable. Therefore the proposal must necessarily be a confession of weakness or inconstancy of determination. It was perhaps to avoid any such miscalculation that President Roosevelt called for unconditional surrender. This demand, which was apparently in the form of overcompensation for Wilson's innovation, played into the hands of the raw ego, which, of course, can be happy only with undoubted dominancy.

Unfortunately for the hope of future peace, the exaction of terms of unconditional surrender suffered from two drawbacks. Thereafter all errors of the subsequent peace would come to rest at the feet of the one who had exacted such extreme terms. Secondly, considering the sensitivity of the national ego, exaction of unconditional surrender would lay up a determination in the vanquished one day to have his revenge.

Generosity in victory, such as animated the spirit of Lincoln, would pave a smoother road to a "lasting peace" than the exaction of humiliating terms. The latter demand, long the standard, was reminiscent of two adolescents who in a fistic altercation could hear shouts from the sidelines urging equally on each of the combatants: "Make him cry uncle!" In other words, "Do not give up, and demonstrate your superior force and skill." The same sentiment might alternatively have been expressed by the urging: "Rub his nose in the dust."

These exhortations were straightaway from the raw ego, and as observed previously, an act of ill-will may be expected to provoke a response in kind—unless the respondent has prepared a different variety of reaction. Such a response might be one of restraint and would seem unnatural by the prevailing standard. It would indeed owe its temperance to the restraint instituted by the mind. It would represent a purposive amelioration of the ego's natural inclination, and could arise only from the generosity of the stronger combatant.

Considering the "heat of passion" under which the ego is constrained to respond under the exultation of victory or anticipation of victory, the restraint that would offer soft terms and exact no tribute or reparations from the vanquished is readily recognized as virtually superhuman.

Yet, how else mitigate the burning emotions that are provoked simultaneously by humiliation and a thirst for revenge?

If the victorious ego cannot be prevailed upon to forego the temptations of victory to dominate and humiliate the vanquished, how could the passions of war, the craving for revenge and the hatred of the victor ever be expected to be dissipated if not wholly dissolved? Surely the initiative must lie with the victor. If he exhibits magnanimity, the possibility of abating the acerbity or acrimony of humiliation would be given its only opening.

Generosity in victory can only be gained by curbing the raw ego which delights in strutting and crowing and swelling with unseemly pride, and further by renouncing some of the fruits of dominancy. This is the same as withholding from aggression the very object of its activity!

What a reversal of the *natural* order! Would any red-blooded human being subscribe to such backboneless behavior? Is man not a vertebrate by heritage? Why then dissolve his backbone in ignominious solutions that would ally him with the jellyfish which is a distinctly inferior form of life?

What statesman after Woodrow Wilson's debacle would expose himself to the catcalls, mockery, and contempt of the masculine world, well knowing that he would be despised by his countrymen should he espouse the weak-kneed principles of non-vindictiveness and later awaken to the fact that the erstwhile enemy, taking advantage of the reprieve extended by the victor, had acted in treacherous and ungrateful fashion?

Yet, which way is man to turn if he is confronted for the first time in history with the grim fact that he possesses the veritable power to destroy the world?

If he does not veer sharply from his ancestral forms of reaction, if he does not rise above his primary will-forces and the demands of his raw ego and curb his reaction to frustration and his predilection for domination, he courts disaster.

Here indeed is a categorical imperative! To be sure it is not in the habiliments of Kant's famous formula, but it towers over man's destiny with a categorical warning.

Is man capable of heeding it?

That is the question of the century that unleashed nuclear destruction. The answer is not self-revealing.

It can easily be concluded that renunciation of force on all sides would provide the answer; but it would only be begging the question. Agreements to outlaw war as an instrument of policy have been reached. While such an agreement may be necessary as a step, it does not supply a guarantee. It does not tame those inner forces of man that, under recurring circumstances in history, have torn asunder all good will, understanding, and friendship. Until these forces are abated, diverted, or redirected, the outlook is not promising.

It goes without saying that a stalemate resting on mutual fear is perhaps the best umbrella for endeavors aimed at defusing man's ego and showing him how to descend gracefully from a high place without executing a crash landing. It will also be urged that if, for example, everyone should live by the principles of Christianity, the defusing would automatically be accomplished. To this there can be no negative reply, but, again, how bring about the universal adoption of the injunction to love others as one loves oneself? Once more, the suggestion begs the question. To say this is not to deprecate the endeavor; it is merely to say that if one set of opposing forces should adhere to that attitude while the other side did not, natural selection would soon supply the answer. The "strong" would in time prevail since they would have little difficulty slaughtering the conscientious objectors.

What then of justice? Of amelioration of the ego? Of education, of family inculcation of self-discipline aimed at understanding of humanity, of the spreading of the gospel of love for fellow man?

In other words, while holding a gun at the head of humanity, with a threat of annihilation, can the solvent of understanding, empathy, kindness, and mutual regard be so universalized that of their own account opponents will simultaneously lower the gun and then not pick it up again?

Does man not learn faster under necessity than under the permissiveness of leisure? The indication is that he does indeed speed his efforts; and as necessity is the mother of invention, an overhanging threat activates the mind at the behest of the primary will-force of fear.

If an international organization is in being, it may serve as an instrumentality for negotiation. Yet it must be clear that neither the existence of the instrumentality for negotiation nor the actual negotiations are the real factors. The question is: How vehement is the demand from the will-forces and the ego? It is they that will tell the tale, not the mind. The mind can help. It can find means of influencing the will-forces and the ego, but it cannot guarantee success in its efforts. The will-forces and the raw ego are notorious for the *hair triggers* that release them.

Even if an international organization were granted plenary powers, so that it could make decisions and enforce them, there would be no assurance that decisions could be reached in view of man's difference of views, difference of interests, and propensity to disagree. The organization might be deadlocked, and if the ruling will-forces and the ego interests of the most powerful member nations were unregenerated or unchastened, the result would be dissension and possibly a breakdown.

Nevertheless, since no guarantee can in any case be provided, the only hope would lie in the endeavor to agree and to make "binding" commitments. Essentially, however, the fortunes of the endeavor must revolve about the question of taming the will-forces and the ego.

The stubbornness of the honor principle would assert itself; and while the principle of honor is not to be deprecated, it can also in the extremities hold tragic consequences. Rigidity between opposing forces has two avenues to a resolution of differences. One is the resort to force, the other, the presence of sufficient wit to permit the admission of flexibility without appearance of retreat. Both avenues are used, but when the second one fails, the first one becomes virtually the only possibility left because of the ego.

Inflexibility assumes a monopoly on wisdom, and no mortal has such a monopoly and only presumption would support such a stance. But man has presumption in abundance. It all comes down to the ego's pull on the heart. The ego cannot on its own motion relinquish its hold on the person. If the grip is to be broken, it must be accomplished from the outside. The ego, as we have endeavored to show, is by nature amenable to reason. It is not incorrigible, although it may appear to be so in some individuals. Some of these are unable to avoid a feeling of dishonesty if they "compromise" their principles.

The resolution of the stalemate in such instances offers some stubborn difficulty. Certainty in the nonphysical field is very elusive, but there are individuals who seek to transfer mathematical or physical certainties into the field of unverifiable opinion. On reaching a conclusion, they have so sublime a faith in their own judgment that they lock the door against contrary opinion and give no one a key to the door. With them the word "shut" has a ring of final, eternal exclusiveness. Not even a ray of light can find an aperture for penetration.

All attempts to change the person's mind inevitably appear to the person to be an assault on his integrity, and he becomes

annoyed at any evidence of persistence. Since he prides himself
on his integrity, he takes an adamant stance. The burden of any
accommodation to be reached with him must necessarily then rest
with his adversary. Unfortunately, much as an aggressive address
arouses animosity in the respondent, inflexibility generates a
temptation to intransigence in the adversary. Honor, which
means the ego's interest, is suddenly again at stake. An atmosphere of tension develops, and the frustration induced by the inflexibility will add its own provoked inclination toward aggression to the milieu. If the person who finds himself frustrated is a
prime minister or a foreign minister, and the adversary is his
counterpart representing another country, the prime minister's
provocation, which is to say, his inclination to burst out in expressions of outrage, will spread quickly to the people of his
country, assuming that no sharp partisan cleavage were present
to divide public sentiment. The people will echo his feeling,
for is he not their spokesman?

Of course, the confrontation of one person by another is not
usually so clean-cut. Inflexibility is not usually confined to one
side. This fact permits the entrance of the *quid pro quo* gambit.

It may be sensed or quite obvious from shrewd observation
that the adversary or opposite number may have a very sensitive
nerve with respect to one or several of the points of difference.
He may have failed to conceal his concern or was too obvious in
his effort to conceal his anxiety over this or that matter under
contention. The opponent, having taken note of this concern,
will in turn hide his discernment of it, the better to exploit the
point to the full—always assuming that he himself has no great
concern about the point himself. He will incline to assume an
air of great concern over it, equal perhaps to that of his
counterpart.

He may, on the other hand, have a great concern of his
own about another point that in turn does not weigh so much
with the other side. He will outwardly exhibit a cool indifference toward that point, all the while pressing hard at the point
which he knows is of most concern to his adversary.

There may be a number of points, some of them possibly
included for diversionary purposes. For each side, there will

quite surely be priorities among the points in terms of importance. A considerable exercise in fencing may engage the parties
in the preliminaries in the hope of gaining clues to the priorities
entertained by the other side.

Because of the gambits employed, the concealment of intentions, exaggerations of interest in one or another point, and the
probing and counterprobes, such diplomatic processes are often
deprecated as games of chess; the players may be pictured as using people and their interests, including the lives of fighting men,
as mere pawns. This is almost surely a cynical assessment about
modern diplomacy but may have had more than a degree of justification in the days of princely and ducal intrigues and wars. The
raw ego is of such a nature that the man in a superior status has
but little feeling or sympathy for the humble members of the
mass and can easily regard them as pawns. Only if the latter have
power over those in superior position will the latter be responsive.

The fact of priorities in what is sought and what, on the
other hand, may be sacrificed with relative unconcern, and the
differences in the scale of priorities between two opposing negotiators makes it possible to reach agreements. One negotiator very
reluctantly will concede a fraction of a point with respect to a
point that he ostensibly but not actually regards as of the highest
importance if his opposite will yield a bigger fraction on another
point. A bigger fraction? Yes, because as the opponent must know,
it is a point of lesser concern. Therefore, since the proffer is of a
small fraction of a point that is so vital to the profferer, the opponent should be willing to sacrifice a large fraction of something
that is much less precious! And, so round and around, all the
while concealing both triumphs and disappointments, the two
sides may come to an agreement that has more gains in the area
of principal concern than losses to each and higher losses in the
areas of secondary concerns and fewer but more meaningful
gains in the important areas.

If news correspondents intrude themselves into negotiations
and make revelations, even if only by drawing inferences of their
own, they may spoil the possibility of reaching a satisfactory
agreement by "tipping the hand" of this or that side. Only by adhering to a code of high responsibility will they overcome their

temptation to exploit journalistically their position as observers.

It goes without saying that not all divisive issues are as simple as the one pictured above; but the possibility of finding a basis for bargaining is seldom absent if continuation of the dispute is not itself of great value to one side or both. In that event, the fencing will be characterized by a series of overtures that will be found by the one side or the other as no more than a ludicrous or insulting offer. In some instances, when no decisive development is visible in the premises, one side may undertake to outwait the other, in the hope that a lack of fortitude in the opponent will cause his retreat or a down-scaling of his terms of settlement.

In maneuvers between two sovereignties, there is a veritable framework of public expectations to guide those who are the responsible spokesmen, as observed earlier. The negotiators are not only aware of these expectations, which may have a very complicated genealogy of their own, but are aware of the penalties that attach to failure to abide by them and to meet them.

Therefore, we should not look so much at the negotiators as we should examine the expectations to which they respond, if we wish to understand a situation and the course of negotiation. What is in these expectations is seldom explicit, but it accompanies the spokesmen and looks over their shoulders. Each opposite is in the same position. Each is aware that the other, too, is not alone, nor a mere person such as Mr. Wilson or M. Clemenceau, or Mr. Stalin or Mr. Churchill. Each knows that the other has history looking at him. Each also knows that the people to whom each is responsive look to him, they know not how, to promote the national interests, whatever these may be, and to preserve the national honor by suffering no insults, slights, or lack of deference or respect.

One of the functions of the correspondents, as they interpret it, is to measure how well these expectations are met. Much of their information, however, must come from secondary sources, and this has often to be made coherent by conjecture and inferences.

If the prospect for abatement of aggressive inclinations, such as may be aroused by frustration of national objectives, is to be assessed, we need only ask what is contained in the public expectations of their spokesmen that would lead them to . . . do what? Yes, that is the question. How must the expectations be modified to produce what effects?

If our desideratum is negotiation to avoid rancor, humiliation, vindictiveness, fear, intrigue, duplicity, treachery, and other reputed characteristics of diplomacy, how must the public expectations be modified? Evidently higher standards of morality must be demanded of negotiators by their own public. This means that the public must first adopt these standards itself. The latter must have become a part of the expectations.

Statesmen permit themselves a level of conduct in the prosecution of foreign affairs that would bring them to disgrace should they conduct their personal affairs in like manner. If the supporting public condones such execrable standards and asks no questions, what but impermanent and unsound settlements can then be expected? If a country's spokesman is denounced abroad by his opposite for his machinations or nefarious schemes, he can be sure that he will be supported at home and that those who attacked him abroad will be roundly taken to task.

This assurance reflects what is virtually a universal attitude of the people at home. It is for this reason that the public is not as innocent as it is often pictured. The people are perhaps innocent in the sense that they are unaware of the force of their contribution to the climate—the moral climate—in which foreign affairs are conducted, but this innocence does not reduce the damage.

The difficulty is that even if they were aware of it, they would not know what to do about it, for the very good reason that no one knows how to change public opinion except perhaps in narrow sectors. We know all the less about how to bring about a major change in the moral climate on the level of public expectations.

Yet, such changes do occur, very slowly though they come about. The process may indeed be accelerated by the categorical imperative of the nuclear threat. There is little question that one of the fundamental needs is a change in the public attitude toward the conduct of foreign affairs, namely, a pulling away from the raw ego; nor can there be much doubt about the painfulness of the process, the utter unwillingness to accept new attitudes that would express a radical toning-down of the national ego.

So difficult would be the process that a virtual martyr's willingness to reap the most unpleasant consequences would be an indispensable quality for advancement in the field. This would include social ostracism and vehement and raucous denunciation, and there is perhaps no more unpleasant punishment short of imprisonment or physical torture than ostracism by one's fellow beings. Who, then, would be the volunteers? And what would they undertake to do? Present-day methods of changing public opinion consist of marches, picketing with signs, public exhortation, a variety of obstructions to public convenience, and other distasteful and irritating deployments designed to attract attention. However, the methods stir so much ill-will that the good will that is sought may be alienated.

Public education or rather re-education is the obvious answer. Yet, such an answer is little better than those previously mentioned. Moreover, the process of education moves at a generation's pace. The fact that the ego's vehemence and stubborn self-promotion are amenable to change, nevertheless offers the most hopeful long-term remedy.

Should the endeavor then call for more Christian missionaries, more ministers of the gospel? While the suggestion may be justified on other grounds, and might be helpful in this undertaking, reliance on it as a radical source of change, as is needed, would be a doubtful course. Missionary work must be voluntary if it is to achieve its ends, and volunteers cannot be produced by conjuration. Leagues and societies offer a variety of approaches to an endeavor of this order, and a plenitude already exists.

The giant obstacle to be surmounted lies in the inescapable fact that peace is negative and does not enlist the positive willforces. It has no pull on the heart. It fires no ambition, incites no heroic deeds, and elicits no lusty greed. It merely provides placid atmosphere in which the will-forces and the ego may pursue their own interests; but they will not be concerned about peace, which is only a medium to them.

This is not to say that the peacemaker is to be despised: mankind is in great need of him and owes him immeasurable gratitude. His presence is indeed a blessing to the society of man. Unfortunately, his admirable attributes have not endeared him to the primitive impulses that fill man's veins. To them he is a halter, a damper, a nay-sayer. He is not of the sanguine countenance that races the pulse or offers adventure and suspense. He is gentle, genteel, meek, and pale-blooded—attractive but not exciting.

The only primary will-force that supports peace and has an interest in it is fear, and fear is negative, defensive, and escapist. Romantic love is a secondary will-force that has an interest in peace but only in the sense of wishing to be left alone.

Fear may, however, be a strong impelling force even if it is negative. This is to say, it may spur man to feverish action dedicated to defensive measures, even if other will-forces are not interested. As observed earlier, avoidance of disagreeable or painful events or conditions may generate as much activity as the promotion of a will-force or ego interest, even if the original motive is negative as fear is negative. Avoidance, moreover, enlists the help of intelligence in the same manner as a positive will-force. It is therefore not without a driving force as is the aspiration to peace itself.

The more threatening a terrifying agent is, the greater the activity to avoid it. Should nuclear attack be completely neutralized, the motivation of peace efforts would quickly slacken unless an equally woeful or worse weapon took its place. As soon as war were rendered much less destructive, the imperative directing its avoidance would lose much of its force. The season for creating peace machinery is at its most fertile period while the threat is in being and hangs overhead at the zenith.

13.

War or Peace?

However, as observed on a previous occasion, memory may be used for projection of thought into the future. Thus, while fear as a response to clear and present danger may disappear when the danger passes, it may be remembered. It may therefore become a base for launching restraining reflections that may ameliorate other will-forces and the ego.

Having, let us say, escaped a veritable threat, which was felt as acute fear, the fear is not forgotten completely during a period of relaxation that follows the passing of the threat. There may linger the realization that the threat may be reconstituted and that it would be prudent to profit by the time gained during the surcease from immediate anxiety.

It is evident that the exercise of reflection, based on memory in this case, represents an activity of intelligence. As we had occasion to remark previously, the memory of the fear will awaken intelligence to the end of avoiding a recurrence. The greater and more terrifying the threat, the greater the onus on intelligence to take preventive measures.

We have now to pull back a little for perspective. What may occur under a canopy of general and frenzied emotional stress in a community, a region, or in a whole country is quite obscure, but some clues are at hand and they may be useful.

We are justified in saying that as common major will-force interests change, remarkable subsidiary changes in outlook may appear. Indeed, far-reaching reorientation may occur, but we do not know the probable direction of change. In a few instances,

300

common experience will provide us with sufficient evidence on which to base tentative conclusions.

Anyone who has lived through childhood into maturity is familiar with the changes wrought by biological development. These developments are changes that modify some of the sources of both primary and secondary will-forces, no less than the ego, and therefore modify the person's "outlook" drastically. What was romantic before may lose its aura and glow. What was heart-filling may now be replaced by emptiness. Bugles and drums may strike the ear with the same timbre and wavelength as before, but the inner reception may be different from the accustomed.

This is the law of inner transformation. Perhaps one of the most nearly universally recognized examples of such transformation, as already indicated, is the change brought about by romantic love—at least so long as it lasts. This transformation shows clearly how a dominant interest may modify the prevailing inner feeling in many directions, when the spell is at its highest. Previous interests and inclinations may be forgotten or relegated to a low priority in choice of activity, while new ones move into their place. We have previously observed the pervasive power of this influence.

One or two supporting examples may be in order. Poetry is often regarded by youngsters and especially by the males of the species as a mode of expression that is not necessary to man's ordinary living processes, but let the subtle transforming breath of romantic love fill the inner precincts and *mirabile dictu,* poetry comes to life. What were dead, enameled words before now melt and as liquid essences permeate the soul. They penetrate where there was only aridity before. Incoming events and stimuli of all kinds, such as come upon everyone, are now given a different reception. Things are "seen" with different eyes, as it were.

The same may be said not only of poetry but also of music, of flowers, and other elements that affect the esthetic sense. They are received by a changed inner medium, and given new meaning and appreciation. Again, referring to the male of the species among the youthful, it may and probably will befall that romantic love will drive to a backseat the erstwhile lust for the "manly" sports, such as hunting and fishing. These pursuits seem to lose their pristine charm. Their attraction may return later, but while the romantic spell is at high noon, there is no place, except perhaps in some obscure corner, in the heart for a secondary interest.

A phenomenon such as this is, of course, observable even in other less extreme inner changes attributable to other causes. A whole people may come under the influence of some consuming interest to the point of obsession, and the minimization of all else occurs. Sometimes the seizure or spell may fall short of an obsession but may yet exert a great influence. The obsession or absorbing interest, like the outflow of a tide, may leave previous attractions "high and dry" like the exposed debris along a coastline, mossed-over skeletons of what were once fresh and warm objects. The interests that were so warm and compelling have been drained of their contents, and are left as shells or empty containers. The new interests dominate the inner chambers.

It is of stuff such as this that morale is built, mystiques are fashioned, and images formed: quite mysterious processes that lie below the surface.

In some instances, the causes of feeling-tones are obvious enough. Certainly the lovelorn youth has little difficulty in recognizing the reason for many of his moods, his odd attachments, and his new aversions. Here there is no mystery. He has difficulty indeed in hiding his emotional attachment. In other instances, the linkage of moods or tones of emotional emanations to particular events, situations, or relations is not so clear. The cause may be hidden or may merely not be identified with the feeling.

Nevertheless, as of interest here, the influence does affect behavior. It shapes attitudes, preferences, aversions, and vague attractions and revulsions. Why does a person who may have a choice of routes from here to there often avoid one route even though it is no longer and has no disadvantages over other routes? He may not know what influences him; but should he be able to retrace his steps, he would no doubt encounter some association with unpleasant emotional experience in the past.

Such psychic coloration, traceable to the will-forces and the ego, may conveniently be referred to as psycoloration. The phenomenon is widely recognized and assumes many practical forms. Much of the force of advertising which is designed to influence the behavior of the consuming public is aimed at psycoloration.

As previously observed, the control of the minds of people is one of the instrumentalities of modern "imperialism" such as communism. The vast propaganda efforts of governments seeking to inculcate beliefs, to win the minds of people and to win them to their side reflect recognition of this principle.

Here it becomes necessary to draw a distinction in the source of coloration.

Consider what is one of the simplest influences that determine how we receive external stimuli, which is to say, the manner in which the outer stimuli "strike" us. A whiff of smoke rising from a grill on which a steak is broiling comes to us on a breeze. If the stomach is empty, the odor evokes a vision of the steak and we can think of nothing more pleasing than sitting down to feast on broiled steak. On another occasion, the experience is repeated, but we have only just now sated our appetite on a steak. The smoke will not now produce the same effect as before. Our inner receptive condition has changed. The will-force represented by hunger is not interested. The condition that calls it forth, namely, an empty stomach, is not present. Therefore the whiff of smoke "strikes" us in a different manner.

Hunger, as when a person is in a truly famished condition, becomes an obsession. This haunting and driving obsession was described by Knut Hamsun in *Hunger*. The one will-force filled the whole inner being. The whole world was seen through this medium. Nothing else mattered.

Yet when such hunger is sated and if the person eats regularly and to his satisfaction without again feeling the pangs of hunger, he finds it difficult even to recall the exact feeling. He remembers it, yes, but he cannot recapture the actual quality of it, just as the quality of romantic love escapes us once it has died. We may describe it, but cannot resurrect it. Sometimes, when the spell is moribund, a strain of music or notes of a song may momentarily bring it back, but only fleetingly.

When the will-force has been drained, it no longer has a moving force. The face that launched a thousand ships can now not launch even a canoe for us. What a change! The time was when life was not reckoned worth living without the object of affection.

In this phenomenon of ephemeralism lies a significance to human behavior that may be worth examining. In other words, how we feel now, perhaps even vehemently, represents nothing absolute or eternal. The wind may change direction and bring us different aromas and scents. We may look back later with little comprehension of our present obsession. We should therefore be careful not to legislate too far into the future without providing a mechanism of repeal.

Just as we discerned a distinction between the primary and secondary will-forces and between the raw and the refined ego, we may distinguish now between the inner feelings that owe their awakening to the will-forces and the ego, on the one hand, and those that are of mental origin on the other.

We say, for example, that we "like" someone. This means that our affection has been or is kindled by someone because of some affinity of personality, some aspect of appearance, bearing, mode of speech, or the like—such as like-mindedness and like interests. We are pleased with the presence of the person; we like to exchange ideas or to banter with the individual. We cannot explain why this should be so. It is simply a fact. On the other hand, we may not have a distinct liking for another person, but we may *admire* him. We may in fact have no affection for him. Our admiration is a mental response, and we have a reason for our admiration. The man is a man of his word, he is courageous and just, always fair even if he is austere. His qualities do not attract our affection, but we take mental note of his virtues. As previously hinted, virtues are singularly devoid in themselves of power to excite affection, but they do evoke admiration.

The distinction between the impelling feelings that move us to action and that sometimes interpret or color the incoming events, and those that arise from mental reflection or consideration lies in the difference between substance or flesh and blood implication or involvement, and philosophical or rational reaction.

This difference may be discerned when we observe the interest and the feeling of a plaintiff or defendant in a suit at law compared with that of the judge. The one who brings the case to court has a direct stake in the dispute. It may be a matter of money owed or property taken away. Let us say, in any event, that the plaintiff's interest is economic. His feelings are aroused by the simple fact that he does not wish to be deprived of his property. The property in turn supports his comfort, perhaps even his food needs and other very personal needs or desires. Even his ego may have an interest, and it may be a double interest. Loss of the property or money would, let us say, affect his economic and social status or even his ambition to progress to higher economic levels, but the winning of the suit or the loss of it might also reflect on him and thus impinge on his ego.

Because of his direct interest, his will-forces would be aroused to a high pitch if the amount of property or money at stake were of a high magnitude in relation to his total property or income, and particularly if the case were doubtful as to outcome, and all the more so if the doubt arose because not all the facts could be clearly presented for lack of previous carefulness.

The feelings would be a compound of fear of loss, of regret and of hatred of the defendant who, we shall assume, had committed a wrong. The compound would burn in the plaintiff's breast or, as it might seem, in the very bowels of the distraught seeker after justice.

Compare his feeling with that of the judge. We assume that he has a judicial temperament and as a judge would not allow his feelings to become implicated lest he render a biased decision.

The judge's feeling would be one of intellectual aloofness, untouched by the personal considerations of the plaintiff. Should he indeed find himself implicated in that sense, he would be obliged in good conscience to vacate his seat while another judge sat in his place.

Looking upon the same facts, the feeling of the plaintiff would be very different from that of the judge, and, we may be sure, from that of the defendant as well.

Each of the three, the plaintiff, the defendant, and the

judge, would "see" the case in a different light because in each
the facts were sifted through a different set of will-forces and ego
interests or psycoloration.

The defendant, assuming once more his unjust behavior,
would feel a fear of losing what his greed had led him to reach
for despite the injustice involved in his act. He would feel a regret from his ego, and again, this would be of a double nature.
His ego would feel "let down" for not finally achieving the possession that would have enhanced his status, but it would also
fear the consequences of being found guilty of fraud or under-
handed methods. A verdict against him would lower the esteem
of him by his friends; it would embarrass him before his family
and in general would lower his repute as a neighbor and a citizen,
and therefore affect his economic and, possibly, his social
standing.

We see here how a given set of identical facts would be
entertained by the three principal participants in the case in a
wholly different manner. Where would the truth lie? If the
truth were simply a matter of physical fact, such as would be
represented by the filching of so many thousands of dollars by
an act of fraud, the case would be relatively simple, but assume
a misunderstanding between the plaintiff and the defendant in
their previous relations before the suit was filed; or a different
interpretation by each of the character of their relationship,
made yet more complicated by earlier failure to agree specifically
on this point or that, so that intent to defraud by the defendant
were in doubt. The case would be more complicated, and it
would not be easy to pluck justice from the midst of the disputed
circumstances. Cases are not often so clearcut in the attendant
circumstances, so far as these can be satisfactorily ascertained, to
make possible a ruling that would meet the theoretical demands
of justice. Under these circumstances, the play of the feelings of
the two sides, as exhibited to the judge, would place him in a
quandary. At his most honest effort, he would be forced to depend on his own limited powers of insight. His sympathy might
incline him to the one side or the other. These sympathies, in
turn, would be traceable to his own past experiences and possibly
his prejudices.

Thus, the limitation of human justice is exposed on its seamy side, revealing human weaknesses and fallibility. The judge, had he honest powers of introspection, which are most difficult to develop, might perceive that his judgment was biased by his feelings, and he would find that the light of true justice was obscured within himself. Moreover, his own temperament might lead him to a conclusion that was far removed from an objective judgment.

There was a motion picture called, if memory serves correctly, *Leave Her to Heaven.* The situation was so complicated that from external appearances human insight was unable to penetrate to the intent of the accused person and therefore unable to determine guilt or innocence. The conclusion was an admission of human fallibility, and this could be traced in part to the operation of the will-forces or the ego and their obscuration of objective fact.

Another example of the influence of feeling on mental objectivity may be found in the experience of a person who had grown to maturity in a family environment in which he was exposed emotionally to one or another political belief, without benefit of "objective" weighing of the differences between the one belief and its opposite. Later, let us say, the person, after exposure to the opposite belief, made a study on his own responsibility and experience, and reached a conclusion at variance with his "inherited" belief. His mind would then be reoriented, so to speak. Such a person might discover that it would be some years before he could bring his "feeling" into consonance with his mental shift. On the eve of an election, his mind would hope for a victory by the side that represented his new view. He would, however, find himself beset inwardly by a secret hope that the party of his old allegiance would win. His mind would not yet have pulled his will-forces about into support of his mental position. He would outwardly cheer according to his new allegiance, but his heart would not support him. Should he continue in his new attachment, time would work the necessary inner transformation of his feelings, but it would not happen overnight.

Within the United States in recent years, numerous southerners have been enmeshed in an emotional complex of feeling against their positive intellectual conclusion with respect to civil rights. Mentally they were ready to support civil rights, but emotionally they were southern. This struggle was not made easier by denunciation of their erstwhile or "inherited" attitude from the outside. Even so emancipated a person as the late William Faulkner, renowned novelist from Mississippi, confessed that in a critical contest he would have been forced to cast his lot with the unemancipated white southerners. Not only were his emotions or feelings, which is to say, the turn of his will-forces, involved, but also his regional ego and heritage. In all honesty, what he confessed was that his mental judgment had not yet risen to a state of domination over his emotion nor achieved the power of redirecting his inner feeling in keeping with his mental judgment.

From an understanding of such a dilemma, it may be concluded that "pressure" from the outside, impatiently applied, may harden a resistance that was already on its way to a silent reassessment and on the verge of being forsaken. By arousing the ego and its pride and reawakening prejudices that had been subdued or at least overridden, interference from the outside may generate a reaction of self-justification and rejection of the denunciation heaped upon practices that were themselves no longer mentally condoned. Under such circumstances, old attitudes are reawakened, and while they may be overridden, after an inner struggle, the spontaneity and satisfaction of self-purgation will be lost to the ego. At best a grudging support may be extended to the effort of the invading challenge. The wounded ego, rejecting the better-than-thou implications of the external attack, may, on the other hand, become very stubborn. An unsolicited tender of help from beyond the regional borders will almost certainly be resisted as a rude intrusion into local affairs. All the more will obtrusive methods arouse resistance and bitter ill-will. Not only will the regional ego react sharply, but the inclination to repel an invasion will be stimulated. A feeling of local outrage will meet the different feeling of outrage harbored by the outsiders who seek to eradicate what to them appears as a shameful social injustice.

To transcend the double feeling of outrage calls for a high degree of self-discipline over the will-forces and the raw ego. This is seldom at hand. The local and regional inhabitants will view the interference from the outside as an aggression that must be resisted. It is in the nature of territorial aggression and arouses similar responses.

Assuming that the sympathy expressed from the outside toward allegedly oppressed minorities located elsewhere arises from a sincere regard for their state of deprivation, the concern may be looked upon as a highly commendable reaction. It might be regarded as an involvement arising by a roundabout circuit from the precept to love one's neighbor, even if he is a thousand miles away or more.

Intrusion nevertheless opens the way to a reaction the character of which is not difficult to predict as it has already been noted. If we wish to love one neighbor, it may be questionable whether we should provoke hate in another, even if our sympathy extends to the one because of his oppression and not to the other, who may or may not be one of the oppressors but who will be bracketed with them by implication.

It may also be a useful reflection to muse over the precept of neighborly love to determine what may be involved in it under different circumstances. Presumably it would go better in all directions if our neighbors also love us. This thought should lead us to the conclusion that we should not place too many impediments in the path of the neighbor who may feel himself as also coming under the precept. If we behave despicably toward a neighbor or neighbors, we make it difficult for his love of us to bloom. We should hardly elicit love by obtrusive behavior.

If we wish to enter into the localities of our neighbors to throw stones at them because we do not approve of their behavior, it would be to exact superhuman forbearance of them if we expected them not to cast back some of the stones and perhaps a few additional ones. It might be useful also if the invaders asked themselves how they would respond if the tables were turned. If on some other ground than that of civil rights, for example, an invasion in the reverse direction were mounted and carried out, would the welcome mat be laid out to the invaders? The question is worth pondering if we are bent on loving our neighbors and at the same time are concerned about not placing an excessive burden on our neighbors to reciprocate. If we are concerned only about loving one of our neighbors and not the other and, moreover, make no overture to avoid irritating and annoying him, what will we have gained toward promotion of the total precept by which we are presumably motivated? Should we perhaps examine our motive with an eye to its true origin? Is it based on revenge of some variety? Or some future advantage? If our conscience cannot rest if we believe someone is oppressed, we are properly sensitive; but how far would our afflicted conscience carry us if there were no reward, either direct or indirect, at the end of the line?

Assume that by invading and demonstrating far away from our own locality we might improve the lot or hope to improve the lot of the oppressed elsewhere, but should leave the place in a shambles (1) because there were not a sufficient number of people in the premises or localities invaded by us who were able to rise to so high a level of understanding of our sincere motive, to be able to hold in check the natural reaction of the primary will-forces and the raw egos among the invaded, with the inevitable results that violence would flare; or (2) because among ourselves were some who had other motives than the sincere ones guiding most of us, and by their conduct should exacerbate feelings already running at high tension: would the love of neighbor be able to communicate itself, or would resort to force become inevitable if the will of the invaders were to prevail?

Is it possible to promote good will and love of neighbor through invasion of premises, voicing of demands, offending local usages, causing irritation by the mere fact of invasion without invitation and against any evidence of welcome reception?

The precept of neighborly love possibly did not contemplate this style of propagation. Accusation is not the door to good will. It begets countercharges by arousing the raw ego and the will-forces of the accused.

As previously noted, to expect the accused to absorb a charge of social obtuseness, callous disregard of the precept of neighborly love, or some other imputation of disrepute or subhuman behavior without exhibition of ill-will or provocation is possibly asking more of him than we, the accusers, could ourselves achieve.

If love of neighbor is to be propagated, a different address, one designed to awaken good will would be more conducive to achievement of the objective than a frictional introduction.

If the purpose is to *force* a change, a different address would, of course, be in order. This would, however, represent a confession of failure of the precept itself or admission that the motivation is of a different kind, one in which the object might be to produce a change regardless of the harshness of the means. Such an approach would resemble pure aggression even if it were not so intended, and the response could be expected to be in kind.

It is, of course, not necessary to assume that love of neighbor is the moving impulse in the civil rights "movement." The motives, as is usual, may be mixed and even contradictory. Those who march or demonstrate together may have a diversity of motives. We have dwelt on the outsiders as the object of consideration, not those on the ground who are the object of solicitude from the outside. They, the object of the conflict, the minority, would have the usual motive of the oppressed.

Among the invaded, in this instance the southern whites, there is also a great diversity of attitudes. Some of the citizens, we may be sure, feel sympathetic toward the unprivileged Negroes; but, again, they live in communities in which the ruling sentiment is to the contrary. Who from the outside is to demand of them that they should turn on their own neighbors to welcome the invaders? The question might again appropriately be asked of the invaders what their own attitude would be at home toward invaders who were bent on upsetting the social customs and attitudes that prevail and have long been accepted as normal. We may be sure that they would exhibit as little inclination as their southern neighbors to turn on their fellow citizens and fellow townsmen to welcome those who came among them not with words of good will and good tidings but as deprecators and revilers, holding themselves on high as representatives of a higher moral order.

In making these observations, the intent is to show how we may look to others when we presume to crusade against them. It is not the purpose to exculpate the southern dominance by the whites over the colored people among them. This dom-

inance was principally of an economic origin and of doubtful enlightenment as an economic instrument. The deprivation of
rights represented the withholding of the instrument of emancipation. It is demonstrably better economics today to have an
educated citizenry disposing of the higher skills and productivity
demanded by advancing technology than to rely on unskilled
labor of a low order of productivity. Wealth-creation is badly
shackled today when the workers are "held down." Typically,
the limited wealth accompanying low productivity was concentrated in relatively few hands; but it bears saying that it is not
necessary to travel to the southern states of America to find the
worst examples of such maldistribution of wealth.

The outbreak of violence has been at a minimum, and this
fact of itself reflects a high order of forbearance among the invaded communities. Considering the nature of the provocation,
control of the counteraggressive impulses should be the subject
of commendation rather than stigmatization and the occasion of
hurling epithets of infamy.

However civilized a people may be, they may yet be quite
deficient in competence to spread civilization en masse to other
people. This is in the nature of the case. Assumption of moral
superiority is implicit in the enterprise, and such assumption of
itself provides sufficient irritation to beget resistance. It is only
necessary to reflect on the nature of primary will-forces and the
raw ego to appreciate the incongruity of the endeavor. Exogenous
pressure induces endogenous resistance. Imposed conversion is
of a different order from induced conversion promoted by
enlightment.

The amelioration of the ego proceeds by the transformation
of mental attitude. The taming of primitive impulses is not accomplished by onslaught but by enlightenment that takes its cue
from human understanding and the propagation of kindly regard
for the troubles and torments of others and to which all mortals
are subject.

The incipience of kindly regard, as we undertook to demonstrate, lies in initial selfishness. First there is the looking inward
and then, perceiving the unpleasant feeling produced by injury
of oneself, extrapolating the experience to others. This repre-

sents the sequence. The first step, to repeat, came when this extrapolation was extended to those who were most closely linked by affection to the perceiver of injury. He extended the memory of his pain to the person for whom he had affection or close friendship. He hoped that the latter might be spared the pain he himself had experienced. This regard is translatable into the word "love." The precept of loving one's neighbor as oneself represented a universal extension of this principle.

The hope of this extension inevitably comes to rest on an actual inner feeling, so far as its most satisfying effects are concerned. However, human limitations, in terms of spatial separation or territorial dispersal, render the true, intimate feeling impossible beyond a relatively few individuals. The desiderated "love" beyond that limit must rely on the secondary will-forces and the tamed ego. It becomes more intellectual, as admiration and justice are intellectual, rather than affective or emotional. The love becomes a disembodied love, and it does not demand throwing one's arms around a nonacquaintance.

The hope of peace in the world is readily seen as resting on an insecure foundation. Man is so easily aroused into an ugly mood that the burden on the peace-keeping interests within him, which are really of no mean magnitude, would be expected to be cumbrous indeed. Since, however, the maintenance of peace is not today in the nature of keeping two individuals from fighting each other, we are plunged into a different order of considerations from those that govern an outbreak of violence between two persons or among small, local groups.

In large wars, killing of enemy military personnel is an impersonal undertaking. Even in close combat, the killing of an enemy combatant is not an act of murder; for even though the intent may indeed be to kill, the necessity of killing is not a personal choice. Often it is an outright act of self-defense. In all cases, it is under command of those whose function it is to conduct the war.

It must be clear, therefore, that a mere lack of desire to kill others does not constitute a renunciation of war. It would seem wholly safe to say that no American soldier who does battle in Vietnam has the least desire in his own heart to kill Vietnamese.

Nevertheless he does so. His action cannot, however, be imputed to the same aggressive impulse that might induce one of these Americans upon return to the United States to engage in personal combat with another person.

Once soldiers have seen comrades in arms fall dead or wounded, they may indeed feel the impulse of revenge. This, however, does not represent unprovoked aggression. They begin to hate the enemy in a personal fashion, but the hatred is not of a particular soldier named Ngo or Sai or Han. His name is not known and there is no interest in knowing it. Why should they be interested? They have never seen him before and have no desire to see him again. There is not so much a desire to kill as to put the opponent out of the way, to eliminate him, and in so doing, to save oneself.

The cause of modern war can hardly be attributed to hatred of one people for another. Wars have changed too frequently from one enemy to another while alliances have also shifted too readily to permit permanent hatreds to develop. To be sure, there have been great hatreds between two peoples, but these have had so many times to be forgotten and shifted elsewhere that the notion of a permanent enemy became somewhat ludicrous.

As previously indicated, a former enemy may quite soon begin to "look good" when a new enemy is encountered. The change in attitude toward the former enemy will occur if he too is unfriendly to the new enemy and has reason to wish him defeated. The proneness to alliance that we noted earlier in the will-forces and the ego will come into play. After some overtures, the former enemies may find themselves on the same side against the third force.

If popular enmity were the cause of war, shifts of this character would hardly occur. England and France were chronic enemies, and yet subsequently they became allies to fight a new common enemy. Popular feeling of the two people toward each other could therefore not be regarded as the determining factor. Rather it was the assumed interests of each country as interpreted by their statesmen.

We are moving toward the paradox to which reference has already been made. Leaders find themselves in the position of inducing their people who do not wish to fight other people to do so nevertheless—not indeed for the leader but for themselves.

The leaders or statesmen are the managers who have been selected by the people to make the necessary determination (assuming the absence of usurpation, seizure of power, or other non-democratic accession to power). To understand this relation of the people to the leaders and of the leaders to the people is to dissolve the paradox. The people do not wish to go to war but will do so at the behest of their statesmen, whom they have entrusted with the responsibility of making the decision.

What becomes now of the so-called aggressive instinct of man? Where do we look to find it?

It is not found to reside in the ordinary citizen as he goes about his routine of earning a living. No foreign citizen has stepped on his toes or spat in his face or otherwise offended him. There is no occasion for evocation of aggressive impulses.

However, as noted earlier, the citizen going about his routines is not as innocent as he might appear to be. He has assigned the function of defending his national interests to his political leaders whom he has helped to elect. Instead of his speaking for himself, he becomes quite far removed from the conflicts and contentions that are of everyday concern to the elected spokesmen and their helpers. The citizen is thus left free to devote his own time to the processes of overcoming the scarcity of the goods he needs for the satisfaction of his needs and desires. He helps to guide his statesmen by means of the expectations that he and other nonofficial members of his society lay upon the statesmen. These expectations may be reflected in the press and other media of expression and in the selection of candidates for election.

Does the citizen drive his leaders to aggressive action against another country or group of countries? Or does he leave the leaders to their own devices? He is, with few exceptions, unknown to the chief executive and his ministers, and is seldom even an acquaintance of his own legislative representative.

Nevertheless, in a roundabout way the citizen lets his leaders know what he expects of them. A leader would have great difficulty waging war if he were not supported by the majority of his public, unless he were a repressive dictator, in which case he would, of course, suppress dissension and exert full powers of propaganda through a one-party or official press. By manipulating the source of news, he would keep his public in the dark and either believing what they are told or not knowing what to believe, and therefore offering no effective opposition.

Not so under a democratic form of government, although the temptation to manage the news is very impelling and needs constant public vigilance to prevent it. Both the government and the press engage in news management, and when the two are in agreement, the public may be the victim, much as in a totalitarian country. War hysteria may be fanned to the point of ready combustion on the eruption of an incident.

However, in the absence of such contrived hysteria, the people having vested their leaders with the power to manage relations with other countries and normally going about their private interests, absorbed deeply in their own problems, maintain a running commentary on the actions and policies of their chosen leaders, informal as well as formal. This is not to say that each person stands on a street corner addressing those within earshot and thus venting his opinion, although this expression is not totally absent. Rather the commentary is left to those who have made their way in their profession as publicists such as editors, commentators through the written or spoken words, who use the available media to express opinion and generally to debate public questions, stirring discussion and controversy. In recent years the polltakers of public opinion through sampling methods have been added to those who undertake to bring public opinion to bear on the current statesmen. The leaders and various levels of political spokesmen in turn woo public opinion or seek to influence it. Thus an interplay, mutually influencing each other to varying degrees, is carried on.

The legislative branch may bring forward resolutions designed to inform the executive leaders of the sentiment of the lawmaking branch.

The leaders are able by consulting the many expressions of opinion to gain some idea of the climate of opinion, not as an accurate measure but as an approximation.

We may now repeat the question. Where do we look if we would find the source of national aggression?

The people, left to themselves, would have no belligerent feelings toward other people, with the exception of those living on the frontiers who might develop points of contention with their opposites, or those engaged in fishing at or near the line of territorial waters.

It would therefore appear that war would not only be avoidable but that it should be difficult to begin one.

Obviously something is wrong with this assessment. A people may not wish to fight and may recoil inwardly from the rigors, hardships, and frightfulness of war, but they *will* consent to go to war, in some instances perhaps even eagerly, if they are convinced by their leaders that there is so much at stake that only a recourse to arms can settle the differences; or that they must defend themselves against unacceptable losses if they are attacked.

In various degrees of intelligence, the people will understand that something vital is at stake, some strategic strait, pass, point, or other position of military advantage; or a vital resource or an approach to such a resource, an approach, moreover, that might be cut off if it were not effectively held against one or another possible enemy. Such a resource might be a basic food source or a vital mineral or fuel.

Should a people under these circumstances then return a "So what?" reply to their leaders? If they did, they would probably soon lose something that they regard vital to their mode of life, and it might be something more than material resources.

What indeed might be at stake? If it were merely a strategic point, what if some other people did control it? If it were a food, mineral, or fuel resource, would it not be possible to trade peacefully for these needs? There is no fully self-sufficient country in the world. Why not allow trade to overcome such deficiencies? Some of the smaller countries are dependent on outside sources for as much as 40 or 50 per cent of the needs of the people. Yet, they do not starve, and some of them are in the forefront of the industrial world. If the small countries are able to endure under these circumstances, why should not the larger ones be able to do so?

The question opens the way to an assessment of the national will-forces and ego considerations. Since nations are composed of people, their behavior arises from human nature and human aspirations. These cannot be expressed through any medium other than individuals.

Individuals will go to great lengths to obtain food, since life depends on it. Lack of food could therefore readily be understood as a cause of both human attack and defense. The same could, of course, be said of water or any of the other goods that are indispensable to the meeting of man's need. In cold latitudes this would include body-covering, shelter, and fuel for warmth.

Man will also exert himself to an extraordinary degree to satisfy his ego and the ambitions that express his ego.

The ego, contrary to the behavior of the primary will-forces, does not subside when the primary needs of man are satisfied. Were it so readily satisfied, and were the secondary will-forces so easily satisfied, human society would still be at a subsistence level.

The ego is at the root of the saying that the more a man has, the more he wants still more. Surely Napoleon's conquests beyond a certain radius had no explanation beyond his insatiable ego. He was able so to dominate the French people that he succeeded in converting them into the instrument of his ambitions. His lieutenants, of course, participated in his military victories and therefore shared in his aspirations. However, no one could charge Napoleon's wars to the aggressive instincts of the French people. Hitler's domination of the German people also made of them an instrument of his megalomania.

The ego cannot be dismissed as a minor influence in the determination of belligerency as opposed to peace. The ambitious leader is able to a great degree to infect his people and to imbue them with his ambitions, but his conversion of them is quite temporary, for the national ambition collapses with his defeat or collapse.

The substance of national ambition may be ever present in a people, but it will not mobilize itself. If it is to express itself it must *be* mobilized—by someone in whom it burns intensely. This need not be a single individual but might be a group or class, a military clique, or the like.

Beyond the primary will-forces and the ego as sources of aggression, which is to say, breaking across boundaries to attack other people, *belief* must be given a place of prominence as a cause of war. However, belief may be buoyed by the ego and by mixed aspirations, some of them of an ulterior character. Religious wars were often far from pure in motive, but the mixture was no doubt of the common variety, in which different individuals may have quite diverse reasons for participation in a campaign, a movement, or a common endeavor.

How belief may be converted into a desire for action calculated to bring the belief to consummation, is not always clear.

A belief is not a will-force, nor is it a facet of the ego. However, to beget action it must enlist one or both of these sources of motive power. Belief is mental in origin and requires a judgment to give it content.

In the physical field a belief must lie this side of certainty, because the supporting evidence falls short of proof. In this field belief may give rise to differences of opinion and therefore to controversy, sometimes bitter enough to break into violence. One difficulty contributing to uncertainty and to differences in belief may lie in questions about the evidence itself. Disputes of some magnitude may develop over the value or authenticity of particular evidence. Some may question its genuineness while others affirm it. Others may say that the evidence is good as far as it goes but is insufficient for proof. Yet others may question the relevance of the evidence in whole or in part.

However, the substantive aspect is the subject of the thing under dispute. How important is this subject? How does it bear on will-force or ego interests? If someone believes that Bacon wrote the plays of Shakespeare, not much is at stake. Belief in life on other planets is a subject of little practical import today but may at some time in the future assume a different color. Differences of opinion, based on conflicting evidence, might become very important because of their bearing on national policy and national commitment to this or that undertaking.

Belief of this variety is, however, different from belief about nonphysical subjects. The latter are matters of opinion and faith, precisely because no proof is possible. The question, to repeat, is how the will-forces and the ego can be implicated. There is nothing at stake of *direct* interest to the primary will-forces. No food, no granaries, no fisheries; no minerals or waterways or fuels— nothing that would meet any of man's material needs is at stake.

The secondary will-forces may indeed be implicated. Moral beliefs fall into this field. Equity and justice, including "social justice," are the subjects of belief, and wide differences of opinion are common. Belief in democracy, in monarchy, in socialism, capitalism, and communism divides people.

Insofar as beliefs have a bearing on material well-being, such as belief in capitalism or socialism, the will-forces, both primary and secondary, are drawn into the arena. As the opinion of people may differ, the ego also becomes implicated.

Religious belief, although not directly concerned with food, clothing, and shelter, nevertheless makes a connection with the considerations through man's relation to man, and these relations are of the deepest concern to religion.

If the belief, moreover, includes an affirmation of immortality in one form or another, and if, further, it holds to a system of rewards and punishment related to the fidelity or infidelity of the individual's mundane behavior to the belief, not only are the will-forces interested, but also the ego.

If future happiness is based on the quality of behavior on earth, and if the alternative is eternal damnation or eternal bliss, the quality of this behavior will become of the utmost concern— particularly to those who are far-seeing, sensitive and inclined to goodness and therefore to obedience.

To such a person his belief becomes the *ne plus ultra*. No material desire beyond that needed to maintain life can weigh as much as fidelity to the person's faith. The world's most precious and entrancing wealth would avail nothing if their possession and enjoyment spelled loss of the soul. It is not surprising therefore that all other aspirations must pale in a contest with the final reward.

It is also understandable that the will-forces and the ego would rally to the support of the culmination of life's very purpose. Further, it is understandable that much anguish and even torture and, among the most deeply attached, martyrdom would be suffered in behalf of the final reward of eternal happiness.

Strangely enough the tendency to defend such a faith might easily, in the absence of true reflection, lead to violence and actual violation of the tenets of the faith itself. The desire to have others adopt the same belief also inclines to run to excesses, as many religious wars of history have demonstrated. Even though the belief may represent a renunciation of materialism, man is so constituted that he has to resort to material elements to instill in others his belief in the nonmaterial. His only other instrument is example as a means of conversion, and this method may be regarded as too slow and uncertain to satisfy the eager will-forces. Therefore, he inclines to violate the very teachings he has sought to propagate. The Crusades were not good examples of the best means to propagate a religion that eschews violence and conquest but, on the contrary, exhorts man to love his enemy. Proper reflection would have renounced this method of propagation of a faith that is directed toward the taming of the will-forces and the ego.

Thus it is that belief is a source of conflict and aggression through its harnessing of the will-forces and the ego to do its bidding.

Belief in communism verges on religion in its belief that it has the key to the conquest of human poverty. In this belief, the faithful will even renounce the usual precepts of morality, assured that any means used for the propagation of the philosophy are justified by the end.

Fanatical belief and judiciousness of mind are, of course, incompatible. If two beliefs, supported by fanatical followers, meet each other, neither will know how to behave if they are mutually frustrative, other than to drive the other out of the way. In this world, the only known way of doing this is to use force. If then the supporters of the opposing belief are equally attached to their belief, a test of physical power is inevitable, and this means a violent clash.

Such clashes will continue to be inevitable not only in the field of belief but also in economic encounters so long as the will-forces and the ego call the signals. These will insist as they must, because of their very nature, on having their way; and they will have it if superior intelligence, numbers, and strength support them. *These forces were not made for retreat, for compromise, or agreement. The elements of mitigating behavior must come from other sources.*

As previously observed, the will-forces and the ego are indeed amenable to training, to education, and to amelioration. So also is belief, but only through taming of the will-force and the ego. These may then temper the expression of belief. *There is nothing in belief that cannot exist alongside other beliefs harbored by others if the will-forces and the ego are brought under the restraint of understanding*—a restraint that a particular belief itself may foster and devoutly hope to instill.

What different individuals and different groupings of individuals seek and expect is perhaps the leading determining factor in human relations. Beyond the primary needs, which, of course, all human beings are obliged to seek to satisfy, there is a great variety of ends sought by different persons and different people; but these *non*primary ends on earth *are not absolute. On the contrary, they are variable to the point of possible complete turnabout.* This is true, with the exception of certain incapacities, physical and mental, of all man's aspirations. They are not absolute so far as earthly objectives are concerned. Even a fanatic may be converted into a reasonable person or into a fanatic of the opposite persuasion from his previous fixation or attachment. Men *can* learn to love their enemies or at least to befriend them. Whole nations accomplish such a turnabout without the bother of an apologia, as history has shown.

Fanaticism, in any case, is a footnote to temperament rather than a mortgage on eternal truth.

Freedom of religion is obviously one of the great pacifiers of man. This freedom has gained enormous ground without sacrificing religion itself. It is a matter of mental attitude, of tolerance.

The bugbear today is economic interest and the fanatical beliefs attaching to it, no less than the national egos that are nourished by the accidents of history. Certain terrestrial advantages and disadvantages have shaped people into diverse cultures and civilizations. Some are proud because God, though harsh, was good to them by giving them the discipline of wintry cold and ice; others feel backward and therefore sometimes offended because God was warm and smiled on them and their land but did not lay the hand of harsh wintry discipline on them.

We recall nature's peculiar insistence on withholding many of her most precious gifts to men, exacting as the price of possession physical exertion to the point of variable perspiration and mental application, both to the natural revulsion of unwilling brains and the rebellion of the impatient will-forces. This is the field of economics.

With the gifts of nature in the raw, sometimes completely hidden from view, all variously scattered throughout the world in unequal proportions, some abundant, others sparse; with man eagerly in pursuit of a happiness that he largely equates with the enjoyment of the goods wrung from nature only by dint of sometimes cruel exertion, the play and contest, not to mention the rivalry and clash, of intent and purposive will-forces and ego ambitions, moving, pulling, and driving men everywhere to garner and work and possess—to have and to hold and to enjoy—how would this melange be expected to act, react and interact? Altogether peacefully?

Or must there be overseers, referees, lawgivers and enforcers? And also peacemakers, comforters, and inspirers? Teachers, philosophers, and prophets? Must there not also be a place for healers and hopelighters, laugh-inducers, singers, and dancers? Wits would be needed, too, and music-makers, poets, and raconteurs to offset scoffers and arrant pragmatists; discoverers, concealers, and inventors, to introduce newness and to prevent sodden monotony; persuaders, debaters, and advisers, as guiders and misguiders—all mixed and moving or standing, sitting or recumbent; all looking, listening, thinking, reflecting, talking, complaining, or working; some aloof, others attentive or prying; some happy, or moody, or weeping, others gay, angry, or serene; yet others agitated, or slow, or hasty; among them the sour, the kind, and sweet, or harsh; others busy or indolent, dozing or alert—and all else that man can be—all having to get along together, brave and timid, intelligent and stupid, high-minded, low-minded, or wayward and straight, direct and roundabout—all alike in fundamentals and all different in detail, distinct in size, age, weight, and height or in color, temperament, taste, and ambition; different also in attitude, experience, and in hopes, and fears, and sorrows—altogether, the populace, here, near, and far away, closely bunched or dispersed; intermingling, working together, travelling, going back and forth or congregating, or going their way, each nursing his whole world of personal concerns and personal history—these, all constituting mankind, differentiated and alike, alien and kindred, all having to get along with one another at multiple points of relation and contact. This is the pluralistic society of man.

A wonder indeed that order is so prevalent, and turmoil really the exception! Evidence that the amelioration of the ego and the restraint of the will-forces have progressed most remarkably is overwhelming. It is precisely because man is highly sensitive to disturbance, jostling, and violence, and vastly prefers peaceful pursuit of his routines that the impression of universal turmoil can gain credence. Were the disruptions of life, the hardships and privations, inconveniences and discomfitures, the common state of affairs, we would not be so impressed with them. Moreover, the more placid and comfortable living becomes, the greater loom the few moments of pain, annoyance, and dissonance that must always be inevitable.

Man has indeed moderated his behavior in relation to his fellow beings, and this very fact supports the hope that he is capable of refining his relations ad infinitum. However, as he does so, the small irritations, hurts, chafings, and discomforts that once passed unnoticed will loom as great impositions and horrors.

Man cannot be satisfied on earth because his expectations, kindled by his will-forces and ego, will always outrun what life can deliver to him. Therein may be seen the footprints of progress.

It seems safe to say that the will-forces and the ego cannot change themselves. Except as they are changed by the different stages of life, they must *be* changed by influences external to themselves, even if these influences are themselves internal within the individual.

The impulses to aggression can be changed only (1) by treating the differences and conflicts encountered in meeting the needs and desires of man by more suitable methods than the primitive ones upon the occasion of frustration—for frustration is inevitable, or (2) by modifying the mental attitude toward the desires and needs, and the beliefs that play on them and abet them in this or that fashion, as if they were absolutes. Only the primary needs are absolute, but even they permit a variation in *method.* The others are not peremptory and may make way for the fact that other inhabitants also occupy terrestrial space with us, far and near.

If diverse religions have learned how to live together, so may diverse economic and political beliefs. Economic considerations are on the practical, measurable level, and differences can be tested, superiority or inferiority established, by the visible fruits. Religious beliefs cannot be tested in this fashion insofar as they relate to the post mortem destiny of man; but economic systems in time test themselves before our very eyes. If religious freedom is possible, economic freedom within the confines of operational discipline should be all the more feasible.

The notion of imposing economic systems on peoples who adhere to a different system springs from political motives, ulterior in character, and may arouse defensive measures in proportion. The motive is to derive a benefit from the imposition, and this benefit would be expected to flow from the economic control that would result. This would extend to resources of soil, minerals, habitable acreage, or strategic advantage.

These were allowable notions despite the attendant violence before the categorical imperative of modern weaponry pressed its horrors upon us. Now the will-forces and the national ego must bow to a higher law, and this they have always been able to do when the mind was able to dominate the scene. Had the primitive impulses not thus been amenable to moderation, man would have been doomed long before now and would be certain of early doom under present circumstances.

We may be sure that man will continue to be born with aggressive instincts or tendencies. When his desires and aspirations are frustrated, these tendencies will assert themselves. As repeatedly asserted herein, these impulses will not restrain themselves, but they may bow to mental considerations, possibly moral or religious in character, or even merely pragmatic. The latter, subsidized by fear of destruction, may be the most powerful of all.

Since man will continue to be born with what might appropriately be called an original inclination to sin, and since he will inevitably meet frustration in many of his endeavors and desires, he will be better prepared for his earthly pilgrimage if he learns how to cope with frustration and bafflement—the earlier in life, the better. For this there is always adequate opportunity in the ordinary vicissitudes of growing up. Of importance is avoidance of the notion that youngsters must not be frustrated or that they must be led by the hand over all hurdles. Such a course would represent poor preparation for the inevitable encounters in later life.

To be sure, they might be helped on their way by a sharpening of their intelligence through parental or other oversight, but they should not be protected against the *pièce de resistance* with an excess of solicitude and concern lest their will-forces or ego be bruised. A fear of meeting life's rebuffs leads away from self-reliance and resourcefulness, both of which represent a state of readiness and alertness that will stand the individual in good stead. A bloody nose may provide a better education than a pat on the shoulders, if the bloody nose was honorably achieved. Aggression loses its attraction if its reward is physical pain, but physical pain borne in behalf of defensive measures represents an answer to the primal need of self-preservation. Memory of the pain may, however, bring a greater reliance on calmness and good sense.

We have said that the impulses that would eventuate in aggression if left to themselves are absolute only if they represent primary needs. The latter, of course, include self-preservation. Nevertheless, the *method* employed and the intensity of pursuit of reaction are not fixed necessities even with primary need fulfilment. Just as the secondary needs are not absolute or peremptory, the action that is dedicated to meeting primary needs, whether it is positive or negative, which is to say aggressive or defensive, is subject to variation. It is not confined to only one method or degree of intensity. In the lower animals, action is indeed determined by the character of the stimulus. There is little if any flexibility or variation since there is no reflection on possible alternative responses.

As we have observed more than once, man has been released to some degree from the blind force of instinct or what goes by that term. Even though he must eat as a condition of continuing mundane existence, and even if he is famished, he is under no peremptory command from nature to imitate a hungry specimen of the porcine species. The study of eating habits and inclinations has indeed taught us not to gulp our food as if this mouthful were the last one. The stomach needs a little notification to get the digestive fluids properly deployed for optimum performance of their function.

Responses made in the line of meeting a primary need may possibly enjoy a higher probability of success if sufficient restraint is exercised to permit intelligence to intervene as a friend of the court, so to speak, offering counsel. Not all "impulsive" actions go awry, but a sufficient number of them have undoubtedly done so in the history of man and under the observation of onlooking eyes so that the impulsive man is regarded with a degree of nervous misgiving. If the particular event or stimulus that calls for a response is trivial in nature, a quick answer that hits the mark is applauded, but it is a different matter if much is at stake. A more calculated or thoughtful response is then greatly preferred.

We may also say then that so far as *method* is concerned, none of our responses is under the sway of the absolute, including those elicited by the primary needs; nor is the method and intensity of address, overture, or onslaught under an unvariable decree. We have choices, and these may be precious. The starling continues its efforts to break a peanut shell by seizing it in its beak and striking the shell on the ground, or even on the snow, unable to profit by observation of the much more effective methods used by the blue jay, the titmouse, and the sapsucker, which pick the peanut (in shell) off the ground and repair to a tree branch, where they clamp the tuber securely between their claws and, using beak as a pick, soon extract the nut. Unlike the starling and all other birds, which are equally attached to their own methods, man does learn from observation and is able to modify his method. His responses are not fixed within the narrowest limits. It is true that individuals among human beings rely on imitation in a very high degree, but having before them a variety of possible responses originated by rare innovators and discoverers over the years and preserved by observers and imitators, they have optional responses.

Intelligence, by playing on those options over long periods of time, has established some responses as superior to others, and, naturally, others as inferior or perhaps even foolish or perilous. The fruits of the recorded observations take the form of craftsmanship, folk knowledge, or even of wisdom, recorded in literature, texts, and so on.

Phenomena that are not understood but that hold power over man in mysterious fashion may become the subject of superstition, and in some instances the superstition may exert great influence over human behavior. It represents a failure of intelligence to provide a rational explanation of observed phenomena. The prevalence of superstition among ignorant people, and the extent to which superstition may be played upon by leaders who harbor ulterior motives aimed toward the promotion of self-glory merely accents the need for education of the masses.

Means of education have been widely developed and diffused. Man has sufficiently mastered the processes of making nature yield her goods to make it possible to free sufficient time for placing children in school. Enlightenment of the citizenry is most important for propagation of civilization, which calls for taming of the will-forces and the ego. Enhancement of the power of the mind over behavior represents the most clearly marked avenue to the institution of the necessary restraints.

It may be argued that today man does not have time to await the ameliorating and restraining effects of education, and that some accommodation must be reached before the slow process of education can be expected to do its work. Furthermore, not all education would necessarily in any case lead to the end that is here posed. The content of education is of the utmost concern, especially since mass education is moving more effectively under centralized control as a result of the new means of teaching and inculcating ideas.

Meantime man will either be tempered by his fear of nuclear disaster or he will fail to respond adequately. If fear holds him to appropriate restraint, it will also accelerate the promotion of appropriate restraints of man's primary will-forces and his raw ego, thus enabling the mind and moral forces to gain the needed ascendancy.

The aggressive instinct of man is not so formidable that it cannot be controlled if what Lorenz has called *militant enthusiasm* can be controlled. We have referred to it as general community, regional, or national emotional stress or hysteria. The principal question is how to instill a growing decency in human relations so that rudeness, aggression, deception, hauteur and the silly pretensions of the ego, will become marked for what they are, namely, the enemy of man as man, and primitive holdovers from lower levels of life.

It is true that economic objectives, like beliefs, as assignments or charges of the will-forces and the ego, will remain objectives until they are reached or not, regardless of the obstacles. It is the function of the will-forces and the ego, with the aid of intelligence, to prevail over the opposition. Should belief change, of course, they will be discouraged of their function in the particular instance.

The usages of social prestige, of community sanction and the bases of group esteem, may upon examination yield very fruitful suggestions for the modification of human behavior. Behavior of the kind that is the raw material of human relations may be turned in one direction or another because of the flexibility mentioned just now. If certain styles of behavior are frowned upon more generally and made the cause of social displeasure, behavior will be influenced.

This is not a counsel of intolerance. Conformity, on the other hand, is not a virtue if departures from the norm are either harmless or regarded as necessary for good reason.

An example of the lack of a code will demonstrate in all its crudity what human behavior may be when it expresses the raw will-forces and the ego without the benefit of reflection, and without the adoption, perhaps unconsciously, of considered responses, which may form the basis of social sanctions.

We have only to observe street, cross-street, or merging highway traffic. Automobile driving was thrust upon the twentieth century inhabitants of the globe in a haphazard, unrehearsed and unheralded fashion. Man had little to go on. His course in this field was not prepared by a long lineage of refinement and politeness. There was no aristocracy of the road, no example of good breeding to imitate.

Each individual was free to behave and to express himself in keeping with his temperament, his upbringing and his wayward inclination of the moment. No restraining hand reached out from the office of social usage and laid on his shoulder, and no voice cried out, "It is not done in this manner." When the driver was on the verge of launching a succession of heated ejaculations, there was no inner or outer voice to say him nay—no echo of a voice from his father or his mother or from a friend, an uncle, or a teacher. He was his own master. If he acted rudely, no one would berate him for his behavior. Therefore his raw ego had nothing to fear. His good standing in the eyes of those with whom he lived and associated would suffer no erosion. If a voice from the back seat remonstrated, he could quell it by asking who should cast the first stone. Why then should he restrain himself? No etiquette of the road or street traffic had been born.

If such an etiquette was to germinate, it must be voiced by someone who could foresee the unhappy consequences of rudeness, of the tendency to blame the other driver if there was an encounter, a mishap, a bad turn, a failure to stop, or a collision.

The etiology of genealogy of a custom is commonly lost in obscurity. In this instance it is not lost in antiquity, since many people still living witnessed the development of the atrocious manners that are still unedifyingly characteristic of motorists after more than half a century of motoring.

It was unfortunate that an etiquette was not made the subject of reflection and study when the automobile first made its appearance. On the golf course, decent usage was already established before the game left its status as a sport of the few. The many who later went on the links were introduced to the etiquette by the veteran players who had already bowed to the accepted usage. A new player gained access to the course by becoming a member of a club, and unless he played by the rules and obeyed the etiquette, he was marked as something less than a gentleman or, later, as women entered the list of players, something less than a lady, if he or she strayed from the line of accepted usage. Such a player knew the penalty. It was a risk no one was greatly tempted to take because of the probability not only of being barred from further playing but of being treated to some of the hints of ostracism. The ego then exerted a discipline of its own on the player.

The oversight, the negligence, and failure of someone of sufficient prestige and status to introduce rules of etiquette and accepted usage into the world of motoring was indeed a lapse that still exacts its toll in human wear and tear, in shattered dignity and good will. A monument to the shame of the traffic jungle is long past its time.

The onus is on the drivers of the so-called prestige vehicles to lead the way as a bell-wether. Prestige attracts imitation. Decency itself begets imitation, but particularly if it is noted in a person of prestige. Then it is at its apogee as a model. Decency is humanity at its best, and man aspires to be man and to move away from the beasts in his behavior. If he is made self-conscious of the marks of bestiality and is properly disposed by family or community attitude, his ego will take pride in the distance its owner puts between his behavior and that of the savage, which is nearer to the animal level than to civilized usage.

If two drivers approach each other and one must give way, which one will have the grace to say "You first?" If one of the two is the driver of a prestige vehicle, the gesture should occur to him, assuming that noblesse rides with him. Yet, as common observation will reveal, the driver who in all else is of genteel behavior may be indistinguishable from the ordinary bully in a traffic stalemate or vexing maneuver.

A deferential driver is virtually an oddity, and he may have the exquisite experience of hearing from his riding companion an impatient intonation, such as only words can achieve under certain circumstances, almost automatic: "Don't be a fool—you have the right of way!"

"Yes," the retort might echo a difficult attitude, "but someone must first *act* the fool so that wisdom may have its turn!"

So would be exemplified one of man's greatest needs: to stir more decency into the ugly ego. The rules of soportsmanship were no doubt established by the few who had the prestige of inherited wealth, and therefore the time and leisure to refine noneconomic forms of competition into contests of strength, skill, nimbleness, and wit, as lovers of sport for itself, which is to say, as amateurs. They could *afford* the luxury. The rules of fair play and generous attitude represented the strain of decency in man without which civilization would have a bleak future.

That the strain of decency is not sterile is perceptible in the everyday gentility that is encountered despite the persistence of thoughtlessness, boorish behavior, and even rudeness. That decency and politeness *could be* introduced into the manners of motorists cannot be questioned. Commendable progress has already been made, and the day may yet come when drivers will become as much concerned about their manners on the road and streets as they are about their behavior in the drawing room, in business conferences, or at a soiree. It is in the escalation of decent behavior that conformity assumes the aspect of virtue. Nonconformity is mere unruliness or obstreperousness when it is practiced for its own sake or in opposition to orderly processes that help to meliorate human relations and make the behavior of people more tolerable to each other.

To make good motoring manners fashionable would be a noble endeavor even if it should come on the scene at this late date. The opening scene for its greater hope of success should be laid at home, in the family, and in school.

The bearing of this subject on the aspect of human aggressiveness that leads to war is not as remote as it might seem on superficial examination. Man does learn from experience. His efforts at avoidance of pain, unpleasantness, and calamitous events are based in his senses. These efforts are far-reaching and enlist man's highest intelligence. The unpleasantness of execrable and abominable manners of motorists is, on reflection, hardly to be compared with the pain, privations, and anguish of war, and for that reason has not received the solicitous attention as the efforts to prevent war. Nevertheless, the changing of motoring manners requires a change in attitude and of social sanctions no less than does the establishment of peace.

If people as people do not seek war but nevertheless are the ones who suffer the consequences of defeat or enjoy the benefits of victory, how may they, the people, affect the desideratum of peace?

That people prefer peace to war in modern times can hardly be doubted, where life is reasonably pleasant. Why then can they not bring about peace? We have seen that the division between the people and their governors is not as steep and absolute as it appears to be. In other words, people desire peace but will also consent to war under certain circumstances, and will engage in it wholeheartedly once they are convinced that war is in their interest.

The question must then arise: Is war in the interest of any people?

Essentially, war is the penalty man must pay for want of sufficient intelligence to obtain from nature or from others of his kind what he needs without the violence of combat. Fundamental to this assertion are two conditions in the relation of man to nature that must be taken as given: (1) Nature does not provide man freely with what he needs in the form he needs or desires it. (2) Nature's goods are neither equally scarce in all areas nor do they require an equal amount of effort to convert them into usable form everywhere.

Equally fundamental is the fact that man does depend on nature for his sustenance. This dependence, however, is absolute only so far as the primary needs extend, and with respect to them there may be, to repeat, a variety of means by which the needs may be met. The goods that are desired to meet the secondary needs usually require more refinement and elaboration than those that cater to the primary needs. Desire for them implicates the ego no less than the secondary will-forces.

Since man's primary needs drive him at the pain of extinction for failure to meet his needs, he has no choice, for self-preservation is one of the most potent of all man's sources of motivation.

Assume primitive tribes living in the same area, and sufficiently near each other to be within reach of one another by pedestrian movement. Assume, further, a calamity of nature, caused by a pest or extreme drouth or other untoward event, and a famine as a consequence. Not enough food is at hand or within reach to feed more than one tribe. However, if one tribe could secure for itself the food held by another or available to it, the first tribe might survive or suffer less attrition from starvation than if it sought to rely solely on its own food supply. It would therefore seek to "take" the food supply of the others.

Since the primary will-forces of both tribes would be frustrated by the condition of acute scarcity, the intelligence at the disposal of each would be enlisted to find the least costly and least painful means of achieving satisfaction. The obstacle in each instance would be the other tribe.

It would be the purpose of the primary will-forces nevertheless to achieve their ends. Obviously the obstacle standing in the way must be removed or circumvented.

How to do this? Since each tribe would be in the same circumstance, neither could help the other even if the desire to do so existed, and, of course, it would not. The only possible remedy would lie in taking by force what would obviously not be surrendered voluntarily.

The chiefs of each tribe and a small number of their leading men would be aware of this. The other tribal members, the older and broken ones, the women, adolescents and children, would perhaps have no desire to go to war. If the question were left to them (with some exceptions), they would give a negative reply to the chief. Yet, their own interests would be at stake. Should their chief listen to them, the whole tribe might be beaten and their means of livelihood taken from them. Their lot would be extinction or slavery, or a combination of the two. The stronger ones might be spared for the work they could perform while the remainder would be dispatched with club or spear. The food supply must at all odds be protected to the greatest possible extent.

Would there have been any other course open to intelligence? Combining forces would not have increased the food supply.

Modern man has encountered similar situations. Polar expeditions have faced starvation, and expedition members did indeed starve. They, however, *were in the same group together.* Yet their gnawing starvation did not induce them to fight each other, with individual exceptions. They had as much reason to seek to take from each other what each needed as did the members of the tribes. Why then did they not choose sides and decide to contest for the food that remained?

Evidently the mental situation was not conducive to such strategy. If the idea occurred to someone, the basis of conspiracy was nevertheless lacking. The expedition members were at close quarters, and the necessary secrecy could hardly have been achieved or maintained. Also, there was no natural division such as the tribal form offered. There was no natural polarization or rallying point about separate leaders. In the other situation, the separate tribes were already in existence, and mutual hostility and suspicion needed no special stimulation. Within the exploring group, there was no prevailing idea that would have suggested a contest. Like the starlings, men act according to the guiding idea in their heads. The birds continue beating the peanut on the ground because they cannot learn a better method. Man at least *can be* taught.

In the modern world, some characteristics of the primitive situations remain. In place of tribes (although some of these continue to exist), most of mankind is divided into national states. These retain more than vestigial tribal characteristics. Each looks to itself, even as did the separate tribes. Each is utterly selfish (with some recent exceptions) and regards the others with suspicion or dubious friendship.

In recent times, famines have attracted actual proffers of help and these have been accepted. Help in the form of food has been extended without exacting slavery or subjugation as the price or even the least territorial cession.

Yet, much of the primitive attitude remains. Racial differences and cultural diversity are formidable. Different degrees of
success attained in the struggle with nature in the production
and distribution of wealth have created cleavages that evoke national egos and considerable sensitivity. Feelings of superiority
and inferiority face each other across boundaries or oceans, and
these are highly fertile sources of misunderstanding and ill-feeling. Who is entitled to what can become questions in which
justice and equity may be embroiled in insoluble contentions.
Only decency of heart can make its way in these entanglements;
and when there is contest between dominant nations for peoples'
minds and loyalties, decency is always subject to indictment and
caricature. Intrigue and subversion are weapons so familiar from
modern usage that the very notion of the introduction of human
decency into the premises necessarily takes the color of naivete
or even of treason!

Yet here is man: He needs either an increase of intelligence
and wit in order to learn how to meet his needs without combat
or without beggaring his neighbors or he must so reduce the
incidence of scarcity that the contest for goods may subside. A
third possibility lies in the amelioration of human relations
through understanding of the probability that failure to come to
terms threatens man's very existence.

An increase in wit may come from experience and reflection.
Diplomacy learns not to hurl ultimatums, for example, and to
afford the national ego of the opposing nation an escape. "Face-
saving" is the term of common parlance. It is not a peaceful gesture to gloat over a victory or to hold the opposing nation up
to ridicule. Ego-satisfaction for home consumption is a luxury
that may have tragic consequences; for it will only incense the
opposing contenders and put their national ego to test. Even
in the animal kingdom a lion or other ferocious beat will not,
except as driven by hunger, attack unless it is injured or its
escape route is blocked or too closely held. Injury to a national
ego is comparable to physical injury of the beast. Barring of the
escape route is tantamount to shutting the door to a face-saving
device.

Cynicism, it goes without saying, is a supreme enemy of

peaceful relations; but perhaps not much more of a temptation to aggression than is naivete. Where to draw the line is a question for wit, wisdom, and decency. The distinction can be drawn from experience and a "will" to understand rather than to misunderstand. The latter (misunderstanding) is a favorite device of the ego and the will-forces in their design to prevent the mind from overruling them.

As for the possibility of reducing the incidence of scarcity, experienced in the form of poverty, the technological advancement of the means of production offers a partial hope; but the galloping pace of population expansion poses a veritable obstacle that will convert the technological endeavor into an exercise of rainbow pursuit if the pace of population expansion is not slowed to a walk. The equation may be reduced to an either-or form of option: either reduce the pace radically or risk a holocaust that may decimate the living. The cure could be infinitely more calamitous than prudent and effective prevention of excessive birth would entail.

Yet, it must not be thought that meeting the primary needs of man would of itself slake man's inclination to seek more than he currently has for his enjoyment. There remain the secondary will-forces and the ego. Their pressing desires, fired by ambition, would still underwrite aggression; as might belief and the national ego endorsing it.

Therefore the aspirations of people must be examined to determine the nature of the burden they place on their leaders through the medium of the peoples' expectations. *It is not enough to say that leaders must restrain themselves. It is necessary to say that people must curb the demands they place on their leaders.* They must be alert and ready to discourage leaders who take their cue from past values, from historical notions of national glory and heroism. These may now be entirely too expensive and dangerous to be trusted in the present milieu.

A review of historical notions of honor and glory is imperative, so that the people will understand that playing with antiquated notions is as dangerous as it is for children to play with matches in a powder arsenal.

That this is a prescription that is virtually beyond the power of man in view of the continuing ascendancy of the primary will-forces and the raw ego in the sphere of relations between peoples goes without saying. Patriotism is dear to the hearts of any virile people, and it courses in the very corpuscles of the blood.

The author must confess to a deep repugnance to the very idea of abatement of patriotism. He cannot say that the notion is even entertainable in his breast. To seek to eradicate it would no doubt encounter an outright impossibility. People have died for it and continue to die for it. The proposal, were it made, would seem so monstrous that only a martyr's motivation could entertain it.

That the prescription is too alien for present-day man may be accepted without, however, recognizing the danger of patriotism as it has been understood. The deep feeling from which it flows may, however, be rechanneled without sacrificing its undoubted value to human morale. Just as the explorers just now cited did not unleash their aggressive instincts toward each other even though they had as good reason to do so as the two tribes that faced starvation, the *idea* of "squaring off" against one another across national lines may be changed. If the idea is changed it will no longer assert itself as a compulsion. Community or national hysteria will have been subordinated to better sense.

Two colonies of bees will fight each other without giving quarter, but it seems that they are guided by odor. If a beekeeper sprays both colonies with the same scent, the difficulty is said to vanish. Substitute the idea for the scent, and man will lose his pugnacity toward those who are, as matters stand today in this world, nothing other than his neighbors.

Today a man could be ridden out of town on a rail and tarred and feathered in some areas, no doubt, for advancing such a suggestion; but time is on the wing and man is confronted with an imperative that will decide whether he has the wit to survive.

Man has learned the good sense of detours in many departments of his life. *He does not give up his destination. He finds a better way of reaching it.*

After all, two thousand years should not be too short a time to learn the most difficult but most beneficent lesson in the world! Even dunces can be taught by wiser and cooler heads.